NAFTA AND INVESTMENT

NAFTA Law and Policy Series

VOLUME 2

Series Editors

Seymour J. Rubin, B.A., LL.B., LL.M.

Professor of Law, Emeritus in Residence,
Washington College of Law, American University

Dean C. Alexander, B.A., J.D., LL.M.

Director, the NAFTA Research Institute, Washington, D.C.

The book series will include high-quality studies on different aspects of NAFTA, including legal analysis and commentary on the Agreement. Among the numerous areas that will be covered in the series are NAFTA topics as diverse as agriculture, dispute settlement, environment, intellectual property rights, investment, and labor. Contributors will be drawn from the legal profession, business, government, and the academic community. The series is designed to ensure that practitioners, corporate counsel, government officials, academics, and businessmen will gain a thorough understanding of the multi-faceted legal and economic implications of NAFTA.

The titles published in this series are listed at the end of this volume.

NAFTA
and
Investment

edited by

Seymour J. Rubin
Dean C. Alexander

KLUWER LAW INTERNATIONAL

THE HAGUE / LONDON / BOSTON

A C.I.P. Catalogue record for this book is available from the Library of Congress

ISBN 90-411-0032-6

Published by Kluwer Law International,
P.O. Box 85889, 2508 CN The Hague, The Netherlands.

Sold and distributed in the U.S.A. and Canada
by Kluwer Law International,
675 Massachusetts Avenue, Cambridge, MA 02139, U.S.A.

In all other countries, sold and distributed
by Kluwer Law International,
P.O. Box 85889, 2508 CN The Hague, The Netherlands.

Printed on acid-free paper

Printed in the Netherlands

TABLE OF CONTENTS

Table of Contents   v

Introduction
    by Seymour J. Rubin & Dean C. Alexander   vii

NAFTA and Investment - A Canadian Perspective
    by Tim Kennish   1

The Transformation of the Maquiladora Under the North American
Free Trade Agreement
    by Preston Brown & Carolyn Karr   37

Mexico's Foreign Investment Law of 1993, Amendments to
the Maquila Decree, and an Overview of Maquiladoras
    by Dean C. Alexander   65

Foreign Investment in Mexico Under NAFTA
    by Jorge Luis Ramos Uriarte   85

A Critical Analysis of the Post-1994 Elections: Mexican
Foreign Investment Regulatory Scheme
    by Jorge Witker & Rich Robins   111

The Likely Impact of NAFTA on Investment in Selected
Goods and Services Sectors in Mexico, Canada, and the U.S.
    by Dean C. Alexander   147

The Role of the Multilateral Investment Guarantee Agency
(MIGA) in Attracting Foreign Investments to Latin America
    by Luis Dodero   161

The Institutional Bases of the Economic Model and the
Treatment of Foreign Investment in Chile
    by Roberto L. Mayorga   179

Selected United States-Mexico-Canada Cross-Border
Investment and Trade Deals: 1992-1993
    by Kent S. Foster & Dean C. Alexander   185

Selected United States-Mexico-Canada Cross-Border
Investment and Trade Deals: 1994
    by Dean C. Alexander   207

Text of the Investment Chapter of NAFTA   219

Bibliography NAFTA and Investment
    by Dean C. Alexander   237

About the Authors   243

Index   245

INTRODUCTION

This book provides a forum for the presentation of various views and analyses of the investment chapter of the North American Free Trade Agreement (NAFTA) and related matters. Among the broad topics that the book addresses include: an analytical discussion of the investment chapter of the Agreement, including U.S., Canadian, and Mexican perspectives; a review of maquiladoras and the ramifications of NAFTA on this Mexican investment tool; a history of the regulation of foreign investment legislation in Mexico and recent developments; the political implications of NAFTA and distinct aspects of doing business in Mexcio; an examination of the likely impact of NAFTA on investment in selected goods and services sectors in the U.S., Canada,. and Mexico; a description of the role of a multilateral investment guarantee institution in attracting foreign investment in Latin America; a discussion of the foreign investment regime in Chile, the next NAFTA partner; a highlight of cross-border investment and trade deals among international firms in the NAFTA nations between 1992 and 1994; and a bibliography on NAFTA and investment.

In *NAFTA and Investment - A Canadian Perspective*, Canadian attorney Tim Kennish addresses numerous issues, commencing with a review of existing Canadian, Mexican and U.S. foreign investment laws and policies. Next, Mr. Kennish discusses the general investment provisions of NAFTA. Subsequently, he analyzes the investor dispute resolution mechanisms in the investment chapter of the Agreement.

Next, U.S. attorneys Preston Brown and Carolyn Karr provide in *The Transformation of the Maquiladora Under The North American Free Trade*

Agreement a multi-level address of maquiladoras and the impact of NAFTA on this border investment scheme. First, the authors relate the history of the maquiladora, followed by a discussion of the structure of the maquiladora. Subsequently, the authors describe how Mexican laws have regulated the maquiladora, including discussing regulations before and up to the 1989 Maquiladora Decree. In the next portion of their chapter, the impact of NAFTA on maquiladoras is addressed as well as 1993 Mexican regulations modifying the 1989 Maquiladora Decree. Afterwards, the authors provide a discussion of other factors, including real estate and taxes, that are relevant to maquiladoras.

Following this piece, U.S. attorney Dean C. Alexander highlights a number of topics in *Mexico's Foreign Invesment Law of 1993, Amendments to the Maquila Decree, and An Overview of Maquiladoras*. In the first portion of the chapter, Mr. Alexander describes Mexico's new foreign investment law of December 27, 1993. Subsequently, a discussion of the December 24, 1993 Maquila Decree, which revised the Decree for Development and Operation of the Maquila Export Industry, takes place. Lastly, a description of the current status and breadth of the maquiladora industry is given.

Another perspective on foreign investment in Mexico and NAFTA is offered by Mexican attorney Jorge Luis Ramos Uriarte in *Foreign Investment in Mexico Under NAFTA*. The chapter discusses the legal framework and history of Mexico's foreign investment rules. Also, it examines Mexico's 1993 foreign investment law. Next, Mr. Ramos addresses the investment chapter of NAFTA.

A timely piece authored by Mexico-based attorneys Dr. Jorge Witker and Rich Robins, *A Critical Analysis of the Post 1994 Elections: Mexican* Foreign *Investment Regulatory Scheme*, provides a multi-faceted discussion of: Mexico's economic conditions; the role of NAFTA as a catalyst for reform; positive and negative aspects of doing business in Mexico; and of specfic goods and services sectors in Mexico.

Following this chapter, Dean C. Alexander's *The Likely Impact of NAFTA on Investment in Selected Goods and Services Sectors in Mexico, Canada, and the U.S.* highlights the findings of a leading U.S. government study on the probable impact of NAFTA on the levels of investment in particular goods and services sectors in Mexico, Canada, and the U.S.

Next, Spanish attorney Luis Dodero provides in *The Role of the Multilateral Investment Guarantee Agency in Attracting Foreign Investments to Latin America* a critical discussion on this important investment guarantee agency and its utility in promoting and safeguarding foreign investment. Initially, the chapter describes MIGA's role in attracting foreign investment to developing nations. Moreover, it relates the manner in which the Latin American nations can profit from the activities of the Agency. In a helpful annex, the author provides a list of MIGA Contracts of Guarantee Outstanding for Projects in Latin American Countries as of January 31, 1994.

Afterwards, Chilean attorney Roberto L. Mayorga details in *The Institutional Bases of the Economic Model and the Treatment of Foreign Investment in Chile* a number of the basic norms known as public economic order. More specifically, Mr. Mayorga describes these norms, including Chile's: property regime, the enterprise regime, the state regime, the social market economy, and the constitutional entities.

Following this chapter, U.S. attorneys Kent S. Foster and Dean C. Alexander in *Selected United States-Mexico-Canada Cross-Border Investment and Trade Deals: 1992-1993* set out a number of trade and investment transactions that occurred in Canada, Mexico, and the U.S. during 1992-1993. In the subsequent chapter, Mr. Alexander in *Selected United States-Mexico-Canada Cross-Border Investment and Trade Deals: 1994* details various deals in the NAFTA nations that occurred during the first year of the Agreement. The text of the investment chapter of NAFTA is made available in the next chapter. In the last portion of the book, Mr. Alexander provides a bibliography on NAFTA and investment, with a particular focus on foreign investment in Mexico.

> Seymour J. Rubin
> Dean C. Alexander
> The Editors
> November 1994
> Washington, D.C.

NAFTA AND INVESTMENT - A CANADIAN PERSPECTIVE

by Tim Kennish[*]

1. INTRODUCTION

The Investment Chapter of the North American Free Trade Agreement ("NAFTA") entered into between the United States, Canada and Mexico (collectively, the "Parties") considerably enhances the opportunities for foreign investment among the three countries, while at the same time improving the security of such investment.[1] NAFTA reflects the Parties' recognition that liberalization of host country investment restrictions is as important as the elimination of trade barriers.

The Investment Chapter is essentially a compromise of the conflicting objectives of the Parties but there are positive elements for all three countries. The Investment Chapter of NAFTA represents something of a victory for U.S. investment policies, which befits the United States' role as the dominant foreign investor in both Canada and Mexico. In the negotiations, the United States sought an "open book" approach to provide greater predictability and security for investment and was rewarded by securing general agreement on a number of investment principles. Accordingly, while NAFTA generally preserves the existing non-conforming investment restrictions of the local law, including the

---

[*]   Partner at the law firm of Osler, Hoskin & Harcourt in Toronto, Ontario, Canada. He has written extensively on NAFTA and Investment.
[1]   NAFTA's Preamble states that the three governments are resolved *inter alia* to "ENSURE a predictable commercial framework for business planning and investment".

general investment screening legislation in both Canada[2] and Mexico,[3] NAFTA places significant constraints on how such laws may be applied to NAFTA country investors. Moreover, in a related development which occurred substantially concurrently with NAFTA's coming into force, Mexico undertook a significant overhaul of its investment screening legislation, proposing as its replacement a substantially more relaxed Foreign Investment Law. As well, while NAFTA will encroach further[4] on Canada's ability to apply restrictive policies to NAFTA country investors through its Investment Canada legislation, in the time since the implementation of the Canada-United States Free Trade Agreement (the "FTA") in 1989, Canada has unilaterally relaxed some of its most restrictive foreign investment policies relating to upstream oil and gas[5] and book publishing.[6] This was undoubtedly brought about by a combination of U.S. pressure for such changes, positive Canadian experience under the FTA and some recession-induced host country realism.

These developments are highly significant given that foreign investment controls have been featured elements of the international posture of both Canada and Mexico. The United States, by contrast, has generally adopted an uncompromising stance on the provision of open access to foreign investment with only relatively few strategic industry exceptions (such as with respect to licensing of the production of nuclear material and the control of U.S. air carriers).[7] At the same time, it must be acknowledged that foreign investment

---

[2]   Investment Canada Act (Canada), R.S. 1985, ch. 28 (1st Suppl.), *as amended* by 1988, ch. 65 and Investment Canada Regulations SOR/85-611, *as amended by* SOR/89-69.

[3]   All references are to the Foreign Investment Law of the United Mexican States published in the Official Gazette (*Diario Oficial*) of the Federation on December 27, 1993 and in force as of February 28, 1993. This law repealed the Law to Promote Mexican Investment and to Regulate Foreign Investment published in *The Official Gazette of the Federation* on March 9, 1973; and Regulations of the Law to Promote Mexican Investment and to Regulate Foreign Investment published in *The Official Gazette of the Federation* on May 16, 1989.

[4]   Beyond that provided for in Chapter 16 (Investment) of the Canada-U.S. Free Trade Agreement.

[5]   In March, 1992 the so-called *Masse Policy*, which prevented foreign acquisitions of control of financially healthy Canadian-controlled upstream oil and gas businesses, was rescinded with the result that such investments are now considered on the same basis as other investments requiring clearance under the Investment Canada Act. The Investment Canada Act was also amended in June, 1993 to remove the restriction for oil and gas previously applicable in cases involving American investors with the result that the Act's higher thresholds for American investors also apply in this area (S.C. 1993 c. 35).

[6]   In January, 1992 the Canadian federal government announced significant modifications of its so-called *Baie Comeau Policy* on book publishing, which considerably relax the degree to which foreign investment in this industry had been restricted under such policy.

[7]   See: *North American Free Trade Agreement: Summary and Analysis* by Paul, Hastings,

in the United States has not raised the same sovereignty concerns that it has posed for Canada or Mexico.

Mexico's principal gains under NAFTA were the preservation of its existing, non-conforming foreign investment laws including, in particular, those relating to the key constitutionally-protected areas, such as oil and gas and basic petrochemicals. The concessions made by Mexico in the investment area, both through its acceptance of the general investment principles set forth in the Investment Chapter (Chapter 11) and its related initiative in replacing its highly restrictive Law to Promote Mexican Investment and to Regulate Foreign Investment and Regulations with its new Foreign Investment Law, represent significant new departures.

Canada's original purpose in participating in the NAFTA negotiations had been largely defensive *viz.*: to protect gains achieved in the FTA. There was a concern that if the United States entered into bilateral agreements with countries such as Canada and Mexico, it would effectively establish a "hub and spoke" system favoring it as the central party to each such arrangement and making it the logical situs of investment by companies seeking to participate fully in the benefits of free trade in each market. Although its initial motivation in entering into NAFTA may have been defensive and its appreciation of the potential represented by the 85 million-person Mexican market was slow to develop, Canada's gaining access to the such market through the liberalization of its foreign ownership and trade restrictions is now seen as a bonus. Prior to NAFTA, Mexico was largely closed to Canadian exports and investments. While, under the FTA, Canada had already taken significant steps to liberalize its investment restrictions, the provisions of NAFTA's Investment Chapter go beyond the FTA (e.g., obligating Canada to refrain from imposing performance requirements on foreign investments of another Party).

2. EXISTING CANADIAN, MEXICAN, AND U.S. FOREIGN INVESTMENT LAWS AND POLICIES

It may be helpful to an understanding of the NAFTA provisions bearing on investment (which also include the investor dispute resolution provisions of

Janofsky & Walker (Matthew Bender 1992) at pp. 52-53.

Chapter 11),[8] to provide some general background regarding the foreign investment laws and policies which currently exist in each of the three countries.

2.1   HISTORICAL BACKGROUND

(i) Canada. Canada has a variety of federal and provincial legislation regulating foreign investment or ownership on a sectoral basis, covering such activities as banking and other financial institutions, transportation, publishing, and communications. The general approach taken under such laws is to impose separate individual and aggregate foreign ownership limits (10% and 25%) on companies engaged in these activities. However, the cornerstone legislation is the *Investment Canada Act* ("ICA"), which has general application to foreign investment (primarily acquisitions) in Canada.[9]

The changing investment policies of the Canadian government have from time to time reflected ambivalent public opinion concerning this type of investment. Concerns have been expressed that high levels of foreign investment have contributed to Canada's seeming over-specialization in raw materials extraction. It has also been argued that the prevalence of branch plants has had the result that, as compared with the United States, high level professional and managerial positions are under-represented in the Canadian work force. Concern has also been expressed that foreign direct investment may negatively affect Canada's balance of payments, both because of dividend outflows and by reason of its adverse effect on exports due to inherent restrictions preventing foreign subsidiaries competing with their parent and affiliate companies for export markets. Finally, it is often asserted that the proliferation of wholly-owned foreign subsidiaries has given rise to a shortage of quality public equity investments in Canada's capital market. However, the evidence does not universally support such a negative view of foreign investment. Several studies have shown, for example, that there is little difference between the performance of foreign and domestically-owned Canadian firms.[10]

---

[8]   Neither NAFTA's Investment Chapter nor this paper deals with the subject of investment in the financial service area, which is a subject unto itself and is covered in NAFTA in a separate chapter (Chapter 14).

[9]   *See* note 2 *supra*.

[10]   See Alan M. Rugman and Joseph R. D'Cruz: *New Visions for Canadian Business Strategies for Competing in the Global Economy* (1990) at p. 31 and *Fast Forward: Improving Canada's International Competitiveness* (1991) at p. 31; and Investment Canada Working Paper No. 9 (October 1991) entitled *"International Investment and Competitiveness"* at

Allegations that foreign investment has not always benefited Canada economically are easier to assess objectively than claims that American investment has tended to erode Canadian culture and identity and Canadian political sovereignty and independence. The influence of these latter factors on public policy in Canada should not be underestimated. Public opinion data suggests that Canadians are more concerned with American influence on the "Canadian way of life" than they are with American influence on the Canadian economy *per se*.

While historically Canada has been an extremely hospitable country for American direct investment, the Canadian government has often appeared indecisive on whether further foreign investment and, in particular, American investment, ought to be encouraged. In the 1960s, the political and regulatory climate was relatively welcoming. However, concerns about United States economic influence helped fuel Canadian economic nationalism to the point where, in 1974, a high watermark was reached with the enactment of the Foreign Investment Review Act ("FIRA") and the establishment of its administrative arm, the Foreign Investment Review Agency. That was followed six years later with the National Energy Program, one of the stated objectives of which was to reduce foreign ownership (and, in particular, American ownership) in the oil and gas industry. This nationalist mood waned during the recession years of 1982 and 1983, when the Liberal government streamlined the Agency's screening procedures. The new policy direction continued after the election of the Conservative government in 1984. The government replaced FIRA with the ICA, thereby instituting a narrower review process administered by Investment Canada, and declared the country to be once again "open for business".

Canada was formed in 1867 through a confederation of several British North American colonies having an inward orientation towards investment and trade. Historically, Canada erected trade barriers through high tariffs to achieve its economic goals of protecting existing domestic producers and encouraging foreign parties to invest and establish manufacturing operations in the country. While discouraging imports, particularly from the United States, these tariff barriers fostered foreign investment in Canada in the late 19th century as multinationals established a Canadian presence to secure positions behind the tariff wall.

Prior to the First World War, foreign investment in Canada was primarily sourced from Great Britain, often in the form of loans as opposed to equity

pp. 37-45.

investments. By the late 1920s, the United States had replaced Great Britain as the key source of foreign investment in Canada. American investment in Canada has traditionally been in the form of equity participation in subsidiaries. This sort of U.S. investment has been so significant that concern has frequently been expressed that it has resulted in a "branch plant" economy effectively truncating Canadian industry. From its inception, Canada was the most logical country for American industry to invest in when it was ready to expand internationally. High tariffs, coupled with close geographical proximity and similar consumer tastes, created an investment environment to which American companies could readily adapt. Indeed, many American entities do not consider their Canadian business as part of their "international operations" but, rather, as being within the purview of domestic (U.S.) management.

(ii) Mexico. Concerns respecting the need to protect the integrity of Mexican sovereignty have so dominated the Mexican political and economic agenda that exclusive Mexican government control over the following sectors or activities is entrenched in the Mexican Constitution:

- Petroleum and all hydrocarbons
- Basic petrochemicals
- Electricity
- Nuclear energy and radioactive materials
- Telegraph and radio telegraph services
- Satellite communication
- Railroads
- Mail service
- Money issue and coinage

Under the Law to Promote Mexican Investment and to Regulate Foreign Investment passed in 1973 (and more recently amended in 1989) much of the area remaining open to foreign investment (in addition to those areas exclusively reserved to the Mexican government, there are additional specific areas of investment which are exclusively reserved to Mexican firms not having foreign investors) had been limited to aggregate interests not to exceed 49% (or lower ceiling percentages in some industries such as secondary petrochemicals and auto parts) without the specific authorization of the Commission Nacional de Inversiones (National Commission on Foreign Investment). The fairly rigorous application of such limitations had resulted in extensive joint venturing between foreign and domestic Mexican companies. A significant exception, in respect of which 100% foreign ownership is permitted, was made for the *maquiladora* industries.

In order to boost economic activity and export sales within the country, Mexico has extensively encouraged foreign investment in Mexico under its *maquiladora* programs pursuant to which defined enterprise zones have been established (many of which are located near the U.S. border) in order to service the production requirements of multinational firms. Under these programs, goods and materials have been permitted to enter Mexico on a duty-free basis provided they are further manufactured into products which are later exported out of the country. In the case of U.S. components which are upgraded by assembly or other manufacture in Mexico, only the Mexican value-added element of the product is then subject to duty upon its export to the United States. As well, much of this material qualifies as "U.S.-made" for entry into Canada under the duty reduced and duty-free provisions of the FTA. The *maquiladora* programs, while dominated by U.S. companies, have also attracted firms from other countries such as Japan, Germany, France, Sweden, South Korea, Hong Kong, Taiwan and Canada.[11]

(iii) United States. As previously mentioned, other than for a relatively limited number of strategic activities declared to be "off-limits" to non-Americans, the policy of the United States towards foreign investment has revolved around the application of the "national treatment" principle, an approach which contrasts substantially with that taken both in Canada and Mexico.[12] Indeed, the most significant feature of U.S. policy in the investment area generally has been its frequent complaining to Canada and Mexico, as well as other countries, about the alleged mistreatment of its nationals investing in those countries. In particular, the United States has remonstrated long and hard about the deprivation of its citizens' and companies' rights in respect of Mexican investments. Indeed, the specific dispute resolution provisions contained in Subchapter B of Chapter 11 (which had no direct counterpart in the FTA) were seen by the United States as an imperative in any agreement with Mexico. In this connection, it is to be noted that Mexico's adherence, since the mid-19th

---

[11] *Canada-U.S.-Mexico Free Trade Negotiations: The Rationale and the Investment Dimension* (Investment Canada, December 1990) at pp. 15-16 and 31-33.

[12] See International Investment Policy Statement released by the White House in September 1983 quoted in *The Investment Provisions of the Free Trade Agreement: A United States Perspective* by Steven C. Nelson in a paper prepared for an ABA National Institute on the Canada U.S. Free Trade Agreement held in Washington in January, 1988 entitled "United States/Canada Free Trade Agreement: The Economic and Legal Implications" at pp. 55-56.

Century, to the *Calvo Doctrine* which effectively requires foreign investors to disavow any international legal rights or remedies (including diplomatic protection) they might otherwise assert, as a condition of their being authorized to invest in Mexico, has caused particular irritation to the United States, to say nothing of its investors.[13]

U.S. legislators have generally resisted temptations to enact legislation restrictive of foreign investment activity, notwithstanding concerns from time to time expressed regarding corporate takeovers in the United States by various Japanese, European, Canadian and Australian investors and in spite of the lack of reciprocity in such countries with respect to foreign investment access or national treatment. Now such access and national treatment are being provided as part of the price for a free trade agreement.

2.2   NATIONAL LEGISLATION

(i) Canada. Canada screens foreign acquisitions of control of Canadian businesses over certain monetary thresholds and requires disclosure of all other foreign acquisitions of Canadian businesses and certain new foreign investment under the ICA.[14] The ICA does not apply to portfolio investments. The stated purpose of the ICA is to encourage investment in Canada which contributes to economic growth and employment opportunities and to provide for the review of significant investments in Canada by non-Canadians in order to ensure their net benefit to Canada.[15]

Under the ICA, the requirement for government review and approval of investments by non-Canadians is largely limited to acquisitions by non-Canadians of significant-sized Canadian businesses. Review may also be required for certain smaller business acquisitions and for establishments of new businesses by non-Canadians. In this regard, industries identified as important to Canada's "national identity" or "cultural heritage" are subject to review if the federal Cabinet, on a case-by-case basis, considers such a review to be in the public interest. Where government review is required, the test that must be

---

[13] Steven C. Nelson: *NAFTA Provisions for Settlement of Investment Disputes: A Commentary* (American Conference Institute Program on NAFTA, December 1992) at pp. 7 and 8.

[14] ICA, ss. 14, 14.1 and 15.

[15] ICA, s. 2. In general, a "non-Canadian" means an individual who is neither a Canadian citizen nor a permanent resident of Canada or a corporation that is controlled or deemed to be controlled by one or more non-Canadians.

satisfied is whether the investment will bring a "net benefit to Canada."[16] Even where the ICA does not require review of an investment, non-Canadians must notify the Canadian government of any Canadian business acquisition (falling below the dollar thresholds requiring review) and of any new business establishment which is unrelated to business being carried on in Canada by the non-Canadian person.

The FTA adjusted the thresholds for the ICA review requirements where either the purchaser or the business to be acquired is a U.S. person or is controlled by a U.S. person. For instance, the threshold for review of a direct acquisition by a non-Canadian of a Canadian business is normally triggered if the business has gross assets of $5 million or more, but for direct acquisitions by U.S. companies the threshold for review is $150 million or more in constant 1992 dollars.[17] Such special rules, however, are not applicable to acquisitions of Canadian businesses in any of the following "Sensitive Sectors" for which the normal review thresholds apply:

- production of uranium or ownership of a producing uranium property
- a financial service business
- a transportation service business
- a cultural business[18]

The normal rules applicable to investments by non-Americans (described below) apply to such Sensitive Sector Investments.

The ICA currently delineates three categories of foreign investment: (i) that which is exempt from the notification and review provisions;[19] (ii) that which merely requires notification;[20] and (iii) that which is reviewable.[21]

The ICA exempts from its application a number of specific investments. These include acquisitions by securities dealers in the ordinary course of business and by venture capitalists, acquisitions of Crown corporations and of charities, realizations of security and the acquisition of securities in connection with financing arrangements. Involuntary acquisitions arising in connection with the devolution of an estate or by operation of law are also exempted, as are

---

[16] ICA, ss. 21 to 23 (both inclusive).
[17] ICA, s. 14.1(2) and (3). Currently, this number is $153 million.
[18] ICA, s. 14.1(9).
[19] ICA, s. 10.
[20] ICA, ss. 11 and 12.
[21] ICA, ss. 14 and 15.

farming business acquisitions. Finally, there are exemptions for corporate reorganizations in which the ultimate control of the corporation carrying on the Canadian business does not change. Where applicable, these provisions operate to exempt a non-Canadian making such an investment from both the review and notification provisions of the ICA.

Notification is the procedure initially to be followed for investments by non-Canadians which are not otherwise reviewable under the ICA but which fall in the "national identity, cultural heritage" category[22] (a "NICH Investment"). A NICH Investment otherwise subject only to notification by virtue of being a new business establishment or a business acquisition below the review thresholds may be reviewed if the federal cabinet so determines and provides notice of such determination to the investor within twenty-one days of receipt of such notification. This category is defined to include the publication, distribution or sale of books, magazines, periodicals, newspapers or music in print or machine-readable form, and the production, distribution, sale or exhibition of film or video products or audio or video music recordings. NICH Investments will only be reviewed if the federal cabinet, on the recommendation of the Minister, considers it in the public interest to do so.

The investments in Canada by non-Canadians, *other than non-Sensitive Sector Investments made or controlled by Americans,* which require review and approval under the ICA are as follows:[23]

- The direct acquisition of a Canadian business which has gross assets of $5 million[24] or more;
- The indirect acquisition of a Canadian business which has gross assets of $50 million or more;
- The indirect acquisition of a Canadian business which has gross assets of $5 million or more but less than $50 million, where the Canadian assets acquired represent more than 50 percent of the aggregate gross asset value of all businesses acquired, directly or indirectly, in connection with the transaction; and
- The establishment of a new Canadian business, or the acquisition of a Canadian business the assets of which are below the above-mentioned reviewable acquisition thresholds and which falls within the NICH

---

[22] ICA, s. 11 and Regulations s. 8 and Schedule IV.

[23] ICA, ss. 14 and 15.

[24] Except where otherwise indicated, the dollar figures throughout this paper refer to Canadian dollars.

Investment category, if the federal Cabinet orders a review and so notifies the non-Canadian.

A "direct" acquisition is one which involves the acquiror directly acquiring the shares or other voting interests of the corporation or other entity carrying on the Canadian business or all or substantially all of the assets and property used in carrying on such business. An "indirect" acquisition, by contrast, involves the acquisition of control of a corporation or other entity which controls the corporation or other entity which actually carries on the Canadian business.

Investments (other than Sensitive Sector Investments) *involving the direct or indirect acquisition of control by an American of a Canadian business, or the acquisition of a Canadian business which is controlled by an American,* which require review and approval under the ICA are as follows:[25]

- the direct acquisition of a Canadian business the gross assets of which aggregate $150 million or more in constant 1992 dollars; and
- the indirect acquisition of a Canadian business has been, since January 1, 1992, completely exempt from review where the assets of the Canadian business indirectly acquired represent less than 50 percent of the aggregate gross asset values of all business assets acquired, directly or indirectly, in connection with the transaction; if the Canadian assets represent 50 percent or more of such aggregate asset values, the direct acquisition thresholds apply.

Where an investment is reviewable, the non-Canadian making the investment must file an application in the prescribed form with Investment Canada. In the case of reviewable indirect acquisitions, the application may be filed at any time prior to the implementation of the investment or within thirty days thereafter.

The Minister has forty-five days from the date of receipt by Investment Canada of a completed application to decide whether the investment is likely to be of net benefit to Canada. This forty-five day period may be extended for a further thirty days or such longer period as is agreed upon between the applicant and the Minister.[26] If no notice is sent to the applicant within the forty-five day (or longer) period, the investment is deemed to be approved.

In connection with certain reviewable transactions (typically the larger or more sensitive cases), written undertakings may be required to be given by an

---

[25]   ICA, s. 14.1(1), (2) and (3).
[26]   ICA, s. 22.

applicant in order to satisfy the Minister that the acquisition will be of net benefit to Canada. Such undertakings could relate to matters such as new capital investment, employment, research and development expenditures, reinvestment of earnings, the employment of Canadians and their involvement in management and equity ownership of the business, and exports. More often, however, acquisition proposals are assessed solely on the basis of the applicant's plans for the business proposed to be acquired.

As mentioned above, a reviewable investment by a non-Canadian will be permitted only if the investment is likely to be of "net benefit" to Canada. The following are the factors[27] that, where relevant, are to be taken into account in making this assessment:

- The effect of the investment on the level and nature of economic activity in Canada;
- The degree and significance of participation by Canadians in the Canadian business;
- The effect of the investment on productivity, industrial efficiency, technological development, product innovation and product variety in Canada;
- The effect of the investment on competition within any industry or industries in Canada;
- The compatibility of the investment with national industrial, economic and cultural policies, taking into consideration industrial, economic and cultural policy objectives enunciated by the government or legislature of any province likely to be significantly affected by the investment; and
- The contribution of the investment to Canada's ability to compete in world markets.

These factors may be given different weight in different circumstances and vary according to the nature of the proposal, the industrial sector in which the investment is to occur, the geographic region in which it is to be made and other circumstances which are special to each case.

The ICA is limited in its application to acquisitions of the voting interests of a Canadian business or of all or substantially all of the property used in carrying on such a business.[28] The ICA specifically provides that the acquisition of less than one-third of the outstanding voting shares of a company (whether public or

---

[27] ICA, s. 20.
[28] ICA, s. 28(1).

private) is not considered to constitute the acquisition of control of such a company.[29] However, the acquisition of one-third to one-half of the voting shares of a company is presumed (subject to rebuttal) to constitute the acquisition of control of a Canadian business. In the case of the acquisition of voting interests in non-corporate business entities (partnerships, joint ventures and trusts), the relevant presumptions (which are non-rebuttable) are that control of such entities is acquired when a majority of such voting interests is acquired and that it is not when the acquired voting interests aggregate less than a majority.[30]

The federal government and many of the provinces in Canada have legislation that restricts the number of shares in regulated companies operating in defined areas, such as loan and trust companies, that may be acquired or owned by non-residents. A non-resident is generally defined in terms similar to the definition of a non-Canadian under the ICA. Typical restrictions on foreign ownership limit the number of voting shares that may be held by non-residents to not more than 10 percent by a single non-resident and not more than 25 percent by all non-residents in aggregate. Restrictions on non-resident ownership of shares are found at the federal level in the area of federally chartered financial institutions such as banks, insurance companies and loan and trust companies as well as in connection with institutions involved in culture and communications.

(ii) Mexico. As mentioned above, in conjunction with the coming into force of NAFTA, Mexico has recently completed a major modification of its foreign investment legislation. Under the new Foreign Investment Law there will continue to be foreign ownership restrictions. However, many of the areas which have been "out of bounds" for foreign investors have been opened up under the new law. The new law has been described[31] as "a radical move to attract foreign investment".

Under the new law the governmental approval threshold for an acquisition of more than 49 percent of a Mexican enterprise is set at U.S. $25 million initially and will increase to U.S. $150 million over the first ten years following NAFTA's coming into force. Investment in domestic air transportation, hitherto completely foreclosed to non-Mexicans, is now permitted up to 25 percent,

---

[29]   ICA, s. 28(3)(d).
[30]   ICA, s.28(3)(a) and (b).
[31]   Lourdes Gonzalez/Miguel Badillo: "Mexico Opens the Door to Foreign Investment", at pp. 14-15 of April 19, 1993 issue of *El Financiero Internacional.*

more in line with foreign investment limits in other countries. Foreign ownership restrictions in relation to secondary petrochemicals (previously capped at an aggregate maximum of 40 percent) are being lifted altogether under the new law. Investments by non-Mexicans of up to 49 percent may now be made in respect of basic telephone services, fishing, the manufacture and sale of explosives and fireworks, newspaper publishing, agricultural, livestock or forestry companies, cable television, auto parts, construction, extraction of minerals, oil and gas well drilling, marine transport, air navigation services, private education and legal services.[32] In many of these cases, higher levels of investment may be undertaken if authorized by the National Foreign Investment Commission.[33]

Investments to which foreign investment prohibitions or maximum aggregate foreign investment percentage limits do not apply and which also fall below the above-mentioned monetary thresholds may exceed 49 percent without any requirement at all for governmental approval.[34] Similarly, no authorization by the National Foreign Investment Commission is needed for foreigners seeking to invest in new areas of business or to manufacture new products (except in respect of those activities referred to above to which specific foreign investment prohibitions or limits are applicable).[35]

Finally, the 14 foreign investment approval criteria required to be applied by the National Foreign Investment Commission under the previous legislation have been reduced under the new Foreign Investment Law to only three, namely: (i) the impact of the investment on employment and training; (ii) the contribution of the proposed investment to technology; and (iii) the contribution of the investment towards enhancing the competitiveness of Mexico's productivity.[36]

(iii) United States. As mentioned above, the United States has no general comprehensive legislation restricting, limiting or controlling investments by non-Americans in the United States which is in any way comparable to Canada's ICA or the Foreign Investment Law of Mexico. The principal foreign ownership

---

[32] Foreign Investment Law (Mexico) - Title One, Articles 7 and 8.
[33] Foreign Investment Law (Mexico) - Title One, Articles 8 and 9.
[34] Foreign Investment Law (Mexico) - Title One, Article 10.
[35] Foreign Investment Law (Mexico) - Title Five, Article 23.
[36] Foreign Investment Law (Mexico) - Title Seven, Article 39.

restrictions under U.S. law, outside the financial services area,[37] include the following:

(A)   a license to transfer, manufacture, produce, use or import any facilities that produce or use nuclear materials may not be granted to a foreign party under the Atomic Energy Act;[38]

(B)   Federal Aviation Administration certifications are required in respect of foreign aircraft repair stations performing work on U.S. aircraft; and

(C)   Under the Federal Aviation Act, domestic air services may only be owned or controlled by U.S. citizens (interpreted as limiting aggregate foreign ownership of voting securities to 25 percent).

2.3 THE CANADA-UNITED STATES FREE TRADE AGREEMENT

Under the FTA, which came into force on January 1, 1989 (and effective January 1, 1994 was replaced by NAFTA), Canada and the United States agreed to provide "national treatment" to investors from each other's country in relation to the establishment of new businesses, the acquisition of existing business (subject to certain monetary thresholds discussed above), and the conduct, operation and sale of established businesses.[39]

As an exception to the national treatment principle,[40] each country was entitled to accord investors of the other country different treatment provided that:

-   the difference in treatment is no greater than that necessary for prudential, fiduciary, health and safety, or consumer protection reasons;

-   such different treatment is equivalent in effect to the treatment accorded by the country to its own investors for such reasons; and

-   prior notification of the proposed treatment is given in accordance with the terms of the FTA.

---

[37] For a listing of U.S. foreign ownership restrictions in regard to financial services, see Part A to Annex VII (Schedule of the United States) to NAFTA.

[38] See Annex I Schedule of the United States to NAFTA (Vol. V of September 6, 1992 draft of NAFTA Text).

[39] FTA, Article 1602(1).

[40] FTA, Article 1602(8).

The FTA also provided that the parties were not to impose, as a condition of permitting an investment or regulating a business, requirements to export a certain amount of goods or services, to achieve a certain amount of domestic content, to undertake to give preference to local sourcing, or to effect import substitution on investors from the other country.[41] Additionally, the FTA provided that neither country should impose any of the foregoing performance requirements on an investor from a third country where meeting the requirement could have a significant impact on trade between the two countries.[42]

Under the terms of the FTA, Canada was required to amend the ICA[43] by increasing review thresholds for United States direct and indirect acquisitions and ultimately by eliminating them in the case of indirect acquisitions (this has now in fact occurred). These higher thresholds, which are described above, did not apply to sensitive sector investments. It was also agreed, in the case of certain industries, such as upstream oil and gas and uranium production, that American business acquisitions in those fields would be regulated by published policies to be implemented through the review process under the ICA, provided that such policies were not more restrictive than those in effect on October 4, 1987. As contemplated by the terms of the FTA, Canada and the United States exchanged letters setting out those policies as they apply in the oil and gas and uranium industries. However, as mentioned above, the Canadian policy in respect of the former was unilaterally abrogated by Canada in March, 1992.

The FTA also provides that neither country would adopt policies requiring minimum levels of equity holdings by their nationals in domestic firms controlled by investors from the other country[44] or requiring forced divestiture (subject to exemption of cultural industries).[45]

Neither country was permitted directly or indirectly to nationalize or expropriate an investment in its territory by an investor of the other country except for a public purpose, in accordance with due process of law, on a non-discriminatory basis, and upon payment of prompt, adequate and effective compensation at fair market value.[46] The FTA provided for the free transfer of profits and other remittances subject only to certain exceptions relating to bankruptcy, criminal offences, reports of currency transfers, withholding taxes,

---

[41]   FTA, Article 1603(1).
[42]   FTA, Article 1603(2).
[43]   FTA, Article 1607(3) and Annex 1607.3.
[44]   FTA, Article 1602(2).
[45]   FTA, Article 1602(3).
[46]   FTA, Article 1605.

trading or dealing in securities or ensuring the satisfaction of judgments.[47]

However, the two countries also agreed that all existing laws, regulations and published policies and practices or continuations or renewals not in conformity with any of the obligations under the Investment Chapter of the FTA were to be "grandfathered" (i.e., exempted from the application of the new rules to the extent that they are non-conforming).[48] This included the ICA as amended in its application to American investors as described above.

The dispute resolution mechanism established by the FTA did not apply to a decision made by Canada under the ICA as to whether to permit an acquisition that is subject to review.[49] Each country and its investors retained their respective rights and obligations under customary international law with respect to portfolio and direct investment not covered by the Investment Chapter of the FTA.[50] It was also agreed that the FTA Investment Chapter would not affect the rights and obligations of either party under the GATT or any other international agreement to which both countries were parties.[51] The FTA Investment Chapter also did not apply to any new taxation measure or any subsidy provided that such non-application did not constitute a means or arbitrary or unjustifiable discrimination between investors of the two countries or a disguised restriction on the benefits accorded to investors under the Investment Chapter of the FTA.

Cultural industries were exempted from the FTA in general,[52] including those provisions relating to regulation of foreign investment in Canada. The definition of excluded cultural industries[53] was generally consistent with the existing NICH Investment category under the ICA (although the words below were not contained in the ICA's NICH Investment definition). A "cultural industry" includes an enterprise engaged in any of the following activities:

- the publication, distribution, or sale of books, magazines, periodicals, or newspapers in print or machine readable form but not including the sole activity of printing or typesetting any of the foregoing;
- the production, distribution, sale or exhibition of film or video recordings;

---

[47] FTA, Article 1606.
[48] FTA, Article 1607.
[49] FTA, Article 1608(1).
[50] FTA, Article 1608(2).
[51] FTA, Article 1608(3).
[52] FTA, Article 2005(1).
[53] FTA, Article 2012.

- the production, distribution, sale or exhibition of audio or video music recordings;
- the publication, distribution, or sale of music in print or machine readable form; or
- radio communication in which the transmissions are intended for direct reception by the general public, including all radio, television and cable television broadcasting undertakings and all satellite programming and broadcast network services.

Canada and the United States agreed that each could take measures of "equivalent commercial effect" in response to actions taken by the other under the authority of the exclusion for cultural industries but which would otherwise have been inconsistent with the FTA.[54] This might possibly have included retaliation by the United States under Section 301 of the Trade Act of 1974 which requires the President to take appropriate action against foreign regulations which place an unreasonable burden on United States' commerce.

Canada also undertook, in the event that the divestiture of a United States' controlled business in the cultural industry sector was required, to offer to purchase the business at a fair, open market value as determined by independent assessment.[55]

The United States, while acknowledging Canadian sensitivities to its cultural heritage, reaffirmed the importance it attaches to ensuring that Canadian policies do not constitute discriminatory barriers to United States trade with Canada. In this connection, it reiterated its understanding that, in return for exemption of certain cultural areas from the agreement, Canada's cultural policies are not to impair the benefits the United States would otherwise expect under the FTA.

[54] FTA, Article 2005(2).
[55] FTA, Article 1607(5).

3. GENERAL INVESTMENT PROVISIONS OF NAFTA

3.1 APPLICATION

The provisions of Chapter 11 apply to investments[56] made in one NAFTA country (a "Party") by investors of another such country (including an enterprise formed under the laws of such a country, whoever owns it).[57] Chapter 11 is divided into two subchapters: A, containing general rules concerning investment, and B, which provides a procedure for the resolution of investor disputes. Subchapter B is discussed in Section IV, below.

The term "investment" for the purpose of Chapter 11 is defined comprehensively in Article 1138. This definition essentially embraces virtually all forms of ownership and interest in a business enterprise, including both majority and minority interests, intangible property and contractual investment interests. There is, however, an exception for debt obligations of state enterprises. A further exception states that investment for this purpose does not include claims to money that arise solely from commercial contracts for the sale of goods or services (trade obligations) by a national or enterprise in the territory of one Party to an enterprise in a territory of another Party or the extension of credit in connection with a commercial transaction (trade financing). The provisions of Chapter 11 (Investment) do not apply to financial services to the extent they are covered by Chapter 14 (Financial Services).

---

[56] The term "investment" for the purpose of Chapter 11 is defined comprehensively in Article 1138. This definition essentially embraces all forms of ownership interests in a business enterprise, including both majority and minority interests, controlling and portfolio investments, intangible property, and contractual investment interests.

[57] Article 1139 of NAFTA defines "*investor of a Party*" as "a Party or state enterprise thereof, or a national or an enterprise of such Party, that seeks to make, is making or has made an investment" and further defines "*investment of an investor of a Party*" as an investment owned or controlled directly or indirectly by an investor of such Party". The term "*enterprise of a Party*" is defined in the same Article to mean an enterprise constituted or organized under the laws of a Party and a branch located in the territory of a Party and carrying on business activities there. It is to be noted, in regard to this last definition, that an enterprise of a Party need not be controlled by one or more citizens of that Party, provided it is constituted, organized or located under the laws, or in the territory of such Party. Given that the term "investor of a Party" also comprehends and extends to an "enterprise of a Party", effectively this means that most of the investor protections provided in Chapter 11 will extend to non-NAFTA controlled or owned enterprises that are based in another NAFTA country. However, under Article 1113, a Party may deny the benefits of Chapter 11 to a non-NAFTA controlled/owned enterprise where the non-NAFTA investors who control the enterprises have no substantial business activities in the territory of the Party under whose law it is constituted or organized.

3.2   NATIONAL TREATMENT

Canada, Mexico, and the United States have agreed, under Article 1102 of
NAFTA, to accord "national treatment" to investors from each country in
relation to the establishment, acquisition, expansion, management, conduct,
operation, and sale or other disposition of investments. In other words, each
Party is to accord to investors of another Party treatment no less favorable than
it accords, in like circumstances, to its own investors with respect to such
investments. The same rule extends to the investments of investors of another
Party within the territory of the host country. With respect to a state or
province, such state or province is required to provide treatment no less
favorable to the investor than the most favorable treatment accorded in like
circumstances by that state or province to investors and to investments of
investors of the Party of which it forms a part. As a corollary of the national
treatment principle, paragraph 4 of Article 1102 provides that no Party shall
impose on an investor of another Party a requirement that a minimum level of
equity in an enterprise in the territory of the Party must be held by its nationals,
other than nominal qualifying shares for directors or incorporators of
corporations. In addition, no Party is to require such an investor, by reason of
its nationality, to sell, or otherwise dispose of, any investment in the territory
of the Party.

3.3   MOST-FAVORED-NATION TREATMENT

Article 1103 of NAFTA obligates each Party to accord to investors of each
other Party treatment no less favorable than it accords in like circumstances to
investors of another Party or of any non-Party with respect to the establishment,
acquisition, expansion, management, conduct, operation, or sale or other
disposition of investments. The same principle also extends to the investments
of investors of another Party. The effect of this provision is to ensure that any
more favorable investment rules accorded by one NAFTA country to investors
of third countries are similarly extended to investors of the other NAFTA
countries; thereby ensuring that NAFTA country investors have true most-
favored-nation status.

3.4   Non-Discriminatory Treatment

A third principle (set forth in Article 1104) requires each Party to accord to investors of another Party, and to the investments of investors of another Party, the better of national treatment and most-favored-nation treatment which, for the purposes of NAFTA, is defined as "non-discriminatory treatment".

3.5   Treatment in Accordance with International Law

Article 1105 requires each Party to accord investments of investors of another Party treatment in accordance with international law, including fair and equitable treatment and full protection and security. This Article effectively gives the Parties a further means of enforcing international law principles under the aegis of NAFTA.

3.6   Performance Requirements

In common with the approach taken in the FTA, NAFTA contains provisions in Article 1106 prohibiting the imposition of significant trade-distorting performance requirements by a NAFTA country in connection with any investments in its territory. The prohibited performance requirements include those relating to export levels, domestic content, local sourcing, trade-balancing, technology transfers, and product mandating.

The restrictions relating to performance requirements which tie the volume or value of imports into, or sales within, a territory to the volume or value of exports from the host country or to its foreign exchange earnings, as well as provisions relating to technology transfers and product mandating, represent additions in NAFTA over and above what was contained in the FTA. Such additions are understood to reflect concerns about the application of such practices in Mexico and, in particular, in regard to requirements relating to its *maquiladora* programs. At the same time, Canada has, from time to time under the ICA and its predecessor, FIRA, influenced foreign investors to provide undertakings in regard to product mandates (another performance requirement now prohibited under NAFTA). Canada was successfully challenged (by the United States) under GATT for its insistence upon foreign investors providing undertakings to give preference to local Canadian sources for goods and services.

Article 1106 of NAFTA *prohibits the enforcement* of any commitment or undertaking to such effect, as well as the *imposition* of such commitments or undertakings. Even though the basic structure of the ICA is preserved under NAFTA, it would appear that, once NAFTA becomes effective, Investment Canada will be unable to *enforce* any undertaking or commitment of the type described in Article 1106. However, there is an exception to this general prohibition. Clause 12 of that part of Annex I which reserves the non-conforming aspects of the ICA states that Article 1106 (Prohibition on Performance Requirements) shall not apply to any such requirement, commitment or undertaking enforced, in connection with a review under the ICA, to locate production, carry out research and development, employ or train workers, or construct or expand particular facilities in Canada.

In keeping with the same principles, Article 1106(3) prohibits a Party from conditioning the receipt or continued receipt of an advantage by investors of a Party or the investors' compliance with performance requirements concerning preferential sourcing of goods, minimum domestic content levels, or trade-balancing.

3.7   SENIOR MANAGEMENT AND BOARDS OF DIRECTORS

Article 1107 forbids a Party requiring that an enterprise of another Party appoint individuals of any particular nationality to senior management positions in that enterprise's investment in the country. However, a NAFTA Party may require that a majority of the board of directors, or of any committee of the board of such an enterprise, must be of a particular nationality or resident in the territory of the Party, so long as that requirement does not materially impair the ability of the investor to exercise control over its investment.

3.8   RESERVATIONS AND EXCEPTIONS

Article 1108 provides that the principles of Articles 1102 (National Treatment), 1103 (Most-Favored-Nation Treatment), 1106 (Performance Requirements) and 1107 (Senior Management and Board of Directors) do not apply to any existing non-conforming measure that is maintained by a Party at the federal level, as described in Annexes I and III. They similarly do not apply to any such measures of any state or province, provided that, after two years from the date that NAFTA becomes effective, only those measures of a state or province which are identified in a schedule to Annex I will continue to be exempted. However, all non-conforming measures of a local government are exempted without any requirement for their publication in such an annex.

The approach of requiring all existing non-conforming legislation ("measures") which are to be protected from the application of the Chapter's investment rules to be specifically reserved in an Annex to NAFTA represents a significant departure from the FTA which essentially grandfathered all such non-conforming measures. This technique also has the merit of giving some publicity to these non-conforming and reserved measures.

One measure which is prominently reserved on Canada's Annex I is the ICA and while the benefit of its special NAFTA Party provisions extend to "investors of a Party", clause 9 of that portion of the Annex which reserves the ICA specifically states that notwithstanding the definition of "investor of a Party" in Article 1139 (which would otherwise include non-NAFTA controlled investors who are only incorporated or organized in a NAFTA country), "only investors who are nationals or entities controlled by nationals as provided for in the ICA, of Mexico or of the United States may benefit from the higher review threshold" stipulated in respect of business acquisitions involving a NAFTA investor.

Annex I explicitly acknowledges that when selling or disposing of an equity interest in, or the assets of, an existing state enterprise or an existing governmental entity (such as in a privatization), Canada and each province has the right to impose limitations on the ownership of such interests or assets and on the ability of owners of such interests or assets to control any resulting enterprise, by investors of another Party or non-Party or their investments. In addition, Canada and each province will continue to have the right to adopt or maintain any measure relating to the nationality of senior management or members of the board of directors. These provisions are specific qualifications on the application of the national treatment (Article 1102) and senior management and board of directors (Article 1107) provisions of NAFTA.

Non-conforming legislation which is included in the Annex I reservation list can never be made more restrictive and if liberalized to a less restrictive state may not thereafter retreat to a more restricted state. This is in contrast to Annex II reservations in respect of which each Party has the right to increase its restrictions at any time.

Canada has also reserved its right to abridge the national treatment and most-favored-nation treatment principles in regard to non-resident ownership of uranium mining properties (which is limited to 9% at the first stage of production). Similarly, Mexico's new Foreign Investment Law, is also exempted from the application of most of these provisions.

The national treatment, most-favored-nation treatment, and senior management principles are expressly stated not to be applicable to government procurement of goods and services or subsidies and grants provided by a Party, including government-supported loans, guarantees, and insurance (Article 1108(8)). Chapter 10 (Government Procurement) specifically deals with these subjects.

The prohibitions on performance requirements are also inapplicable to:

- qualification requirements for goods or services with respect to export promotion and foreign aid programs;
- the procurement of goods and services by a Party or a state enterprise of that Party; and
- the requirements imposed by an importing Party related to the content of goods necessary to qualify for preferential tariffs or preferential quotas (Article 1108(9)).

3.9   SOCIAL SERVICES

Article 1101(4) and Annex II to the Investment Chapter expressly permit NAFTA Parties themselves to provide services and perform functions such as:

- law enforcement
- correctional services
- income security or insurance
- social security or insurance
- social welfare
- public education
- public training
- health
- child care

provided that this is done in a manner which is not inconsistent with Chapter 11.

3.10 TRANSFERS

Article 1109 obligates each Party to permit transfers and international payments relating to an investment of an investor of another Party in the territory of the first mentioned Party to be made freely and without delay. Such transfers include:

- profits, dividends, interest, capital gains, royalty payments, management fees, technical assistance and other fees, returns in kind, and other amounts derived from the investment;
- proceeds from the sale of all or any part of the investment or from the partial or complete liquidation of the investment;
- payments made under a contract entered into by the investor or its investment, including payments made pursuant to a loan agreement; and
- expropriation payments and awards made pursuant to dispute resolutions effected pursuant to Subchapter B of Chapter 11.

These provisions effectively prevent a NAFTA Party from taking steps to block the transfer of funds out of the country. In addition, NAFTA investors will be able to convert local currency into foreign currency at prevailing rates of exchange for any such transfers. Each NAFTA country is responsible to ensure that such foreign currency may be freely transferred. This will enhance the security of investments by other NAFTA Party investors in NAFTA countries, as they will be assured that, even if their investment is expropriated, the compensation paid for such forcible taking will not be tied up in a blocked currency.

There is also a provision (Article 1109(3)) preventing any Party from requiring its investors to transfer, or from penalizing its investors who fail to transfer, the income earnings, profits, or other amounts derived from, or attributable to, an investment in the territory of another Party. In the early 1970s, when the United States was experiencing a critically adverse balance of payments situation, that country sought to compel repatriation to the United States of foreign earnings of controlled American subsidiaries located abroad. Article 1109(3) would effectively prevent any such requirement.

An exception to the foregoing principles is provided in Article 1109(4) which provides that, notwithstanding such principles, a Party may prevent a transfer through the equitable, non-discriminatory and good faith application of its laws relating to: (a) bankruptcy, insolvency or the protection of the rights of creditors, (b) issuing, trading or dealing in securities, (c) criminal or penal offences, (d) reports of transfers of currency or other monetary instruments; or (e) ensuring the satisfaction of judgments in adjudicatory proceedings.

3.11 SPECIAL FORMALITIES AND INFORMATION REQUIREMENTS

Article 1111(1) sets forth a further exception to the national treatment principle which permits a NAFTA host country to impose a requirement on investors of other NAFTA countries that they must be residents of the host country and that investments made by such investors must be legally constituted under the laws of the host country (e.g., be held in a locally-incorporated corporation), "provided that such formalities do not impair the substance of the benefits of any of the provisions" of Chapter 11. In addition, the Parties are expressly permitted to require, from an investor of another Party or its investment, routine business information to be used solely for informational or statistical purposes concerning that investment (Article 1111(2)).

3.12 EXPROPRIATION AND COMPENSATION

Under Article 1110, no NAFTA Party may nationalize or expropriate an investment of an investor of another Party in its territory, directly or indirectly, except for a public purpose, on a non-discriminatory basis, in accordance with due process of law and international law and upon payment of compensation. Compensation is to be equivalent to the fair market value of the expropriated investment immediately prior to the expropriation, without reflecting changes in value occurring as a result of the expropriation. Valuation criteria are to include going concern value, asset value, and other criteria as appropriate to determine fair market value. Article 1110 stipulates that compensation is to be paid without delay and shall be fully realizable. Interest on the amount of compensation is to be paid at a commercially reasonable rate for the currency in which it is paid and is to be calculated from the date of expropriation until the date of payment. Upon payment, compensation is to be freely transferable, as stipulated in Article 1109.

3.13   ENVIRONMENTAL MEASURES

Article 1114 states that nothing in Chapter 11 is to be construed as preventing a Party from adopting, maintaining, or enforcing any measure that it considers appropriate to ensure that investment activity in its territory is undertaken in a manner sensitive to environmental concerns. In addition, the Parties recognize that it is inappropriate to encourage investment by relaxing domestic health, safety, or environmental measures (e.g., by becoming a pollution haven to attract investment). In this connection, the Parties have agreed to consult with one another if one of them considers that another may have offered such encouragement.

In August 1993, the Parties entered into a side agreement entitled "North American Agreement on Environmental Cooperation".[58] This agreement requires each Party effectively to enforce its environmental law through appropriate government actions. The agreement provides a mechanism for the resolution of disputes concerning environmental law compliance. A trinational council is authorized to require consultations in an effort to resolve such disputes. If, however, the Council is unable to resolve such dispute due to a Party's persistent failure effectively to enforce an environmental law in certain circumstances, any Party may request the establishment of an arbitral panel. If such a panel is established and determines that a Party has engaged in a persistent pattern of failure to effectively enforce its environmental law and no mutually satisfactory action plan to remedy is agreed upon, the panel may establish its own action plan and may also make a determination on the imposition of monetary enforcement assessments on the offending Party. In the case of Canada, enforcement of such assessment and action plan is limited to recourse to the Canadian courts, while in the case of Mexico and the United States, the complaining Party may suspend NAFTA benefits, which may involve the imposition of duties based on the amount of the assessment.

---

[58] North American Agreement on Environmental Cooperation, August, 1993, Government of Canada: Background Information (Press Release, Ministerial Statements, Trilateral Summaries, Highlights of the Labor and Environmental Agreements).

3.14   OTHER EXEMPTED MATTERS

(i) Cultural Industries. By virtue of Article 2106 and Annex 2106, Canada preserves, under NAFTA, the same exemption for cultural industries[59] that is provided under the FTA. As in the FTA, each NAFTA country reserves the rights to take measures of equivalent commercial effect in response to any action regarding cultural industries which would have been a violation of NAFTA but for the cultural industries exemption. These compensatory measures will not be limited by obligations imposed by NAFTA.

(ii) National Security. Under Article 2102, NAFTA does not limit a Party's ability to take actions which it considers necessary for the protection of its essential security interests:

- relating to the traffic in arms, ammunition, and implements of war and to such traffic and transactions in other goods, materials, services, and technology undertaken directly or indirectly for the purposes of supplying a military or other security establishment;
- taken in the time of war or other emergency in international relations; or
- relating to the implementation of national policies or international agreements respecting the non-proliferation of nuclear weapons or other nuclear explosive devices.

(iii) Annex II Exemptions. Annex II to Chapter 11 contains specific exemptions from the national treatment (Article 1102), most-favored-nation treatment (Article 1103), performance requirements (Article 1106), and nationality requirements for senior management or members of boards of directors (Article 1107) for a number of specific industrial sectors. These include aboriginal affairs, social services, communications, government finance (securities), minority affairs, and air and water transportation. There are also reservations in Canada's Annex II listings in respect of communications and air and water transportation.

With regard to communications, in addition to a number of other existing

---

[59] Cultural industries are defined as the publication, distribution, or sale of books, magazines, periodicals, or newspapers; the production, distribution, sale, or exhibition of films or video recordings or audio music recordings; the publication, distribution, or sale of music; and radio communication in which transmissions are intended for direct reception by the general public, any radio, television, or cable television broadcasting undertakings or any satellite program and broadcast network services.

measures detailed in Annex II, Canada reserves the right to adopt or maintain any measure relating to investment in telecommunications transport networks and telecommunications transport services, radiocommunication and submarine cables, including ownership restrictions and measures concerning corporate officers and directors and place of incorporation. With reference to air transportation, in other specific existing measures detailed in the Annex, Canada reserves the right to adopt or maintain any measures that restrict the acquisition or establishment of an investment in Canada for the provision of specialty air services to a Canadian national or to a corporation incorporated and having its principal place of business in Canada, its chief executive officer and not fewer than two-thirds of its directors as Canadian nationals and not less than 75 percent of its voting interests owned and controled by persons otherwise meeting these requirements. In regard to water transportation, in addition to a number of specific items of existing legislation detailed in Annex II, Canada has reserved the right to adopt or maintain any measure relating to the investment in or provision of maritime coastal services.

Mexico's Annex II reservations from the national treatment, most-favored-nation and/or senior management principles relate to such matters as:

- the ownership of bonds, treasury bills or other securities of various Mexican federal, state and local governments
- measures relating to investment in or provision of broadcasting
- investments in or the provision of air traffic control and other telecommunication services relating to air navigation
- telecommunications transport and telecommunications transport services
- legal services
- public law enforcement and correctional services and other social services for a public purpose.

United States' Annex II reservations include the following:

- cable television (reciprocity basis)
- telecommunications transport networks, telecommunications transport services and radio communications
- public law enforcement and correctional services and other social services provided for a public purpose
- provisions providing rights or preferences to socially or economically disadvantaged minorities
- legal services

- daily newspapers (reciprocity basis)
- monitor transportation services

In regard to all measures covered in Annex II reservations, unlike those reserved under Annex I, they may be made more restrictive at any time.

4. INVESTOR DISPUTE RESOLUTION

4.1 GENERAL

Subchapter B of Chapter 11 (Investment) sets out a comprehensive code for the resolution of investment disputes involving a breach or an alleged breach of NAFTA (Subchapter A) investment rules by a NAFTA country. A NAFTA investor may either seek monetary damages through binding investor-state arbitration or remedies that are available in the domestic courts of the host country.

The FTA contained very few provisions which dealt with investor disputes. Under the FTA a number of existing rights are preserved (i.e., exempted) as for example Canadian decisions under the ICA, existing rights under customary international law with respect to portfolio and direct investment and rights and obligations of either Canada or the U.S. under GATT or any other international agreement. However, the FTA contained no provisions specifically enabling investors to require the resolution of investment disputes with a host country directly. This situation is remedied in NAFTA by the investor dispute resolution provisions contained in Subchapter B of Chapter 11.

4.2 CHOICE OF ARBITRATION OPTIONS

Subchapter B establishes a mechanism to settle investment disputes that assures due process before an impartial tribunal. An investor of a Party has an option either to resolve a claim against a Party for breach of any of the provisions of Subchapter A before the tribunals of the Party where the investment was made, or to submit the claim to arbitration.[60] Three arbitration options are provided: ICSID (International Centre for Settlement of Investment Disputes Convention)

---

[60] NAFTA, Article 1120(1).

arbitration (if the two countries involved are parties to ICSID); the Additional Facility Rules of ICSID (if one country is not a party); or arbitration under the rules of the United National Commission on International Trade Law ("UNCITRAL Arbitration Rules"). Accordingly, the NAFTA investor dispute resolution mechanism does not involve the establishment of a new arbitral process but instead permits investors to seek arbitration for violations of NAFTA investment rules under three existing international arbitration procedures. Currently, only the United States is a signatory to the ICSID Convention. Consequently, the option of arbitration pursuant to that convention will only become available if another Party signs it. However, the Additional Facility Rules of ICSID are intended to deal with investment disputes where one of the parties is not a member of the Convention, but another is. The UNCITRAL Arbitration Rules are rules which international parties can and frequently do choose to have govern disputes arising out of international contracts.

The Subchapter B provisions overcome problems which have been encountered in connection with foreign investment disputes. Generally speaking, international rights are recognized as between states and, where international law is violated with reference to an individual investor from a state, it is the nation not the individual investor that has the right to assert a claim in regard to the injury sustained. Heretofore, individual investors, in dealing with a foreign state, have been constrained in their ability to seek relief directly. Instead, such investors have had to enlist the assistance of their own governmental authorities to present their claims against the foreign state. Moreover, a further obstacle has been that international law requires that a private party must first have exhausted the remedies available to it under the laws of the host state before presenting its claim through the diplomatic channels of its own state. In the case of Mexico, the problem was further exacerbated by the *Calvo Doctrine*, under which foreign concessionaires and investors have routinely been required, as a condition of receiving concessions or being allowed to proceed with investments, to renounce all remedies other than those provided by the domestic law of Mexico, and to waive any right of diplomatic protection of their own government.

The NAFTA investor dispute provisions represent a significant reform in that the process may now be initiated by the investor, without the cooperation or any involvement of its own government, using existing legal procedures for the resolution of international commercial disputes.

4.3 ELIGIBILITY REQUIREMENTS AND PRECONDITIONS TO RECOURSE TO INVESTOR DISPUTE RESOLUTION PROCEDURES

Under Article 1116 of NAFTA, an "investor of a Party" may submit for arbitration under Subchapter B a claim that another Party has breached a provision of Subchapter A and that the investor has incurred loss or damage by reason of, or arising out of, that breach. For this purpose, "investor of a Party" is defined in terms of a national of that Party, as well as the Party itself, and any state enterprise of that Party when it acts as an investor. In addition, Article 1117 provides that "an investor of a Party" may also submit a claim to arbitration on behalf of an enterprise of another Party that is a juridical person that the investor owns or controls, directly or indirectly, alleging that the enterprise has incurred loss or damage by reason of, or arising out of, that breach. The importance of this provision is that it permits the investor to assert a claim in regard to an injury caused to an entity in which the investor is a shareholder or creditor, where the only injury has been sustained by the entity and the investor has himself not been independently or directly injured. Article 1174(4) provides that an investment itself may not make a claim under the investor dispute resolution provisions of NAFTA (i.e., it must be the investor making the claim on behalf of the investment enterprise).

There is also a timeliness requirement for such claims to be asserted. Article 1116(2) prohibits such claims if more than three years have elapsed from the date on which the investor knew, or should have known, of the alleged breach and resulting damage. A similar limitation applies to claims made on behalf of an enterprise. While it is no longer necessary for a claimant to exhaust all of its possible remedies under the local law, Article 1118 provides that the disputing parties should first attempt to settle a claim through consultation or negotiation prior to resorting to arbitration. Article 1119 provides for the disputing party to serve written notice of its intention to submit a claim to arbitration not less than 90 days prior to its submission. Details of the claim, including the name and address of the disputing investor, the provisions of the Agreement alleged to have been breached, the issues and factual basis for the claim and relief sought, and the approximate amount of the damages claimed, are to be set forth in the notice given. Article 1120 stipulates that a minimum of six months must have elapsed since the events giving rise to the claim, before the disputing investor may submit the claim to arbitration.

Article 1121(1)(a) requires a disputing investor to consent to arbitration and waive its rights to initiate or continue the dispute in another forum, except in the case of proceedings for injunctive declaratory or other extraordinary relief not involving the payment of damages.

In a provision unique to Mexico, it has declared in Annex 1120.1 that an investor may not allege that Mexico has breached the Investment Chapter both in an arbitration under Subchapter B and in proceedings before a Mexican court or administrative tribunal. The same is true where an enterprise of Mexico, that is a juridical person owned or controlled by the investor of another Party, makes similar allegations in a Mexican court or Tribunal. In such a case, the investor may not allege the same breach in arbitration under Subchapter B. This has been referred to as a vestige of the *Calvo Doctrine*.[61]

The Subchapter B provisions effectively apply to all industries except for the financial service industry, the procedures and protection for which are governed by Chapter 14. The investment dispute resolution procedures of Subchapter B, however, do not cover disputes that an investor from one NAFTA country may have with private parties in the country in which it invests. Those types of disputes are still required to be resolved before the courts or tribunals agreed upon by the private parties, or which would otherwise have jurisdiction over the dispute.

4.4   ARBITRATION PROCEDURES

Under Article 1123, unless the disputing parties otherwise agree, the arbitration tribunal is to consist of three arbitrators, one to be appointed by each of the disputing parties, and the third to preside over the arbitration, appointed by agreement of the disputing parties. If a Party fails to appoint an arbitrator or the disputing parties are unable to agree upon the presiding arbitrator, the Secretary General of ICSID shall make the necessary appointment from a list of 45 presiding arbitrators agreed upon among the parties on the date NAFTA comes into force (Article 1124). Neither NAFTA nor any of the arbitration procedures which may be elected pursuant to Chapter 11 stipulates that arbitrators must be nationals of the disputing parties. The same is true with regard to persons which may be appointed presiding arbitrators by the Secretary General.

---

[61] Steven C. Nelson: *NAFTA Provisions for Settlement of Investment Disputes: A Commentary*, American Conference Institute Program on NAFTA, December 1992, at p. 13.

4.5   FINALITY AND ENFORCEMENT OF AWARDS

NAFTA Article 1135(1) provides that an award made by a tribunal under Subchapter B is binding on the disputing parties, but otherwise does not have any precedential effect (i.e., beyond the parties to, and limited to the specific facts of, that proceeding). Under Article 1135(5), each Party undertakes to provide for enforcement of the award in its territory. Should a Party fail to abide by, or comply with, the terms of the final award, a Chapter 20 panel may be established. This panel may be requested to determine that the other Party's failure to abide by the terms of the final award is inconsistent with obligations under NAFTA and to recommend that the defaulting Party abide by the terms of the final award. In addition, the disputing investor may seek enforcement of an arbitration award under the ICSID Convention, the United States Convention on the Recognition and Enforcement of Foreign Arbitral Awards (known as the "New York Convention") or the Inter-American Convention.

Chapter 11 says nothing about challenges to investor panel decisions. Since the arbitrations are governed by provisions or the arbitral regimes which may be elected by the Parties, the rules of those regimes would control in this regard. While ICSID Convention procedures have generally admitted such challenges on a fairly routine basis, since only the United States is currently a party to that Convention, this is somewhat academic at the present time. By contrast, the UNCITRAL arbitration rules do not provide for challenges to awards, although they have procedures for interpretations of awards and corrections to awards because of clerical, arithmetic, or similar errors in supplementary decisions. The ICSID Additional Facility is similar in this regard.

4.6   EXCEPTION FOR DISAPPROVED ACQUISITIONS

Article 1137 specifically excludes from the application of this Subchapter the decision by a Party to prohibit or restrict the acquisition of an investment in its territory by an investor of another Party. Thus, the foreign investment screening processes of Canada's ICA and Mexico's Foreign Investment Law are exempted from review or challenge under these provisions. This is supplemented by Annex 1137.2, which specifically states that a decision by Canada, following a review under the ICA, or by the National Commission on Foreign Investment, following a review under the Foreign Investment Law of Mexico, with respect to whether or not to permit an acquisition that is subject to review cannot be subject to the dispute settlement provisions of Subchapter B or of Chapter 20.

5. CONCLUSION

Although NAFTA's Investment Chapter represents a practical compromise of the frequently conflicting attitudes of the Parties toward the appropriate treatment of foreign investment, it clearly is having the effect of liberalizing the more restrictive laws and policies of Mexico and Canada in this area. There is increasing recognition that greater openness towards foreign investment is not only a necessary complement to free trade, but an independently desirable objective in an increasingly internationalized world.

THE TRANSFORMATION OF THE MAQUILADORA UNDER THE NORTH AMERICAN FREE TRADE AGREEMENT

by Preston Brown and Carolyn Karr[*]

1. INTRODUCTION

1.1 HISTORY OF THE MAQUILADORA

In the early 1960s, the region along Mexico's border with the United States suffered from high unemployment and a virtual absence of industrial development. In 1965, the Government of Mexico introduced the Border Industrialization Program[1] ("BIP") to address those concerns. BIP was intended to fulfill three goals: (i) to promote border industrialization--even if that meant

[*]   Preston Brown (A.B. and LL.B., Harvard University) is a partner in the Washington, D.C., office of Curtis, Mallet-Prevost, Colt & Mosle. Carolyn Karr (B.A., University of California Los Angeles, J.D., Stanford Law School), formerly an associate at Curtis, Mallet-Prevost, is an attorney with the U.S. Agency for International Development (AID) in Washington, D.C. Ms. Karr's writing illustrates her personal views and not that of AID. The authors would like to acknowledge the invaluable information and insight provided by: Antonio Prida and Jose Alberto Tamayo of Curtis, Mallet-Prevost's Mexico City Office; Marco Blanco, Harold Ullman and Michaela Vrouwenvelder of the Firm's New York Office (who contributed to the tax section of this chapter); Eugenio Salinas and Brian Elwood Salido of the Embassy of Mexico Trade Office in Washington, D.C.; Robin Ritterhoff and William Barreda of the U.S. Department of the Treasury, Washington, D.C.; and Gerardo Traslosheros and Gabriela Hernandez of the Mexican Secretariat of Commerce and Industrial Development ("SECOFI"). In addition, the authors would like to acknowledge their special indebtedness to Manuel Pacheco of SECOFI for his analysis, comments and assistance.

[1]   U.S. General Accounting Office, *The Maquiladora Industry and U.S. Employment* 1 (July 1993). GAO/GGD-93-129. The Maquiladora Program was later expanded to encompass Mexico's interior regions.

37

permitting foreign investment (which at that time was widely condemned), (ii) to stimulate Mexican industry by providing it with a market--in the form of foreign-owned assembly plants--for commodities and components and (iii) to lower the rate of unemployment along the border.[2]

The maquiladora program (the "Maquiladora Program"), a program to encourage production of articles with foreign source components for export, formally began in 1965 as part of BIP. In fact, however, it had originated before that time in private arrangements that enabled United States manufacturers to conduct assembly operations in Mexico using industrial plants built by Mexican landowners. The practice gained Mexico's official endorsement when, in 1964, the United States canceled its Bracero Program (which had permitted Mexican workers to perform seasonal farm work in the United States) and the Mexican government turned to the Maquiladora Program as a means of combatting the rise in the already high level of unemployment it anticipated in the Bracero Program's aftermath.[3]

The Maquiladora Program was originally designed to promote industrialization in the border region, to create sources of employment and to attract new technology in the hope that it could be integrated into Mexico's industrial base.[4] Other objectives included expanding the tax base and increasing foreign currency reserves.[5]

The Maquiladora Program is essentially a form of duty-drawback program established by the Government of Mexico. As a general matter, a "duty-drawback" program provides for the repayment of import duties on goods or materials used in the production or manufacturing of articles upon the

[2]   Ellwyn R. Stoddard, *Maquila: Assembly Plants in Northern Mexico* 17 (1987).

[3]   M. Angeles Villareal, *Mexico's Maquiladora Industry, Mexico Trade and Law Reporter* 1 (April 1, 1992). (Asian countries were already conducting assembly and processing work for United States companies at the time.) Bracero workers often moved their families from their homes in Mexico's interior regions to the area along the the the U.S. border to make possible more frequent yet less expensive visits. The settlement of these families in the border area exacerbated housing shortages and the scarcity of municipal services in the border towns. *Production Sharing: U.S. Imports Under Harmonized Tariff Schedule Provisions 9802.00.60 and 9802.00.80, 1989-1992*, USITC Publication 2729, at 4-1 (February 1994).

[4]   Cheryl Schechter & David Brill, Jr., *Maquiladoras: Will the Program Continue?*, 23 *St. Mary's L.J.* 697, 700 (1992).

[5]   *Id.* The maquiladora industry has in fact provided Mexico with a major source of foreign exchange, especially during the past decade. In 1992, it generated more foreign currency than tourism. Indeed, the maquiladora industry ranked second only to the petroleum industry during that year. U.S. International Trade Commission, USITC Publication 2729, *supra* note 4, at 3-1.

subsequent exportation of those articles.[6] The word "maquila" refers to an assembly or production process that uses large numbers of semiskilled or unskilled workers to perform machine or manual operations.[7] The setting in which this process occurs is the "maquiladora."[8] In Mexico today, the word "maquiladora" has come to mean a foreign-owned or -controlled plant located in Mexico that imports foreign components, assembles, services or processes them, and then exports finished goods. From a technical standpoint, a maquiladora may be legally defined as a Mexican company that performs such operations under a maquila working program[9] (a "Maquiladora Working Program") approved by the Mexican Secretariat of Commerce and Industrial Development ("SECOFI"). Any product may be assembled, packaged, processed, sorted, transformed or rebuilt; there are no restrictions on what may be produced in a maquiladora, other than on firearms and radioactive materials.[10]

A maquiladora may also import equipment and ancillary items to Mexico free of duty provided that they are re-exported in the event the maquiladora ceases operations. Because the maquiladora operation relies upon temporary importation into Mexico of such items as raw and intermediate materials, production machinery and equipment, including spare parts and auxiliary equipment such as safety and pollution control devices, telecommunications and computer equipment, packaging materials and storage and transportation equipment, the processing of these items at the border prior to the passage of the North American Free Trade Agreement ("NAFTA") has been governed by special customs regulations.[11] While a bond or similar collateral was once required at the border to guarantee the subsequent export of the temporarily imported goods, this practice was abolished. Instead, a maquiladora has been

---

[6]   Ruth F. Sturm, 1 *Customs Law & Administration* § 17.1 (3rd ed., 1993).

[7]   The word "maquila" is derived from the verb "maquilar," which means to grind corn. Historically, corn growers would take their crop to a "maquiladora," who would grind the corn in exchange for a portion of it. Interview with Eugenio Salinas, Counsellor, Embassy of Mexico Trade Office, Washington, D.C., February 10, 1994.

[8]   Stoddard, *supra* note 3, at 1.

[9]   "Programa de Maquila."

[10]   Gonzalez Baz, *Manufacturing in Mexico [Under] The Mexican In-Bond (Maquila) Program: The Most Commonly Asked Questions* (guide issued by the Trade Commission of Mexico).

[11]   *See* Article 78 of the Customs Law (Ley Aduanera).

allowed to provide a "guaranty letter"[12] stating that it will re-export the imported items or pay the applicable duties upon them.[13]

Maquiladoras were at one time subject to stringent exchange controls, but these were eliminated in 1991.[14] Similarly, the condition that a maquiladora maintain a balanced foreign currency account, which had been retained until the passage of NAFTA--will now of course be eliminated as well.

This chapter traces the origins and features of the Maquiladora Program before NAFTA and explores the changes in Mexico's regulation of maquiladoras as a result of NAFTA.

1.2   STRUCTURE OF THE MAQUILADORA

There are three means typically used to structure a maquiladora: the subsidiary maquiladora, or the establishment of a controlled subsidiary; the subcontracting arrangement, or the subcontracting out of all or part of the maquiladora operation; and the "shelter" operation, or the foreign-controlled, but not foreign-owned, entity that conducts the maquiladora operation in accordance with the direction of the foreign company. The subsidiary was the first, and remains the most common, structure used.

In a subsidiary maquiladora operation, the foreign company establishing the operation owns all or a majority of the shares of a Mexican company, typically

---

[12]   This provision is not codified; it is merely customary. Telephone interview with Manuel Pacheco of SECOFI. March 30, 1994.

[13]   Goods produced in a maquiladora using United States components have also enjoyed certain advantages pursuant to the "production-sharing" provisions of the Harmonized Tariff Schedule of the United States ("HTS"). Harmonized Tariff Schedule of the United States (1992), USITC Publication 2449. Under HTS provision 9802.00.80 articles assembled abroad in whole or in part of fabricated components, the product of the United States, which were exported in condition ready for assembly without further fabrication, retain their physical identity and whose value has not been enhanced except by being assembled and except by operations incidental to the assembly process are generally subject to "[a] duty upon the full value of the imported article, less the cost or value of such products of the United States." Similarly, HTS provision 9802.00.60 provides that certain metal products initially manufactured or processed in the United States, then exported for further processing abroad and then returned to the United States for still further processing are subject upon their re-entry to the United States to duty only on the value added by the foreign processing. *See* U.S. International Trade Commission ("USITC"), *Production Sharing: U.S. Imports Under Harmonized Tariff Schedule Subheadings 9802.00.60 and 9802.00.80, 1988-1991*, USITC Publication 2592, at 1 (February 1993).

[14]   Decreto por el Que se Abroga el Decreto de Control de Cambios, *Diario Oficial* (hereinafter *D.O.*), November 10, 1991.

structured in the case of a maquiladora as a "sociedad anonima." Under Mexican law, this kind of entity must have: a minimum of two shareholders, each of whom must subscribe to at least one share; minimum capital stock of 50,000 New Pesos (which must be fully subscribed); and may be of fixed or variable capital and managed either by a sole administrator or a board of directors. All of the entity's shares must be of the same value.

The subcontracting arrangement consists of a Mexican-owned operation to which a maquiladora delegates either elements of or the entire production process. The subcontractor may also export the finished goods on behalf of the maquiladora at the parties' option.

In a shelter operation, a foreign company enters into a contract with a shelter operator, which may be the Mexican subsidiary of a foreign company or a Mexican entity.[15] Pursuant to the shelter contract, the shelter operator provides the foreign company with personnel and administrative support services.[16] If the shelter operator provides the facility, its use may be covered in the shelter contract or in a separate facilities agreement.[17] The foreign company provides a general manager and perhaps other management and supervisory personnel.[18] The foreign company also supplies, and maintains title to, all raw and intermediate materials and finished goods.[19]

2. MEXICAN REGULATION OF THE MAQUILADORA

2.1 REGULATIONS BEFORE 1989

The initial regulations for the Maquiladora Program were promulgated in 1965 in a series of circulars issued by SECOFI and the Department of the Treasury ("Treasury") interpreting a provision of the Customs Code already in effect.[20] Pursuant thereto, the authorized location of maquiladora facilities was confined to specific border regions. In addition, as indicated, a bond was required to be posted to guaranty re-export of the goods imported into Mexico. The formation

---

[15] Alfredo Andere-Mendiola, *Issues in Maquiladora Lending* 3 (1991) (unpublished article prepared by Mr. Andere as a Special Consultant to Luce, Forward, Hamilton & Scripps).

[16] *Id.*

[17] *Id.*

[18] *Id.*

[19] *Id.*

[20] Schechter & Brill, *supra* note 5, at 701.

of a Mexican company was also required, although that company could be 100 percent foreign-owned.[21]

The first formal decree, enacted as a set of customs regulations in 1972, eliminated the geographical restrictions on the location of a maquiladora (with the exception of certain urban areas) and permitted a maquiladora to seek permission to sell a portion of its products in Mexico's domestic market.[22] The second, also enacted as a set of customs regulations, expanded the Maquiladora Program in 1977 to cover operations employing the idle capacity of existing Mexican plants. Such plants, which had not previously participated in maquiladora operations, were required to incorporate a minimum of twenty percent domestic content in the goods destined for export.[23] The third, enacted in 1983, altered the domestic content requirement of the second.[24]

The fourth decree, issued in 1989 (the "1989 Decree")[25] reflected an industrial policy that attempted to integrate the Maquiladora Program with national industry as a whole.[26] For example, maquiladoras were permitted to subcontract out their operations (see above).[27]

---

[21] *Id.*

[22] Schechter & Brill, *supra* note 5, at 703.

[23] *Id.*, citing Reglamento del Párrafo Tercero del Artículo 321 del Código Aduanero de los Estados Unidos Mexicanos para el Fomento de la Industria Maquiladora, *D.O.*, October 27, 1977.

[24] *Id.* at 704, citing Decreto para el Fomento y Operación de la Industria Maquiladora de Exportación (the "1983 Decree"), D.O., August 15, 1983. Schechter and Brill note that the 1983 Decree, issued following the abrogation of the Customs Code on July 1, 1982, was the first decree to stand on its own; it sought to "institutionalize government cooperation," and to promote the industry while promoting investments in high technology and worker training programs as well as to encourage a greater integration of national content. *Id.* at 703, fn. 31, citing the 1983 Decree, Article 16.

[25] Decreto para el Fomento y Operación de la Industria Maquiladora de Exportación, *D.O.*, December 20, 1989.

[26] Schechter & Brill, *supra* note 5, at 704.

[27] Around the same time, the Government of Mexico established two additional export programs in response to the success of the maquiladoras. (We have heard that these programs were established by other ministries to emulate or perhaps to compete with SECOFI.) The PITEX Program, established pursuant to a decree issued in 1990 (Decreto Que Establecer Programas de Importación Temporal para Producir Articulos de Exportación, *D.O.*, May 3, 1990, the "PITEX Decree") was designed to grant to Mexican companies some of the benefits enjoyed by the predominantly foreign-owned maquiladoras. Schechter & Brill, *supra* note 5, at 708.

Under the PITEX Program, if a company exports a certain minimum percentage of its total sales, it may import the raw materials, parts, components, containers and auxiliary materials used for such exported products, as well as fuel and materials consumed in the process of producing them, duty-free. If the company's exports meet a certain higher

The 1989 Decree was Mexico's primary regulatory mechanism with respect to maquiladoras when NAFTA was passed. Despite recent amendments to the 1989 Decree in order to implement NAFTA, the 1989 Decree will in essence remain the foundation of maquiladora regulation. Accordingly, the 1989 Decree is discussed in more detail.

2.2   THE 1989 DECREE

(i) Purposes. The stated purposes of the 1989 Decree are to promote the establishment of enterprises that are totally or partially engaged in maquiladora export production and to regulate the operation of such enterprises by means of a flexible and decentralized administrative process.[28] Subsidiary, subcontracting and shelter arrangements are governed by the 1989 Decree. We should note, however, that a maquiladora seeking to operate pursuant to subcontracting arrangements required further authorization in addition to securing its Maquiladora Working Program.[29]

The 1989 Decree charged maquiladoras with fulfilling the following national purposes:

1. To create sources of employment.
2. To shift the balance of payments by increasing the flow of foreign currency into the country.
3. To achieve greater industrial integration and increase the international competitiveness of Mexican industry.
4. To increase the skills of the work force and to foster the development and transfer of technology in the country.[30]

---

percentage of its production, machinery and equipment intended for use in the production process may also be imported "temporarily" as they are pursuant to the Maquiladora Program. A company operating pursuant to the PITEX Program is granted a Temporary Import Program to Produce Products for Export ("PITEX Working Program").

Similarly, the ALTEX Program (the "ALTEX Program") provides certain advantages for certain companies that directly export or indirectly export certain percentages of their production. Decreto para el Fomento y Operación de las Empresas Altamente Exportadoras, *D.O.*, May 3, 1990.

[28]   Article 1.
[29]   Article 28.
[30]   Article 2.

(ii) Administrative Procedures. With repect to the administrative procedures for establishing a maquiladora, the 1983 Decree had provided that procedures governing application, approval and registration were administered under the auspices of SECOFI through its central or regional offices.[31] However, there was no single source of information available to an applicant seeking to fulfill the procedural requirements for establishing a maquiladora.[32] The process was consolidated in 1987 to provide for a unitary filing window, or "ventanilla unica" vested with the authority to authorize Maquiladora Working Programs for individual applicants.[33] The unitary filing window processes all information to be submitted to the National Registry of Maquiladora Industries, the National Commission of Foreign Investments (if applicable), the Secretary of Foreign Affairs, the Federal Registry of Taxpayers of the Secretary of the Treasury and Public Credit, the Institute of the National Workers Housing Fund (INFONAVIT) and the Mexican Institute of Social Security.[34]

Applications submitted with respect to agro-industrial, mineralogical, forestry and fishery projects were evaluated in accordance with other applicable law, including environmental law.[35] Government officials consulted by SECOFI in that regard were required to respond within ten business days.

(iii) A Maquiladora Working Program. As indicated, the 1989 Decree provided for each maquiladora to operate pursuant to a Maquiladora Working Program, which sets forth information in regard to the maquiladora enterprise, a description of its processes, the characteristics of its product or service, a list of the goods it proposes to import temporarily for use in the maquiladora and other information required by SECOFI.[36] As also indicated, maquiladoras were subject to a simplified customs dispatch process.[37]

Maquiladora Working Programs, once approved, were granted for an indefinite period.[38]

---

[31] 1983 Decree, *supra* note 25, Article 18.
[32] Zack V. Chayet & Eduardo A. Bustamante, *The Mexican Maquiladora Industry: Legal Framework of the 1990s*, 20 *California Western International L.J.* 263, 266 (1990).
[33] *Id.*, citing Ley para Regular la Inversión Extranjera, *D.O.* May 16, 1987.
[34] Article 3.VIII.
[35] Article 14.
[36] Article 3.IX.
[37] Article 4.
[38] Article 7.

(iv) Import Specifications; Export Quotas. A Maquiladora Working Program entitled its holder to temporarily import the following items:

First Group. Materials and auxiliary components, packaging materials, labels and pamphlets to complement basic production processes.
Second Group. Tools, equipment and auxiliary production items to be used for industrial security, environmental protection and safety, such as work manuals, industrial blueprints and telecommunications and computer equipment.
Third Group. Machinery, instruments and spare parts used in the production process, laboratory and testing equipment for the maquiladora's products and quality control procedures, and equipment to train personnel and to conduct managerial operations.
Fourth Group. Trailers and containers.[39]

These items could remain in Mexico for differing periods of time depending on their grouping: items in the first group for an initial six-month period (which could be extended for an additional six months), those in the fourth for three months and the second and third groups for as long as the Maquiladora Working Program pursuant to which their entry was authorized remained in effect.[40]

Following approval of its Maquiladora Working Program, a maquiladora was required to commence operations within one year; a one-time, three-month extension of such term was permitted. Should a maquiladora demonstrate special needs, the extended term could be further extended by SECOFI upon request. Subsequent temporary importation of the items set forth in paragraphs 1 and 2 of Article 10 required further specific authorization from SECOFI.[41]

When under special circumstances the products produced in the maquila operation were subject to export quotas (such as textiles), SECOFI was charged with allocating the quotas among those interested in obtaining them.[42]

(v) Waste and Shrinkage. Under the 1989 Decree, non-hazardous waste (as defined pursuant to applicable Mexican law) was to be returned to the country of origin, destroyed or donated to charitable or educational institutions.[43]

---

[39] Article 10.
[40] Article 10.
[41] Article 11.
[42] Article 12.
[43] The waste disposal process has been very controversial. It has been estimated that

Should the maquiladora wish to sell waste in the Mexican market, it was required to seek the approval of SECOFI, specifying the type, quantity, value and purchaser of the waste and fulfilling the requirements for its permanent importation. SECOFI then submitted notice of its approval (if granted) to the Secretary of the Treasury and Public Credit, which issued the corresponding authorization. Hazardous waste was to be handled in accordance with applicable Mexican environmental law.[44]

The 1989 Decree defined "waste" as the residue of materials remaining upon completion of the production process and "shrinkage" as the portion of materials consumed in the production process whose integration into the product to be re-exported cannot be demonstrated. Both were deducted from computation of the quantities of materials imported. In addition, products rejected by the maquiladora's quality control processes could be counted as waste, as long as SECOFI determined that such waste was normal. The containers and packaging materials used for waste were also treated as waste.[45]

(vi) Certain Obligations of the Maquiladora. In accordance with Article 16 of the 1989 Decree, maquiladoras operating under an approved Maquiladora Working Program were required to agree:

1. To comply with the terms of that Maquiladora Working Program.
2. To earmark the imported goods for the specific purposes for which their importation was authorized and to use properly the export quotas (if applicable) assigned to them pursuant to Article 12.
3. To hire and to train each category of employee in accordance with applicable law.
4. To comply with applicable tax provisions, labor standards and exchange controls.
5. In the event of suspension of the maquiladora's operations, to notify SECOFI within ten calendar days.[46]

---

notwithstanding applicable requirements, perhaps thirty percent of the hazardous waste discharged by maquiladoras remains in Mexico. *More Muck than Money, Economist,* at 50 (October 16, 1993).

[44] Article 15. While beyond the scope of this chapter, this of course is one of the most complex and controversial issues raised in connection with the debate over NAFTA and its treatment of the maquiladora industry.

[45] *Id.*

[46] Article 16.

Under the 1989 Decree, maquiladoras were also obligated to provide information requested by SECOFI and the Secretary of the Treasury and Public Credit and to cooperate fully with those offices in their supervision of maquila operations.[47] All maquiladoras were also required to comply with all applicable environmental law.[48]

(vii) Sales in Mexico's Domestic Market. Under Article 19 of the 1989 Decree, SECOFI was charged with determining when a maquiladora would be permitted to sell a portion of its products in the Mexican market for two-year periods.[49] Article 20 provided that products sold in the Mexican market could not exceed fifty percent of the total value of goods exported during the prior year. Maquiladoras seeking permission to sell goods in the Mexican market were also required to comply with provisions pertaining to their balances of foreign currency.[50]

Goods sold by the maquiladora in the Mexican market were exempt from being required to have obtained a prior import permit if such a permit would not otherwise be required.[51] Import taxes were assessed upon foreign components at the applicable rate for goods destined for the Mexican market. Pursuant to the 1989 Decree, a maquiladora could pay duty at the tariff rate applicable to the domestic content of an article if it met a minimum domestic content requirement.[52]

Pursuant to the 1989 Decree, maquiladoras desiring to sell their products in the Mexican market were also required:

1. To maintain the same control over and quality of products destined for the Mexican market as those established for their exported products by law and by regulations promulgated by SECOFI.
2. To pay the general import tax imposed in accordance with Article 22 of the 1989 Decree.
3. To comply with other applicable legal requirements.[53]

---

[47] Article 17.
[48] Article 18.
[49] Article 19.
[50] Article 20.
[51] Article 21.
[52] Article 22.
[53] Article 23.

Maquiladoras that had been granted approval to sell their products in the Mexican market were also allowed to avoid exporting and then re-importing such products. The 1989 Decree accomplished this by allowing the maquiladora to deem such products exported and then re-imported upon conditions determined by SECOFI and Treasury in each case.[54]

(viii) Transfers; Immigration. The export of goods by a party to whom goods had been transferred by a maquiladora required the prior authorization of Treasury, acting upon the prior opinion and determination of SECOFI. In making its determination, SECOFI was required to take into account the maquiladora's compliance with applicable obligations, to consider the export an indirect export to be carried out in United States currency or another foreign currency and to exempt transfers between textile maquiladoras and apparel-manufacturing maquiladoras.[55]

Similarly, SECOFI was required to make a determination (which required Treasury's subsequent approval) in the event of transfers of machinery, tools and equipment from one maquiladora to another and the transfer of machinery and equipment from maquiladoras to their Mexican suppliers. Such transfers could be carried out in the form of commodotatum agreements, leases or purchase agreements.[56]

The 1989 Decree also authorized the appropriate authorities to permit immigration of administrative and technical personnel to conduct the operation of maquiladora enterprises.[57]

(ix) Termination; Sanctions. In the event a maquiladora decided to terminate its Maquiladora Working Program, a thirty-day advance notice to SECOFI was required. SECOFI would grant permission to terminate the Maquiladora Working Program if the maquiladora was found to be current in the fulfillment of its labor and customs commitments.[58]

In the event it violated its Maquiladora Working Program, a maquiladora could be sanctioned or its permission to operate suspended--depending on the gravity of its acts and without prejudice to other sanctions which might be imposed under other applicable law. The repetition of an act or omission on

---

[54] "Exportación virtual." Article 24.
[55] Articles 25 and 26.
[56] Article 27.
[57] Article 29.
[58] Article 30.

which a previous suspension was based constituted grounds for permanent cancellation of an approved Maquiladora Working Program. SECOFI was required to notify Treasury of any sanction imposed on a maquiladora. Prior to the application of sanctions, maquiladoras were granted fifteen business days to appeal the imposition of such sanctions.[59]

3. THE MAQUILADORA AND MEXICAN TRADE POLICY

This section will briefly review the development of maquiladoras in the context of Mexico's historic trade policies and then survey the ways in which NAFTA will affect the regulation of maquiladoras described in the previous section. For the maquiladora, the most significant change in Mexico's trade policy, as reflected by NAFTA, is the increased accessibility of its domestic markets.

It has been said that under NAFTA the Maquiladora Program will be effectively eliminated.[60] This is of course true in the strictest sense with respect to United States- and Canadian-owned maquiladoras. However, the elimination process--in addition to being gradual--has implications of its own.

Moreover, many maquiladoras are not United States- or Canadian-owned. In fact, as of 1990, approximately half of the applications seeking permission to establish maquiladoras were submitted to the Government of Mexico by non-United States--primarily Japanese--parties.[61] By 1992, there were 52 Japanese-owned maquiladoras.[62] It is important to bear in mind that these maquiladoras are governed by the same Mexican regulations. Indeed, as the discussion below reveals, their existence was a significant factor in the negotiation of the tariff provisions of Article 303 and the performance requirements of Article 1106 of NAFTA.

---

[59]   Article 32.

[60]   Mickey Kantor, *It's Time to Puncture the Myths of Treaty's Opponents*, *Roll Call* (September 27, 1993).

[61]   Khosrow Fatemi, *The Maquiladora Industry: Economic Solution or Problem?* 10 (1990).

[62]   USITC Publication 2729, *supra* note 4, at 4-5, citing GAO/GGD-92-131, Sept. 1992, p. 97.

3.1 BACKGROUND

Mexico first established a free trade zone in the border region with the United States in 1861 to discourage its citizens from moving to Texas. The root of Mexico's contemporary border region policies can be traced to 1933, when Mexico established limited free zones in the region as a means of protecting local retail markets and maintaining a higher standard of living for regional residents. By the 1960s, "a dual policy system had emerged: while a strict protectionist stance was taken for the national economy, a fairly liberal policy was established for its border markets, increasing its trade and interdependency with the United States."[63]

It was in this context that the maquiladora industry originated and it is in this context that the changes portended by NAFTA may be most significant for Mexico's domestic economy. As has been discussed, Mexico's border economy is not currently, and until now has not been, integrated into the national economy. Yet the maquiladora, in the process of being altered by NAFTA, may be instrumental in fostering that integration process.

To begin with, the Government of Mexico has not required maquiladoras to be located in the border region since 1972. One reason that many remain there is to minimize their reliance on Mexico's historically uneven infrastructure and communications and transportation systems.[64] United States operations may also wish to contain transportation costs by remaining close to their home markets. For these reasons too, entities that as a practical matter resemble maquiladoras may flourish even after United States- and Canadian-owned maquiladoras have technically ceased to exist--until operations based farther away from the border can, in the judgment of their operators, be sustained.

Second, maquiladora products currently contain, on average, a scant two percent of domestic components or materials.[65] To the extent this is because duty is currently assessed upon Mexican components of the maquiladora's products upon their export into the United States, the elimination of tariffs under NAFTA will gradually eliminate that deterrent to the purchase of materials from

[63] Stoddard, *supra* note 3, at 16.

[64] *See Maquiladoras Will Increase Under NAFTA, Speakers at Conference Agree, BNA Daily Report for Executives* (June 19, 1991). Conversely, location of a maquiladora in close proximity to Mexico's border with the U.S. can facilitate the maquiladora's access to benefits on the U.S. side such as infrastructure, services and technical assistance. USITC Publication 2729, *supra* note 4, at 4-2.

[65] Consejo Nacional de la Industria Maquiladora de Exportación A.C., *Industria Maquiladora: In-Bond Industry* 11 (1993).

Mexican suppliers. This too, of course, will link the border and national economies.

In any case, as Mexico opens its economy to far greater participation by the other NAFTA parties, maquiladora facilities may serve as a launching pad from which United States and Canadian manufacturers may expand into the Mexican market. In fact, access to Mexico's domestic market was an important element of many United States corporate strategies--even before NAFTA.[66]

Even after the maquiladora incentives are eliminated under NAFTA, United States and Canadian companies[67] will probably continue to establish assembly, processing and manufacturing facilities in Mexico because, in addition to the factors just noted, labor costs will probably remain lower there.[68] Indeed, much of the opposition to NAFTA was based on that very premise. Such facilities may, after NAFTA's phase-out provisions have expired, consist of actual manufacturing, in addition to mere assembly and processing, operations. However, the assembly and processing operations typically conducted in maquiladoras may serve as a means of transition into more sophisticated processes as United States and Canadian companies build on their experience and become willing to assume greater risks.

Finally, it is important to bear in mind that United States companies have already made enormous investments in maquiladoras and other industrial facilities; these investments have established industrial linkages that would be costly (and imprudent) to sever.[69]

Thus, NAFTA could well contribute to the integration not only of the economies of the United States, Mexico and Canada but also of Mexico's border and national economies, with the result--although probably not in the manner--that the Government of Mexico originally envisioned when it established the Maquiladora Program.

[66] Sidney Weintraub, *Industrial Integration Policy: A U.S. Perspective*, in *U.S.-Mexican Industrial Integration: The Road to Free Trade* 55 (1991).

[67] As of July 1992, Canadian companies had invested only about $1 billion in Mexico, whereas United States companies had invested more than $100 billion. *NAFTA's Effect on U.S. Trade with Canadians to Be Minimal*, San Diego Business Journal, July 27, 1992, § 1, at 14.

[68] David Voigt, *The Maquiladora Problem in the Age of NAFTA: Where Will We Find Solutions?* 2:323 *Minn. J. Global Trade* 323, 327 (1992).

[69] *See* Weintraub, *supra* note 67.

3.2   NAFTA AND THE MAQUILADORA

(i) Summary of Applicable NAFTA Provisions. Those provisions of NAFTA that will affect maquiladoras most significantly are contained in Chapters 3 and 11, and in their Annexes.[70] Chapter 3 pertains to tariffs; Chapter 11 pertains to investment. Both contain provisions that were drafted with a view to affecting maquiladoras specifically as well as more general provisions that will affect a variety of enterprises, including maquiladoras. This discussion is limited to those specific provisions.

Article 302 is the provision that will phase out tariffs generally whereas Article 303 sets forth specific provisions with respect to duty-drawback programs.[71] Article 1102 accords national treatment to investors of NAFTA parties generally and Article 1109 provides for the free transfer of all profits, dividends, proceeds, etc., in freely usable currency, by such investors. Article 1106 phases out the performance requirements that applied to maquiladoras specifically. Section B of Chapter 11, which provides for the settlement of disputes between a party to NAFTA and an investor of another party to NAFTA, will apply to maquiladoras generally.

Several other provisions of NAFTA merit brief mention. First, the definition of "territory," in Annex 201.1 was designed to ensure that all maquiladoras-- including those located in areas not deemed "territory" for customs purposes-- would be covered by NAFTA's provisions.[72] Chapter 4, which pertains to rules of origin, will of course affect maquiladoras significantly--although it will not in many cases alter their fundamental operation.[73] Article 513 of Chapter 5 establishes a Working Group on Rules of Origin which will study, among other things, the effective implementation and administration of Article 303. Although immigration matters are beyond the scope of this chapter, we note that

---

[70] For a discussion of the effects of NAFTA on the U.S. production-sharing tariff provisions discussed in note 14 *supra, see* USITC Publication 2729, *supra* note 4, at 3-4.

[71] Article 301 provides that NAFTA's signatories will accord to one another national treatment with respect to goods. National treatment means that another party's products shall be treated no less favorably than like, domestic products. This notion, while fundamental in principle, in fact merely reiterates obligations that all three NAFTA parties have already assumed as parties to the General Agreement on Tariffs and Trade. *See* U.S. International Trade Commission, *Potential Impact on the U.S. Economy and Selected Industries of the North American Free-Trade Agreement*, USITC Publication 2596 at 3-2 (January 1993).

[72] Telephone conversation with a NAFTA negotiator on a background basis.

[73] Of course, various sector-specific provisions, such as NAFTA Annex 300-A, which pertains to the automotive sector, will profoundly affect certain maquiladoras. These matters are beyond the scope of this chapter.

Chapter 16, which provides temporary entry for business persons, may be relevant as well.

We should also note that pursuant to the NAFTA Implementation Act,[74] Mexico has been deleted from the list of countries eligible for the Generalized System of Preferences[75] ("GSP").[76] Many Mexican products previously entered the United States duty-free under the GSP.

(ii) Chapter 3. Article 302 phases out virtually all tariffs within the territory of the NAFTA parties by the year 2004. Because the very notion of a duty-drawback program rests upon the existence of tariffs, this provision is clearly fundamental in analyzing the treatment of maquiladoras under NAFTA. However, because the phase-out process is gradual, and, perhaps more importantly, because the further motive underlying the use of maquiladoras by many foreign companies may in any case have been other factors such as lower labor costs, the abolition of tariffs will not by itself eliminate United States- and Canadian-owned maquiladora-type operations in practice.[77]

Article 303 limits the exemption from duty of third-country imports by one NAFTA party on condition that the goods are subsequently exported to another NAFTA party.[78] The specific provisions operate as follows. A duty waiver, reduction or refund that is contingent on the export of an item originating in a third country may not exceed the smaller of: (i) the total amount of the duties paid or owed on the initial importation of the item into North America or (ii) the total amount of the duties paid on the item's subsequent shipment from one NAFTA party to another.[79]

However, were a maquiladora to use North American components, those components, and the products manufactured from them, would remain eligible for duty drawback until tariffs are fully phased out under NAFTA.[80]

---

[74] North American Free Trade Agreement Implementation Act, P.L. 103-182, Dec. 8, 1993.

[75] 19 U.S.C.S. 2441, et seq.

[76] NAFTA Implementation Act, *supra* note 73, Title II.

[77] Obviously, maquiladoras owned by persons of non-NAFTA countries will evolve differently.

[78] USITC Publication 2596, *supra* note 72, at 3-6. Similarly, Article 304 and Annex 304 preclude NAFTA parties from adopting new customs duty waivers that are conditioned upon the fulfillment of performance requirements. In addition, as discussed below, Article 1106 prohibits performance requirements in the area of investments. *Id.* at note 21.

[79] *Id.* at note 22. *See also* U.S. Department of the Treasury, Office of International Trade, *Operation of NAFTA Drawback Formula.*

[80] U.S. Department of the Treasury, Office of International Trade, *Operation of NAFTA*

When tariffs have been eliminated on products of North American origin, no drawback will be permitted on components of such products that originate in third countries.[81] For trade between NAFTA parties to which Most Favored Nation ("MFN") tariff provisions apply,[82] drawback will be permitted only to the extent needed to ensure that duty is collected only once on components originating in third countries.[83]

(iii) Chapter 11. Article 1106 relates to performance requirements and was designed to ensure that NAFTA does not affect any NAFTA party disadvantageously with respect to third parties.[84] Accordingly, Article 1106 phases out the imposition of performance requirements by a NAFTA party both on the other NAFTA parties and on non-NAFTA parties. This is extremely important because, as indicated, all maquiladoras are not United States- or Canadian-owned.

Drawback Formula.

[81] Research and interviews with various Mexican and U.S. parties by the USITC led it to conclude:

> "Japanese and Korean maquilas, particularly those assembling televisions in Tijuana, will be placed at a competitive disadvantage because the rules of origin under the NAFTA favor companies like Zenith, RCA, and Magnavox that make greater use of U.S.-made parts in the Mexican assembly plants. Asian television companies may either (a) open plants in North America to produce picture tubes and other key parts, (b) insist that important part suppliers move production to North America, or (c) shift sourcing to existing U.S. parts producers."

USITC Publication 2729, *supra* note 4, at 3-4.

[82] Article 1103: Most-Favored-Nation Treatment:

1. Each Party shall accord to investors of another Party treatment no less favorable than that it accords, in like circumstances, to investors of any other Party or of a non-Party with respect to the establishment, acquisition, expansion, management, conduct, operation, and sale or other disposition of investments.

2. Each Party shall accord to investments of investors of another Party treatment no less favorable than that it accords, in like circumstances, to investments of investors of any other Party or of a non-Party with respect to the establishment, acquisition, expansion, management, conduct, operation, and sale or other disposition of investments.

[83] U.S. Department of the Treasury, Office of International Trade, *NAFTA Limitation on Drawback, Elimination of Maquila Sales Restrictions and Export Performance Requirements* (1992).

[84] *See* Appendix A.

Article 1106 will, *inter alia*, eliminate the requirements that: (i) a given level or percentage of goods or services be exported, (ii) maquiladoras obtain permission to sell their products in the national market and (iii) goods achieve a given level or percentage of domestic content.

NAFTA Annex I-M-34 of Mexico sets forth a timetable for increasing the percentage of their production that maquiladoras may sell in the Mexican market, culminating with the complete elimination of any such percentage limitation in the year 2001.[85]

Article 1109 provides that each NAFTA party "shall permit all transfers relating to an investment of an investor of another Party in the territory of the Party to be made freely and without delay." As the discussion below demonstrates, this provision will preclude the Government of Mexico from imposing the balance of payments requirements on maquiladoras that it did before NAFTA.

4. THE REGULATION OF THE MAQUILADORA IN MEXICO AFTER NAFTA

4.1   THE 1989 DECREE AS MODIFIED BY THE AMENDING DECREE

As indicated, the 1989 Decree was Mexico's primary regulatory mechanism with respect to maquiladoras at the time NAFTA was passed. On December 24, 1993, the Government of Mexico implemented the provisions of NAFTA relevant to maquiladoras by enacting a series of amendments to the 1989 Decree (the "Amending Decree").[86] The following discussion reviews the Amending Decree. We should note, however, that the Government of Mexico will continue to monitor all maquiladora enterprises and many of the basic interactions between maquiladoras and the Government of Mexico will continue as before.

(i) Definitions. Whereas the 1989 Decree had defined the "maquila operation"[87] as an industrial process or service in which foreign materials

---

[85]   NAFTA Annex I-M-36 encompasses those provisions of the ALTEX Decree, and Annex I-M-37 those provisions of the PITEX Decree, that would violate Article 1106. These annexes also provide that beginning in 2001 entities operating under, respectively, the ALTEX and PITEX Programs will no longer be subject to percentage requirements.

[86]   Decree Modifying the [Decree] for the Development and Operation of the Maquiladora Exportation Industry, *D.O.*, December 24, 1993.

[87]   "Operación de Maquila."

temporarily imported were transformed, elaborated or repaired by maquiladoras or by others engaging in export activities pursuant to the 1989 Decree,[88] the Amending Decree expands the definition of "maquila operation" to encompass both a maquiladora and an entity providing services (such as equipment repair) to either a maquiladora or a company operating under a PITEX Program.[89]

In addition, the 1989 Decree had limited the definition of maquiladora to those enterprises that exported all of their production (with the exceptions noted above). Now that Article 1106 of NAFTA is eliminating performance requirements, however, the definition of maquiladora simply refers to those enterprises that export their production.[90]

(ii) Administrative Procedures. The Amending Decree reduces the procedural burden on the maquiladora by providing that administrative procedures carried out in connection with a Maquiladora Working Program following its initiation are also subject to the unitary filing window provisions.[91]

The 1989 Decree had authorized SECOFI to approve the Maquiladora Working Program of a maquiladora that exported all of its products unless produced with "surplus capacity."[92] In accordance with the expanded definition of "maquila operation" noted above, the Amending Decree augments this provision by authorizing SECOFI to approve the Maquiladora Working Program of an entity that provides services to a maquiladora or to an entity operating under a PITEX Program.

(iii) Sales in Mexico's Domestic Market. As set forth above, under Article 19 of the 1989 Decree, SECOFI was charged with determining cases in which a maquiladora would be permitted to sell a portion of its products in the Mexican

---

[88] Article 3.V.

[89] Article 3.V.

As indicated, NAFTA Annexes I-M-36 and I-M-37 permit the respective continuation of the ALTEX and PITEX Programs in their current form until 2001. At that time the performance requirements imposed by these programs will be discontinued. We have inquired whether the Government of Mexico intends to promulgate any further regulations with respect to either program and have been informed that it has no such plans at present. The Government of Mexico may, however, act before 2001 to lift the performance requirements it imposes on entities operating under the ALTEX and PITEX programs. Telephone conversation with Brian Elwood Salido, Embassy of Mexico Trade Office, February 23, 1994.

[90] Article 3.VI.

[91] Article 5.

[92] Article 5.

market.[93] Article 20 provided that products sold in the Mexican market could not exceed fifty percent of the total value of goods exported during the prior year. Maquiladoras seeking permission to sell goods in the Mexican market were also required to comply with provisions pertaining to their balances of foreign currency.[94]

In accordance the reservations of Mexico set forth in Annex I, I-M-34, of NAFTA, the Amending Decree replaces Article 19's provisions with a schedule phasing out the performance requirements previously placed on the sale of maquiladora products in the Mexican market.[95] The Amending Decree eliminates the fifty percent requirement and currency obligations previously imposed by Article 20 and amends Article 20 to provide for a bimonthly report (the form of which is set forth on Annex 1 of the Amending Decree) of national sales that details the amount and value of such sales and the percentage of the previous year's exports such sales represent.[96]

Also with respect to goods sold by the maquiladora in the Mexican market, both the 1989 Decree and the Amending Decree provide that import taxes shall be assessed upon foreign components at the applicable rate for goods destined for the Mexican market--which, if such goods are of North American origin-- will be phased out in accordance with Article 302 of NAFTA.[97] Pursuant to the 1989 Decree, a maquiladora could pay duty at the tariff rate applicable to the domestic content of an article if it met a minimum domestic content

---

[93] Article 19.

[94] Article 20.

[95] Article 19. Maquiladoras may sell a part of their production in the national market in accordance with the following provisions:

I.   In 1994, up to 55% of the total value of their exports during the previous year.
II.   In 1995, up to 60% of the total value of their exports during the previous year.
III.   In 1996, up to 65% of the total value of their exports during the previous year.
IV.   In 1997, up to 70% of the total value of their exports during the previous year.
V.   In 1998, up to 75% of the total value of their exports during the previous year.
VI.   In 1999, up to 80% of the total value of their exports during the previous year.
VII. In 2000, up to 85% of the total value of their exports during the previous year.

Beginning in the year 2001, sales of maquiladora products in the national market shall not be subject to any limitation; maquiladoras may sell all of their production in the national market.

[96] Articles 19 and 20.

[97] Article 22.

requirement; the Amending Decree deletes this provision, in accordance with Article 1106 of NAFTA.[98]

(iv) Import Specifications; Export Quotas. As indicated, pursuant to the 1989 Decree, a Maquiladora Working Program entitled its holder to temporarily import certain items. The provisions governing which items may be imported by a maquiladora remain unchanged. The provisions governing the lengths of time these items may stay in Mexico have changed slightly, however. Pursuant to the Amending Decree, the items in the first group may remain in Mexico for one one-year term, rather than what was effectively two six-month terms.[99] The items in the second and third groups will now receive a two-year authorization, but may remain as long as the Maquiladora Working Program permitting their entry remains in effect. The items in the fourth group may also remain in Mexico for as long as the Maquiladora Working Program associated with them, but they may not remain for a term exceeding twenty years.[100]

When under special circumstances the goods used in the maquila operation were subject to export quotas (such as textiles), SECOFI was charged with allocating the available quotas among those interested in obtaining them. The Amending Decree provides that these export quotas shall be allocated by federal delegations and subdelegations of SECOFI.[101]

The provision providing that maquiladoras that had been granted approval to sell their products in the Mexican market could deem their products exported and then re-imported has now been derogated in accordance with Article 1106 of NAFTA.[102]

The Amending Decree provides that enterprises subject to export quotas wishing to transfer part of their quota allocation must seek the authorization of SECOFI. Such transfers shall be deemed indirect exports.[103]

(v) Currency Requirements. In accordance with the modification made in 1991 and described above, the Amending Decree eliminates the foreign exchange

---

[98] *Id.*

[99] This change is intended to clarify, rather than to alter, the former provision. Telephone interviews with Gabriela Hernandez and Manuel Pacheco of SECOFI on, respectively, March 25, and March 30, 1994.

[100] Article 10.

[101] Article 12.

[102] Article 24.

[103] Articles 25 and 26.

requirements of subsection 4 of Article 16 of the 1989 Decree. Also, in accordance with Chapter 11 of NAFTA, Article 26 of the Amending Decree deletes the requirements that indirect exports be realized in American Dollars or in another foreign currency. Similarly, the Amending Decree eliminates the 1989 Decree's provisions pertaining to balances of foreign currency.[104]

(vi) Environmental Matters. As indicated, under the 1989 Decree, all maquiladoras were also required to comply with all applicable environmental law.[105] This remains unchanged, although compliance will now of course be far more complicated than it was before. However, a discussion of those environmental measures to which maquiladoras will be subject under Mexican law, NAFTA and NAFTA's side agreements is beyond the scope of this chapter.

(vii) Transfers. As set forth above, transfers of machinery, tools and equipment from one maquiladora to another and the transfer of machinery and equipment from maquiladoras to their Mexican suppliers were permitted upon approval by SECOFI.[106] Pursuant to the Amending Decree, transfers of machinery, tools and equipment between maquiladoras and enterprises operating under the PITEX Program are also permitted.

(viii) Sanctions. In the event that it violated its Maquiladora Working Program, a maquiladora could be sanctioned or its permission to operate suspended for the reasons stated above; maquiladoras were granted fifteen business days to appeal the imposition of such sanctions.[107] While the sanctions remain the same, this period was increased to forty-five days by the Amending Decree. In addition, SECOFI may now cancel a maquiladora's registration if requested by any arm of the Federal Public Administration.

5. OTHER CONSIDERATIONS

In addition to those provisions of Mexican law that specifically pertain to maquiladoras, many other areas of Mexican law apply to their establishment and

[104] Article 20.
[105] Article 18.
[106] Article 27.
[107] Article 32.

operation. We have already noted that environmental, immigration and labor provisions are beyond the scope of this chapter. While also beyond the scope of this chapter, the following areas, and the general ways they will be affected by NAFTA, are briefly noted for reference.

5.1 REAL ESTATE

Under Mexico's previous foreign investment regulations,[108] foreign-owned Mexican companies were free to purchase and sell real estate in Mexico except real estate located in the 100-kilometer strip along the Mexico-United States border and the 50-kilometer strip along Mexico's sea coasts. Under Annex I, I-M-1, of NAFTA, certain limitations on real property ownership by foreigners in the restricted areas will remain in effect.

Before, a foreign-owned company could acquire the right to full use of land in the restricted areas by becoming the beneficiary of a trust, for which the beneficiary chose a Mexican bank to serve as trustee. Such trusts usually had a duration of thirty years, renewable for another thirty years. The beneficiaries' rights pursuant to the trust included full use and enjoyment of the land. It could use, encumber or sell its rights and may receive any income earned from the property. Leases were unrestricted in this regard.

Now, pursuant to the new foreign investment law issued in 1993,[109] the term of these trusts has been extended to fifty years, renewable upon request. Most important for maquiladoras and other foreign-owned businesses, however, is that the prohibitions in the restricted areas with respect to non-residential property have been eliminated.

5.2 TAXES

While tax matters are also beyond the scope of this chapter, we will just briefly note that the two most important bodies of Mexican tax law applicable to

---

[108] Reglamento de la Ley para Promover la Inversión Extranjera, *D.O.*, May 16, 1989. These regulations implement the Foreign Investment Law (Ley para Promover la Inversión Extranjera), which went into effect on May 8, 1973. The provisions in regard to restricted areas originate in Article 27, Subparagraph I, of Mexico's Constitution, the *Constitución Política de los Estados Unidos Mexicanos*.

[109] Ley de Inversión Extranjera, *D.O.*, December 27, 1993.

maquiladoras are the income tax law[110] (the "Income Tax Law") and the asset tax law[111] (the "Asset Tax Law"). In addition, Mexico and the United States recently concluded an income tax treaty (the "Treaty"), which is effective as of January 1, 1994. These three regimes work together in certain ways that affect-- or could affect--maquiladoras.

Mexico has structured its asset tax as a form of alternative minimum tax. Accordingly, the amount of asset tax payable in a particular year or paid within the preceding ten years is reduced by the amount of income tax paid in that year. But because subsidiary maquiladoras are usually structured as cost centers rather than as profit centers, the amount of income tax that they pay is minimal as their profits are marginal. Any income tax that is paid in Mexico, however, is creditable against United States income tax liability. The Mexican income tax paid or accrued will not be reduced by any amount of Mexican asset tax liability for United States foreign tax credit purposes.[112] Further, any Mexican asset tax that has been refunded will not reduce the amount of Mexican income tax paid for foreign tax credit purposes.

The assets and inventory of subsidiary maquiladoras were exempt from the minimum two percent tax imposed on the assets of Mexican businesses by the Asset Tax Law until March 31, 1992.[113] This is because a subsidiary maquiladora's assets and inventory are considered only temporarily imported if the enterprise is not--and it typically has not been--deemed to be a "permanent establishment." These exemptions, however, expired on March 31, 1992. Unofficially, government officials have indicated that they did not intend to eliminate these exemptions. However, the Government of Mexico has taken no formal steps to re-enact the exemption or otherwise alter the current situation. Accordingly, assets which are used by maquiladoras and inventory which is sent by foreign companies to Mexico for processing by maquiladoras would appear to be subject to the two percent tax on assets.

The foregoing notwithstanding, pursuant to the Treaty, Mexico could impose asset and income taxes on subsidiary maquiladoras. The Treaty makes this possible by specifying that the term "permanent establishment" encompasses a dependent agent that habitually processes goods or merchandise owned by a

---

[110] Ley del Impuesto Sobre la Renta of 1980 (as amended).

[111] Ley del Impuesto al Activo de las Empresas of 1988 (as amended).

[112] Rev. Rul. 91-45, 1991-2 C.B.336.

[113] In contrast, Pitex companies are not exempt from the asset tax.

foreign entity on behalf of the foreign entity using assets furnished by the foreign entity or a related person.[114]

Mexico also has a value added tax law[115] (the "Value Added Tax Law") at a general rate of ten percent. Products purchased by maquiladoras in Mexico are effectively exempt because exports of goods and services, which include sales by Mexican residents to maquiladoras, are subject to a zero tax rate. Services provided to the maquiladora are taxable at the zero tax rate as well. Furthermore, all value added tax paid is generally refundable with respect to subsequently exported products.[116]

6. CONCLUSION

A maquiladora-type facility may continue to offer opportunities for United States and Canadian investors for years to come. Perhaps more significantly, however, the Maquiladora Program may serve as a vehicle of integration--both between the national and border economies within Mexico and in North America as a whole through NAFTA.

---

[114] U.S.-Mexico Income Tax Treaty, Article 5(5)(b). The U.S. Treasury Department's Technical Explanation states that this provision simply provides clarification; "it is not meant to create a permanent establishment where one would not exist without this language." U.S. Department of the Treasury, *Technical Explanation of the U.S.-Mexico Income Tax Treaty* 12 (1993).

[115] Ley del Impuesto al Valor Agregado.

[116] Articles 2A and 29 of the Value Added Tax Law.

APPENDIX A

Article 1106 of NAFTA provides, in relevant part:

Article 1106: Performance Requirements

1. No Party may impose or enforce any of the following requirements, or enforce any commitment or undertaking, in connection with the establishment, acquisition, expansion, management, conduct or operation of an investment of an investor of a Party or of a non-Party in its territory:

(a) to export a given level or percentage of goods or services;

(b) to achieve a given level or percentage of domestic content;

(c) to purchase, use or accord a preference to goods produced or services provided in its territory, or to purchase goods or services from persons in its territory;

(d) to relate in any way the volume or value of imports to the volume or value of exports or to the amount of foreign exchange inflows associated with such investment;

(e) to restrict sales of goods or services in its territory that such investment produces or provides by relating such sales in any way to the volume or value of its exports or foreign exchange earnings;

(f) to transfer technology, a production process or other proprietary knowledge to a person in its territory, except when the requirement is imposed or the commitment or undertaking is enforced by a court, administrative tribunal or competition authority to remedy an alleged violation of competition laws or to act in a manner not inconsistent with other provisions of this Agreement; or

(g) to act as the exclusive supplier of the goods it produces or services it provides to a specific region or world market.

. . .

3. No Party may condition the receipt or continued receipt of an advantage, in connection with an investment in its territory of an investor of a Party or of a non-Party, on compliance with any of the following requirements:

(a) to achieve a given level or percentage of domestic content;

(b) to purchase, use or accord a preference to goods produced in its territory, or to purchase goods from producers in its territory;

(c) to relate in any way the volume or value of imports to the volume or value of exports or to the amount of foreign exchange inflows associated with such investment; or

(d) to restrict sales of goods or services in its territory that such investment produces or provides by relating such sales in any way to the volume or value of its exports or foreign exchange earnings.

MEXICO'S FOREIGN INVESTMENT LAW OF 1993, AMENDMENTS TO THE MAQUILA DECREE, AND AN OVERVIEW OF MAQUILADORAS

by Dean C. Alexander*

1. MEXICO'S FOREIGN INVESTMENT LAW OF 1993

1.1 INTRODUCTION

On December 27, 1993, Mexico's new foreign investment law, *Ley de Inversión Extranjera*, was published in Mexico's Official Gazette (*Diario Oficial de la Federación*). This legislation was a dramatic advancement in the regulation of foreign investment in Mexico. Its adoption was part of the legislation required to be adopted by Mexico in order to implement the NAFTA. Some commentators suggest that were NAFTA not adopted, Mexico would have adopted similar legislation in order to demonstrate its commitment to liberalizing its foreign investment regime.

This article provides an overview of the various components of the legislation. Other articles in this volume also address this legislation, its relation to NAFTA, and its ramifications for attracting foreign investment to Mexico. Subsequently, a discussion of the December 24, 1994 Maquila Decree which revised the Decree for Development and Operation of the Maquila Export Industry. Lastly, an overview of the maquiladora industry is provided.

---

* Director, The NAFTA Research Institution, Washington, D.C.

1.2 OVERVIEW OF NEW FOREIGN INVESTMENT LAW (DECEMBER 27, 1994)

The first title of the legislation discusses general provisions, including: the purpose of the law; reserved activities; and activities and acquisitions subject to specific regulation. The second title relates to the acquisition of real property and trusts, such as: acquisition of real property; and trusts as to real property in a restricted zone. The third title covers the incorporation and amendment of companies. The fourth title addresses investment by foreign entities and qualification of foreign firms.

The fifth title covers the complex subject of neutral investment, including: its definition; neutral investments represented by instruments issued by fiduciary institutions; neutral investments represented by special series of stock; neutral investment in firms controlling financial groups, multiple banking institutions, and securities firms; and neutral investment made by international development financial institutions.

The sixth title discusses the national foreign investment commission, including: its structure; the basis for its authority; and the operation of the commission. The seventh title addresses the national registry of foreign investment. The eighth title covers the sanctions that are available under this legislation. Lastly, transitional provisions relate to: what laws are repealed or amended due to this legislation; schedules for various levels of investment; and other relevant matter.

1.3 FIRST TITLE

Chapter I, the objective of the law, includes Article 1 which provides that the purpose of the legislation is to create rules by which foreign investment will flow into Mexico and ensuring that such funds assist national development. Next, Article 2 sets out definitions to a number of key terms that are used throughout the legislation, including, for instance: I. Commission (National Foreign Investment Commission); II. Foreign Investment (a. an investment by foreign investors in any level in the capital stock of a Mexican company; b. an investment by a Mexican company a majority of the capital stock of which is owned by foreign investors; and c. an investment by foreign investors in the activities and actions perceived therein); III. Foreign Investor (an individual or legal entity with a nationality other than Mexican and any foreign entity without legal personality); IV. Registry (National Registry of Foreign Investment); V. Ministry (Ministry of Trade and Industrial Development); VI. Restricted Zone (the portion of Mexican territory, extending one hundred kilometers from the borders and fifty kilometers from the coasts, which is discussed in section I of Article 27 of the Political Constitution of Mexico); VII. Foreign Exclusion Zone (an express covenant or agreement which forms an integral part of the articles of association of a company and establishes that such firm shall not allow, directly or indirectly, as partners or shareholders, any foreign investors or any companies which permit investment by foreign investors).

Article 3 addresses the rule that investments made by foreigners in Mexico which have been granted the status of immigrant shall be treated as Mexican investments, save for investments made in the activities foreseen in the First and Second Titles of this legislation. Furthermore, Article 4 pronounces that foreign investors may invest in any percentage of capital stock of Mexican firms, obtain fixed assets, open new areas of economic activity or make new products, open and operate establishments or expand or relocate existing establishments, aside as noted herein.

Chapter II covers reserved activities. For instance, Article 5 expresses which activities are reserved exclusively to the Mexican State as determined by appropriate laws, they include: I. Petroleum and other hydrocarbons; II. Basic petrochemicals; III. Electricity; IV. Generation of nuclear energy; V. Radioactive minerals; VI. Satellite communications; VII. Telegraphy; VIII. Radiotelegraphy; IX. Mail; X. Railways; XI. Issuance of bank notes; XII. Minting of coins; XIII. Control, supervision and oversight of ports, airports, and heliports; and XIV. Any other areas expressly indicated in the provisions of applicable law.

Article 6 addresses the activities reserved to Mexican nationals. Among the economic activities and enterprises that are reserved exclusively to Mexicans or to Mexican companies having a foreign exclusive clause include: I. National land transportation of passengers, tourism and cargo, excluding messenger and parcel services; II. Retail sale of gasoline and distribution of liquid petroleum gas; III. Radio broadcasting and other radio and television services, except those relating to cable television; IV. Credit unions; V. Development banking institutions, in accordance with applicable law; and VI. Professional and technical services expressly referred to in the provisions of applicable law.

Moreover, Article 6 provides that foreign investors may not invest directly in the activities or type of firms mentioned in Article 6, or through trusts, covenants, partnership agreements or articles of association, pyramid schemes, or any other mechanism by which they may acquire control of an investment, except as noted for in the Fifth Title herein.

Chapter III covers the activities and acquisitions that are subject to specific regulation. More specifically, Article 7 addresses activities in which foreign investment is subject to percentage limits. For instance, foreign investment in the following economic activities and enterprises are limited by the following percentages: I. Up to 10% in production cooperatives; II. Up to 25% in national air transportation, transportation by aerotaxes, and specialized air transportation; III. Up to 30% in firms controlling financial groups, multiple banking institutions, securities firms, and stock exchange specialities; IV. Up to 49% in: (a. Insurance companies; b. Bonding companies; c. Foreign exchange companies; d. Bonded warehouses; e. Financial leasing companies; f. Financial factoring companies; g. Limited-purpose financial companies discussed in Section IV of Article 103 of the Credit Institutions Law; h. Companies referred to in Article 12 Bis of the Securities Market Law; i. Stock which represents the fixed capital of investment companies and operating companies of investment companies; j. Manufacture and sale of explosives, firearms, cartridges, ammunition, and fireworks, excluding the acquisition and utilization of explosives for industrial and extraction activities, or the processing of explosive mixtures for use in connection with such activities; k. Printing and publication of periodicals for exclusive distribution within the national territory; l. Series "T" shares of companies holding agricultural, ranching, and forestry properties; m. Cable television; n. Basic telephone services; o. Fresh water fishing and coastal fishing in the exclusive economic zone, excluding aquaculture; p. Port authority administration,; q. Harbor piloting services for ships engaged in cabotage and domestic navigation, in accordance with applicable law; r. Shipping companies dedicated to commercial for-profit operation of cabotage and domestic navigation services, with the exception of tourist cruise ships and dredging and naval services relating to harbor construction, conservation and port operation; s. Services relating to railways, including passenger services, maintenance and rehabilitation of rail systems, loading and unloading services, tractor and hauling equipment repair shops, organization and commercial trading of unitary trains, operation of domestic cargo terminals and railroad telecommunications; and t. Supply of fuel and lubricants for ships, airplanes, and railroad equipment).

In addition, Article 7 notes that the limitations on foreign investment set out above cannot be overreached directly or through trusts, covenants, partnership agreements or articles of association, pyramid schemes or any other mechanism by which control or participation exceeding that which is stated above can be acquired, except as provided in Fifth Title herein.

Next, Article 8 relates activities in which foreign investment above 49% requires approval of the Foreign Investment Commission. More particularly, a positive determination by the Commission is needed for any foreign investment in a percentage exceeding 49% in the business activities and types of firms noted below: I. Harbor services for ships involved in domestic navigation operations such as towing, mooring, and lighterage; II. Shipping companies dedicated exclusively to transoceanic shipping services; III. Administration of air terminals; IV. Private educational services in pre-school, elementary, junior high school, and high school levels (and combinations thereof); V. Legal services; VI. Credit information companies; VII. Securities rating institutions; VIII. Insurance agents; IX. Cellular telephone services; X. Construction of pipelines for the transportation of oil and oil derivatives; and XI. Drilling of oil and natural gas wells.

Under Article 9, a positive determination by the Commission is required for any foreign investment, directly or indirectly, in an interest in a Mexican corporation (engaged in an activity other than those mentioned in the preceding Articles) in a percentage exceeding 49% of its capital stock, but only when the total value of the assets of such corporation, at the time when the application for the acquisition is submitted, exceeds an amount which the Commission shall determine on an annual basis.

1.4 SECOND TITLE

This title recites the regulation of the acquistion of real property and trusts. Article 10 of Chapter I of this legislation provides that in compliance with the clauses of Section 1 of Article 27 of the Political Constitution of Mexico, Mexican firms which have a foreign exclusion clause (or have obtained the agreement referred to in such provisions) can obtain title to real property in Mexico. With reference to firms whose articles of association include the arrangement discussed in Section 1 of Article 27 of the Constitution, the items below will apply: I. They may obtain title to real property located in the restricted zone which is signified for non-residential purposes, as long as such acquisitions are recorded with the Ministry of Foreign Affairs; and II. They may obtain rights to real property located in the restricted zone which is designated for residential purposes, in accordance with the provisions of Chapter II.

Next, Chapter II relates to trusts as to real property in the restricted zone. Article 11 covers trusts requiring approval by the Ministry of Foreign Affairs. More specifically, it requires the authorization of the Ministry of Foreign Affairs so that credit institutions can obtain, as trustees, rights with regard to real property located in the restricted zone, when the objective of the trust is to permit the use of and earnings from such properties without creating real property rights to them, and the beneficiaries are: I. Mexican firms not having a foreign exclusion clause as provided for in section II of Article 10 of this legislation; and II. Foreign individuals or legal entities.

Article 12 discusses the use of and earnings from real property in the restricted zone. More particularly, it provides that utilization of and profiting from real property situated in the restricted zone means the capacity to use and enjoy the same, including, as the case may be, the benefit of any products or proceeds and, generally, the profits which may occur from the lucrative operation and taking advantage thereof through third parties or the fiduciary institution.

Meanwhile, Article 13 expresses that the term of each trust covered in this chapter shall be a maximum period of fifty years, which can be prolonged at the request of the interested party. Nevertheless, the Ministry of Foreign Affairs reserves the right to verify at any time the fulfillment of the conditions to which the authorizations and registrations referred to in this title are granted.

Next, Article 14 relates to the permit approval process. Assessments of the permits discussed in this chapter are carried out by the Ministry of Foreign Affairs. In doing so, the Ministry takes into account the economic and social benefits that Mexico would obtain due to these operations. It is important to emphasize that every permit application which complies with the indicated requirements must be granted by the Ministry of Foreign Affairs within thirty days subsequent to the date of its submission. Likewise, the recordations discussed in Section 10 of Article 10 have to be processed within a maximum period of fifteen business days after the submission of the application. Otherwise, the permit or the corresponding registration shall be considered granted.

1.5   THIRD TITLE

This title describes the methodology with reference to the incorporation and amendment of companies. For instance, Article 15 sets out that the Ministry of Foreign Affairs must authorize all incorporations of companies. Moreover, the articles of association of such firms must include either the foreign exclusion clause or the agreement provided for in Section I of Article 27 of the Constitution. Also, under Article 16 modification of the incorporated companies' names or change of their foreign exclusion clause necessitates approval by the Ministry of Foreign Affairs.

1.6   FOURTH TITLE

Article 17 of this title recites the qualifications of foreign companies. This article provides that without prejudice to international treaties and agreements to which Mexico is a party, foreign firms that seek to do business in Mexico must obtain the prior authorization of the Ministry for their registration with the Public Registry of Commerce in accordance with Articles 250 and 251 of the General Law of Mercantile Companies. Yet, such applications which comply with the corresponding requirements must be granted by the Ministry within 15 business days subsequent the date of its submission.

1.7   FIFTH TITLE

The Fifth Title discusses the concept of neutral investment. Under Chapter I, Article 18, a definition of neutral investment is provided. More specifically, it is expressed as passive investment that is made in Mexican firms or in authorized trusts with compliance of this Title and which is not to be taken into account in determining the percentage of foreign investment in the capital stock of Mexican companies.

Next, Chapter II, Article 19 covers neutral investment represented by instruments issued by fiduciary institutions. The Ministry may require fiduciary institutions to issue neutral investment instruments which shall only grant, with reference to firms, financial rights to the holders thereof and, if applicable, limited corporate rights, without granting to the holders any voting rights in the firm's ordinary general shareholders' meetings.

Subsequently, Chapter III, Article 20 discusses neutral investment represented by special series of stock. Investments in stock without voting rights or with limited corporate rights shall be signified as neutral investments, as long as the prior approval of the Ministry was acquired and, if appropriate, that of the National Securities Commission.

Chapter IV, Article 21 addresses neutral investment in firms controlling financial groups, multiple banking institutions, and securities firms. More specifically, under this article, the Ministry, after consultation between the Ministry of Finance and Public Credit and the National Securities Commission, may make assessments regarding neutral investments impacted through the acquisition of ordinary certificates of participation issued by fiduciary institutions authorized for such purpose, whose capital comprises of series "B" of the capital stock of firms controlling financial groups or multiple banking institutions or series "A" shares of the capital stock of securities firms.

Next, Chapter V, Article 22 covers neutral investment made by international development finance institutions. More particularly, the National Foreign Investment Commission may make assessments regarding neutral investments which international development financial institutions seek to make in the capital stock of companies, in accordance with the terms and conditions established to this effect by the regulation promulgated under this legislation.

1.8   SIXTH TITLE

This title discusses the National Foreign Investment Commission. Under Chapter I, Article 23, the composition of the Commission is discussed. More particularly, the Commission will be comprised of the Ministers of the: Interior; Foreign Affairs; Finance and Public Credit; Social Development; Energy, Mines and Parastatal Industries; Trade and Industrial Development; Communications and Transportation; Labor and Social Security; and Tourism, each of whom may appoint a deputy minister as a representative. Also, any authorizations with competence in the matters involved can be invited to participate in the sessions of the Commission.

Article 24 notes that the Commission will be chaired by the Ministry of Trade and Industrial Development as well as have an Executive Secretary and a Committee of Representatives to carry out its daily functions. Also, Article 25 relates that the committee of representatives shall be comprised of the public officials designated by each of the Ministers who belong to the Commission. These representatives will have the powers delegated to it by the Commission.

Next, Chapter II discusses the authority of the Commission. More specifically, under Article 26, the Commission shall have the following capabilities: I. To establish policy guidelines regarding foreign investment as well as to craft the mechanisms to promote investment in Mexico; II. To determine, through the Ministry, the merits, and as appropriate, the terms and conditions of foreign investment in the activities or in the situations subject to particular regulation under Articles 8 and 9 of this legislation; III. To provide mandatory consultation in the area of foreign investment for the various departments and agencies of the Federal Public Administration; IV. To establish the criteria for the application of the legal and regulatory provisions in the area of foreign investment through the issuance of general resolutions; and V. Any other authority which would inure to it in accordance with this law.

Next, Article 27 describes the authority of the Executive Secretary. More particularly, the Executive Secretary shall have the following authority: I. To represent the Commission; II. To provide notice of the resolutions to it by the Commission; III. To carry out the studies entrusted to it by the Commission; IV. To submit to the Mexican Congress an annual report of statistics concerning foreign investment activities in Mexico, including the economic sectors and regions in which such investments are made; and V. Any other authority which would inure to it in accordance with this Law.

Under Chapter III, the operation of the Commission is discussed. Article 28 covers the decisions of the Commission. For instance, the Commission must rule on the applications submitted for its consideration not more than 45 business days after the date such application was submitted, pursuant to the terms established by the regulation of this legislation. If the Commission does not make a decision with respect to any application within the specified time, the application shall be deemed to be approved in accordance with the terms thereof. At the express request of an interested party, the Ministry shall issue the corresponding authorization.

Meanwhile, Article 29 relates the factors to be considered by the Commission. For instance, in order to evaluate the applications submitted for its consideration, the Commission shall consider the following criteria: I. The impact on employment and the training of workers; II. The technological contribution; III. Compliance with rules relating to environmental matters as contained in applicable environmental laws; and IV. In general, the contribution to development of the competitiveness of the productive base of Mexico. Furthermore, when the Commission judges an application, it may only institute requirements that do not distort international trade. Of relevance, too, is Article 30 which permits the Commission to prevent acquisitions by foreign investors for reasons of national security.

1.9   SEVENTH TITLE

The Seventh Title discusses the national registry of foreign investment. More specifically, Article 31 notes that the Registry shall not be of a public nature. Moreover, the Registry will be separated into sections established by its internal rules which shall determine its organization as well as the information that should be filed with the Registry.

Article 32 sets out the institutions that must register with the Registry, among them: I. Mexican companies with foreign investors; II. Foreign individuals and entities carrying out commercial activities in Mexico, and branch offices of foreign investors established in Mexico; and III. Stock or partnership trusts, real property and neutral investment trusts in which beneficial rights are held by foreign investors.

It is noteworthy that under the necessity of register is the responsibility of entities and individuals cited above in sections I and II, and with reference to section III, the obligation to register shall apply to the fiduciary institutions. The registration must be made within 40 business days after the date: on which the company was organized or the foreign investment was permitted; on which the formalization or legalization of the documents relating to the foreign company was completed; or on which the respective trust was created or the beneficial ownership interests were transferred to the foreign investor.

With regard to registration receipts, Article 33 provides that the Registry shall issue registration receipts when the data is contained in the application: I. With respect to sections I and II of Article 33 the following information is required: a. Name, firm name or trade name, address, date of organization, if appropriate, and principal business activity to be carried out; b. Name and address of the legal representative; c. Name and address of persons authorized to hear and receive notifications; d. Name, firm name or trade name, nationality and immigation status, if appropriate, address of each foreign investor in or outside Mexico and the percentage of the corresponding investment; e. Amount of capital subscribed and paid or subscribed and payable; and f. Estimated date of the beginning of operations and the approximate amount of the total investment (broken down into a schedule).

Furthermore, Article 33 provides that with reference to section III of Article 32, the Registry shall issue registration receipts when the following data is provided in the application, including: a. Name of the fiduciary institution; b. Name, firm name or trade name, address and nationality of each foreign investor or foreign investor beneficiary; c. Name, firm name or trade name, address and nationality of each foreign investor or desginated trusteee of a foreign investor; d. Date of creation, purpose, and term of the trust; and e. Description, value, function, and, if appropriate, location of the assets held in trust.

If any registration receipts and renewals have been issued, the Registry reserves the right to solicit clarifications with reference to the information submitted. Noteworthy, too, any change of the information submitted in accordance with this Article must be communicated to the Registry in compliance with its internal rules.

Next, under Article 34, instructions to notaries public is provided. With regard to any organization, modification, transformation, merger, split, dissolution, and liquidation of mercantile businesses, civil associations or corporations and, in general, in all legal actions and proceedings where they may appear in person or by representation, notaries public shall demand that such persons (or their representatives) as are obligated to register with the Registry pursuant to the terms of Article 32 of this legislation, submit evidence of their registration with the Registry, and in the event that the registration is still being processed, that they submit evidence of the filing of the corresponding application. If no such evidence is submitted, notaries public may legalize the respective public instrument but shall inform the Registry of such omission within ten business days after the date on which the instrument was legalized.

Meanwhile, Article 35 discusses registration renewals. For instance, persons which are required to register with the Registry must renew their registrations annually, and for such purpose it shall be sufficient to submit a financial and economic questionnaire in accordance with the internal rules of the Commission. Also, under Article 36 the federal, state, and municipal authorities are required to provide the Ministry with the necessary reports and certifications to enable it to comply with its functions in accordance with this law and the regulatory provisions thereof.

1.10 EIGHTH TITLE

The eighth title covers sanctions. Article 37 relates to the revocation of authorizations. More specifically, in the event of actions contrary to the provisions of this legislation, the Ministry may revoke the authorizations granted. In addition, the acts, agreements, partnership agreements or articles of association which are declared to be void by the Ministry, as contrary to the provisions of this law, shall have no legal effect between the parties and shall be unenforceable with respect to third parties.

Under Article 38, other sanctions are discussed. For instance, this Article provides that violations of the provisions of this legislation and the regulatory provisions promulgated below shall be punished as follows: I. If the foreign investor carries out activities, acquisitions or any other act for which a favorable resolution of the Commission is needed, without such authorization having been previously acquired, a fine of 1,000 to 5,000 salaries shall be imposed; II. If the foreign legal entities perform on a regular basis commercial activities in Mexico without having obtained the prior authorization of the Ministry, a fine of 500 to 1,000 salaries shall be imposed; III. If actions in violation of the provisions of this law and the regulatory provisions promulgated hereunder with reference to neutral investment, a fine of 100 to 300 salaries shall be imposed; IV. In the event of an omission, late filing, submission of incomplete or incorrect information with respect to registration requirements, reporting or notification to the Registry, a fine of 30 to 100 salaries shall be imposed; V. If inappropriate activities with the purpose of permitting the enjoyment or sale of real property in the restricted zone to foreign individuals or legal entities or Mexican companies that do not have a Foreign Exclusion Clause, in violation of the provisons of the Second and Third Titles of this law, the violator shall be assessed a fine up to the total amount of the transaction; and VI. Other violations of this law and the regulatory provisions promulgated hereunder shall be punished with a fine ranging from 100 to 1,000 salaries.

For purposes of this Article, salary shall be deemed the minimum general daily wage in effect in the Federal District at the time of the violation. In assessing and imposing sanctions, the affected party must be first heard and, in the event of monetary sanctions, the nature of the violation must be taken into consideration, as well as: the seriousness of the actions, the economic ability of the offender to pay, the lapse of time that ran between the date the requirement should have been complied with and the time of its compliance or regularization, and the total value of the transaction.

The Ministry shall be responsible for imposing the sanctions, save for the violation described in Section V of this article and other violations relating to Third and Second Titles of this legislation, the sanctions for which will be imposed by the Ministry. The imposition of sanctions referred to in this title shall be without prejudice to any other civil or criminal liability, as the case may be.

Article 39 discusses instruction to notaries public. More specifically, notaries public shall report, insert or add to the official file or appendix of the instruments which they prepare, the functions included in the authorizations that must be issued pursuant to the terms of this law. When they legalize instruments in which they do not report such authorizations that must be issued pursuant to the terms of this law. When they legalize instruments in which they do not report such authorizations, they will subject themselves to such sanctions as may be specified in the laws governing notaries public and the Federal Law of Public Notaries.

1.11 TRANSITIONAL PROVISIONS

This section of the legislation addresses the transitional aspects of this legislation. Under Article 1 of the transitional provisons, there is a declaration that the new legislation will come into effect one day after its publication in the *Diario Oficial de la Federación*.

Under Article 2 of the transitional provisions, a number of laws are repealed: I. The Law for the Promotion of Mexican Investment and Regulation of Foreign Investment, published in the *Diario Oficial* on March 9, 1973; II. The Organic Law of Section I of Article 27 of the Constitution, published in the *Diario Oficial* on January 21, 1926; and III. The Decree establishing the temporary necessity of obtaining a permit in order for foreigners to acquire assets, and so that to establish and modify Mexican companies that have or could have foreign partners, which was published in the *Diario Oficial* on July 7, 1944.

Under Article 3 of the transitional provisions, the following items are amended: I. Articles 46 and 47 of the Federal Law on Firearms and Explosives published in the *Diario Oficial* on January 11, 1972; and II. All legal, regulatory, and administrative provisions general in nature that are inconsistent with this law.

Next, under Article 4 of the transitional provisions, during the period the regulations under this law are usually prepared, the regulation under the Law to Promote Mexican Investment and Regulate Foreign Investment published in the *Diario Oficial* on May 15, 1989 shall remain in force to the extent not inconsistent with this law.

Article 5 of the transitional provisions provides that foreign investors and firms with foreign investors which, at the time of the publication of this law, have already established schedules, complied with requirements and made commitments before the Commission, its Executive Secretary or the Executive Office for Foreign Investment of the Ministry, may submit for consideration by such Executive Office an application for exemption from compliance, to which such administrative unit must respond within 45 business days after the date of submission of such application. Foreign investors who do not take the possibility of such exemption must comply with the commitments previously set by the Commission and the aforementioned persons and public entities.

Article 6 of the transitional provisions relates that activities such as international land transportation of passengers, tourism and cargo between points in Mexico, as well as administrative services relating to passenger trucking centers and auxillary services are reserved exclusively to Mexicans and to Mexican companies having a Foreign Exclusion Clause.

Notwithstanding the rest of Article 6 of the transitional provisions, foreign investors may acquire interests in the previous business activities in accordance with the following provisions: I. As of December 18, 1995, up to 49% of the capital of Mexican companies; II. As of January 1, 2001, up to 51% of the capital of Mexican companies; and III. As of January 1, 2004, up to 100% of the capital of Mexican companies without the necessity of obtaining the prior approval of the Commission.

Article 7 of the transitional provisions provides that foreign investors may obtain interests in up to 49% of the capital of Mexican firms devoted to the manufacture and assembly of parts, equipment and accessories for the automotive industry, without prejudice to the provisions of the Decree for the Development and Modernization of the Automotive Industry. Furthermore, as of January 1, 1999, foreign investors may obtain up to 100% of the capital of Mexican companies without the necessity of obtaining the prior approval of the Commission.

Article 8 of the transitional provisions relates that with reference to videotext and telephone switching systems, foreign investors may acquire interests of up to 49% of the capital of Mexican companies. From and after July 1, 1995, foreign investors may acquire interests of up to 100% in the capital of companies dedicated to such services, without the necessity of obtaining the prior approval of the Commission.

Article 9 of the transitional provisions discusses that prior approval of the Commission is required in order for foreign investors to invest more than 49% of the capital of companies engaged in any of the following activities: I. Building, construction, and installation of construction sites; II. Construction of pipelines for the transportation of petroleum and byproducts; and III. Drilling of oil and gas wells.

With reference to the business activities mentioned in section I of Article 9, from and after January 1, 1999, foreign investors may invest in up to 100% in the capital of Mexican companies dedicated to such activities without the necessity of obtaining the prior approval of the Commission.

Article 10 of the transitional provisions relates that for the purposes of Article 9, and while the Commission is determining the amount of the total value of the assets referred to in the above-referenced Article, such amount shall be deemed to be 85,000,000 New Pesos.

Article 11 of the transitional provisions discusses foreign investors and Mexican companies with a foreign admittance clause who, on the effective date of this legislation are the beneficiaries of real properties held in trust in the

Restricted Zone, shall be subject to the provisions of Chapter II of the Second Title, to the extent that they benefit therefrom.

1.12 BIBLIOGRAPHY

Diario Oficial de la Federación of December 27, 1993; English translation of the law by the law firm Carlsmith Ball Garcia Cacho y Asociados, S.C., Mexico City/Los Angeles; English translation of the law by the law firm Bryan, Gonzalez, Vargas y Gonzalez Baz, S.C., Mexico City/New York City; additional English translations and commentaries on the law, including "Foreign Investment" in *Mexico Business: The Portable Encyclopedia For Doing Business With Mexico*, World Trade Press (1994); and U.S. government and Mexican government materials on the subject.

2. AMENDMENTS TO THE MAQUILA DECREE

2.1 INTRODUCTION

Prior to the publication in the *Diario Oficial de la Federación* on December 27, 1993 of Mexico's new foreign investment law, *Ley de Inversión Extranjera*, Mexico published three days earlier revisions to the Decree for Development and Operation of the Maquila Export Industry. These amendments, which included additions and deletions to the Maquila Decree, came into effect on January 1, 1994.

According to the law firm of Bryan, Gonzalez, Vargas y Gonzalez Baz, among the highlights of the changes instituted under the December 24, 1994 revision to the Decree for Development and Operation of the Maquila Export Industry are:

1. The concept of Maquila Operations is extended to include the service activities provided to maquiladoras or to firms with a Temporary Exploitation Program to Produce Articles for Exportation, generally known as PITEX firms.
2. The concept of maquiladoras no longer requires that a firm export all of its production.
3. The materials and components imported for use in a maquiladora may remain in Mexico for a maximum term of one year (and not for six

months, extendable).

4. With reference to the materials, components, tools, and spare parts needed for its industrial operations, the same will currently be permitted into Mexico for a period of two years and the same may stay in Mexico as long as the industrial program for which they were authorized remains in effect.

5. Trailers and containers that are temporarily imported into Mexico may remain as long as the maquila program for which they were authorized continues to be in effect, without their stay being longer than 20 years.

6. With reference to specific export quotas, the Ministry of Commerce and Industrial Development (Ministry) will approve the programs pursuant to the assignment policies of the quantities available, eliminating the concept that the quantities available must be prorated among interested parties. In addition, in the event that the maquiladoras that utilize these quotas require to carry out operations, these must be authorized by the Ministry and such transfer operations shall be deemed indirect exportations.

7. The Exchange Control requirements abrogated in 1991 are eliminated.

8. Maquiladoras may carry out sales into Mexico in the following percentages, pursuant to their total annual value of the exportations made during the preceding year: 1994 - 55%; 1995 - 60%; 1996 - 65%; 1997 - 70%; 1998 - 75%; 1999 - 80%; and 2000 - 85%. From 2001, sales of maquiladoras' products into the Mexican market will not be subject to any limitation. Thus, these plants could sell all of their production to the Mexican market.

9. Maquiladoras must file every 2 months with SECOFI a report of the sales that they carry out in the Mexican market, noting the amount and total value of their exportations during the preceding year, of the sales into Mexico, and the percentage that said sales represent of the total value of their annual exportations that they have carried out during the previous year.

10. The Mexican import duties of the products earmarked for sale into Mexico shall be computed only upon the import tariff corresponding to the foreign parts and components and not upon the total value of the finished product.

11. Article 24 which allowed maquiladoras who were duly authorized to sell into Mexico to elect for the virtual exportation of their finished products under the conditions determined in each case by the Ministry of Treasury is repealed. Such selection is no longer required since this issue is adequately covered by the amendments.

12. Transfer of machinery, tools and spare parts may now be made between maquiladoras and enterprises that have a Program for Temporary

Importation to Produce Articles for Exportation (PITEX), which was not available in the past.

13. For submaquila operations, the limitation that existed for textile products was eliminated, as was the requirement that maquiladoras also be current in the filing of their foreign currency generation report.

14. The Ministry may now cancel the maquila registration granted to an enterprise due to a petition legally supported from another agency of the Federal Public Administration. In additon, the prior term for the application of sanctions by the Ministry during which interested parties may argue what may be to their interest, is raised from 15 business days to 45 business days.

15. The Consultative Committee of the Maquila Export Industry shall also be integrated by the Board of the National Maquiladora Council and by the National Directors representing local maquila associations affiliated to the National Board.

2.2 BIBLIOGRAPHY

Law firm of Bryan, Gonzalez, Vargas y Gonzalez Baz, S.C., Mexico City/New York City, "Amendments to the Maquila Decree," *International Lawyers' Newsletter*, Vol. XVI, No. 2, at 9-10, 1994. *See* Manuel F. Pasero, "The Maquiladora Decree," law firm of Paero, Martin-Sanchez y Sanchez, Tijuana; "Foreign Investment" in *Mexico Business: The Portable Encyclopedia For Doing Business With Mexico*, World Trade Press (1994).

3. OVERVIEW OF MAQUILADORAS

According to the magazine, *Twin Plant News*, as of November 1994 in Mexico there exist 2,134 maquiladoras (maquilas), employing 482,893 people. The largest number of maquiladoras can be found in the following cities : Tijuana, Baja California Norte (529 maquilas, employing 81,599 people) ; Ciudad Juarez, Chihuahua (278 maquilas, employing 100,247 people); Mexicali, Baja California Norte (125 maquilas, employing 19,772 people); Matamoros, Tamaulipas (111 maquilas, employing 41,147 people); Monterrey, Nuevo Leon (95 maquilas, employing 18,221 people); Tecate, Baja California Norte (92 maquilas, employing 7,448 people); Ciudad Chihuahua, Chihuahua (66 maquilas, employing 29,010 people). ["Maquila Scoreboard," *Twin Plant News*,

82 _Dean C. Alexander_

November 1994, at 41. _See_ Don Nibbe, _New Trends Inside Maquiladoras_, Twin Plant News, August 1994, at 28; Muri Carmen Elores, _Are Maquiladoras Near Extinction?_, Twin Plant News, January 1995, at 27; Lucinda Vargas, _Changing Dynamics: Maquilas Enter Consolidation Period_, Twin Plant News, January 1995, at 34.]

Similarly, the number of maquilas and those employed in such plants in the various Mexican states are as follows: Baja California Norte (795 maquilas, employing 112,630 people); Baja California Sur (8 maquilas, employing 662 people); Sonora (196 maquilas, employing 49,104 people); Chihuahua (367 maquilas, employing 137,051 people); Coahuila (170 maquilas, employing 38,124 people); Nuevo Leon (95 maquilas, employing 18,821 people); Tamaulipas (256 maquilas, employing 94,035 people); Durango (50 maquilas, employing 8,118 people); Jalisco (40 maquilas, employing 14,300 people); Yucatan (31 maquilas, employing 5,354 people); Morelos (15 maquilas, employing 1,189 people); Mexico, Federal District (27 maquilas, employing 3,475 people); Sinola (5 maquilas, no statistics available regarding the number of employees); Zacatecas (4 maquilas, no statistics available regarding the number of employees); San Luis Potosi (9 maquilas, no statistics available regarding the number of employees); Aguascalientes (10 maquilas, no statistics available regarding the number of employees); Guanajuato (36 maquilas, no statistics available regarding the number of employees); Michoacan (2 maquilas, no statistics available regarding the number of employees); Hidalgo (13 maquilas, no statistics available regarding the number of employees); Veracruz (2 maquilas, no statistics available regarding the number of employees); and Campeche (3 maquilas, no statistics regarding the number of employees). It is noteworthy that the states with the largest number of maquilas and employees at such sites are those on the U.S.-Mexico border, namely: Baja California North (borders California), Sonora (borders Arizona and New Mexico), Chihuahua (borders New Mexico and Texas); Coahuila (borders Texas); Nuevo Leon (borders Texas), and Tamaulipas (borders Texas). ["Maquila Scoreboard," _Twin Plant News_, November 1994, at 41.]

Others suggest that the number of maquiladoras in 1993 reached 2,205 while employing over 600,000 people. These figures illustrate a dramatic rise over 1988 statistics which found about 1,500 maquiladoras, employing about 500,000 people. In 1993 the maquiladora industry exported $19.8 billion in products, led by electronics, transport equipment, electronic machinery, textiles, and furniture. Exports of electronics and transport equipment each reached over $5 billion in 1993. [Kevin Hall, "Mexico Maquiladoras Face Uncertainity Under Nafta," _The Journal of Commerce_, August 12, 1994, at A1. _See_ Kevin Hall,

Life After Nafta: Steady Trade Gains, The Journal of Commerce, October 17, 1994, at 7A. *See generally* U.S. General Accounting Office, *North American Free Trade Agreement: U.S.-Mexican Trade and Investment Data*, GAO/GGD-92-131 (September 1992); U.S. General Accounting Office, *The Maquiladora Industry and U.S. Employment*, GAO/GGD-93-129 (July 1993); U.S. International Trade Commission, *Production Sharing: U.S. Imports Under Harmonized Tariff Schedule Subheadings 9802.00.60 and 9802.00.80, 1988-1991*, U.S. ITC Pub. 2592 (February 1993); Manuel F. Pasero, "Maquiladoras" in *Mexico Business: The Portable Encyclopedia For Doing Business With Mexico*, World Trade Press (1994).]

FOREIGN INVESTMENT IN MEXICO UNDER NAFTA

by Jorge Luis Ramos Uriarte*

1. INTRODUCTION

On December 17, 1992, Presidents Carlos Salinas de Gortari of Mexico and George Bush of the United States and Prime Minister Brian Mulroney of Canada signed the official text of the North American Free Trade Agreement (NAFTA). "The opening provisions of the NAFTA formally establish a free trade area between Canada, Mexico and the United States, consistent with the General Agreement on Tariffs and Trade (GATT). They set out the basic rules and principles that will govern the Agreement and the objectives that will serve as the basis for interpreting its provisions."[1] The agreement went into effect on January 1, 1994 and it created the biggest free trade area in the world, stretching from Alaska to Yucatan.

NAFTA will eliminate all tariffs on goods originating in Canada, Mexico and the United States over a "transition period." The objectives of NAFTA are "to eliminate barriers to trade, promote conditions of fair competition, increase investment opportunities, provide adequate protection for intellectual property rights, establish effective procedures for the implementation and application of the Agreement and for resolutions of disputes and to further trilateral, regional

---

* Attorney, Ministry of Commerce and Industrial Promotion (SECOFI), Mexico City.
[1] Description of the proposed North American Free Trade Agreement. Prepared by the Governments of Canada, the United Mexican States and the United States of America. Practising Law Institute, 1992, 11.

and multilateral cooperation."[2]

NAFTA has radically changed the protectionist investment rules that have limited American and Canadian investments in Mexico. Also the agreement has transformed Mexico into a more attractive and safer place for investors.

The new Mexican Investment Law (NFIL) was published in the "Diario Oficial", Mexico's Official Gazette, on December 27, 1993. This law was drafted in order to implement the commitments made in NAFTA and in an effort to put Mexico in an advantageous position in international competition for investments.

This chapter discusses the Mexican foreign investment rules and NAFTA's investment chapter. It will also assess the new Mexican Investment Law and will examine the interaction and compatibility between the said law and NAFTA. Part I provides the legal framework and history of the Mexican foreign investment rules. Part II examines the new Mexican Foreign Investment Law. Part III contains an analysis of chapter eleven of the NAFTA.

1.1 LEGAL FRAMEWORK AND HISTORY OF THE MEXICAN FOREIGN INVESTMENT RULES

(i) Constitutional Framework. The Mexican legal system is based on the civil law system which originated in Roman law. The Mexican system has adopted a number of institutions which originated in the French and German laws.

The Mexican Constitution was enacted on February 5, 1917, in the city of Queretaro. The Mexican Constitution contains the basic principles and social aspirations that Mexican revolutionaries struggled to attain. Undoubtedly the most important principle incorporated into the Constitution is the prohibition of the President's re-election. The Mexican Constitution embraces the so-called "garantías sociales" (social guaranties), such as the right to have access to education, to own a home, and a multitude of worker's and peasant's rights. The framers established a federal republic[3] with the division of powers in three branches: the executive branch, invested in the President of the Republic;[4] the legislative branch, invested in the "Congreso de la Union",[5] composed of two

---

[2] Id.

[3] Constitución Política de los Estados Unidos Mexicanos [Constitution of the United Mexican States] [Mex. Const.] Art. 40 (Mexico).

[4] Id. Art. 80.

[5] Id. Art. 50.

chambers, Camara de Diputados (chamber of representatives) and Camara de Senadores (chamber of senators); and the Judicial branch.[6]

(ii) Mexican Investment Rules Prior to 1973. Prior to 1973, foreign investment rules were characterized by an emphasis on increasing exports and protecting existing national industries from domestic competition by foreign investors. There was no investment law, the rules were contained in various decrees issued by the executive branch on a case-by-case basis.

The Emergency Decree of 1944[7] issued by the Mexican Executive granted discretionary control over foreign investment to the Secretariat of Foreign Affairs. The purpose of the Emergency Decree was to avert disruption of the economy caused by the investments of temporary foreign capital. This decree introduced restraints on the creation, modification, liquidation, and transfer of stock of Mexican companies with foreign shareholders that were organized subsequent to enactment of the decree. While it originally affected few and relatively insignificant activities, the Emergency Decree was nonetheless the precursor to more restraints on foreign investment.[8]

Before the enactment of the 1973 Foreign Investment Law, the only restrictions on foreign investment were the provisions of the Emergency Decree and the exclusion of foreigners in nationalized industries.[9] In general, in this period of time due to the lack of an investment law the Mexican government was flexible and the attitude towards foreign investors was one of cautious acceptance.

(iii) 1973 Foreign Investment Law. Prior to the enactment of the 1973 Foreign Investment Law, there was no single investment code. There were many regulations and decrees that made it a legal nightmare for foreign and Mexican counsels. There was an urgent need for uniformity and codification. "The Law to Promote Mexican Investment and Regulate Foreign Investment (FIL), enacted in 1973, was of utmost importance. Its purpose was to codify existing laws, regulations, and policies, and it established the National Foreign Investment

---

[6]   Id. Art. 94.

[7]   Emergency Decree, D.O., July 7, 1944; Sandra F. Maviglia, Mexico's Guidelines for Foreign Investment; the Selective Promotion of Necessary Industries. 80 Am. J. Int'l L. 281, 285 (1986).

[8]   Hope H. Camp, Jr., Foreign Investment in Mexico from the Perspective of the Foreign Investor. 24 St. Mary's L.J. 775, 785 (1993).

[9]   Such as oil, electricity, railroads, and wireless communications.

Commission (FIC)."[10]

The FIL "essentially codifies a plethora of laws, decrees, administrative rulings and unwritten procedures followed by the Ministry of Foreign Relations, the administrative branch formerly in most direct control over the admittance of foreign investments, and the Ministry of Industry and Commerce."[11]

This law was too anti-foreign investor and the international business community did not react positively. "When the 1973 Investment Law was enacted, foreign investors reacted negatively."[12] The FIL contained several prohibitions and restrictions with regard to foreign investment.[13] For example, Article 5 included a 49% maximum foreign ownership limitation in Mexican corporations. Under Article 4, certain activities were reserved to the Mexican government and domestic investors, among them petroleum, exploitation of radioactive minerals, electricity, railroad and telegraphic and wireless communications. Approval from the FIC was required when foreign investors wished to acquire Mexican concerns. Article 12 granted the FIC discretionary authority to decide on the reduction or expansion of the percentage of the foreign investment participation in the different geographical areas or economic activities. This power was broadly used by the FIC in order to attract foreign investment and dilute the protectionist provisions of the Law.

(iv) 1989 Foreign Investment Law Regulations. The Salinas Administration recognized the importance of attracting foreign investment. However, a significant obstacle stood in the way of any proposals to amend the FIL. More specifically, the 49% percent maximum foreign ownership requirement was already almost a taboo.[14] In fact, even among the long-ruling PRI there was

---

[10] Ley para Promover la Inversión Mexicana y Regular la Inversión Extranjera (FIL), D.O., Mar. 9, 1973, translated in Doing Business in Mexico pt. IV, A.4-1 to A.4-53 (1990).

[11] Gordon, The Contemporary Mexican Approach to Growth with Foreign Investment: Controlled but Participatory Independence. 10 Cal. West. L. Rev. 1 (1973).

[12] W. Friedmann & J.P. Beguin, Joint International Business Ventures in Developing Countries, 14, 385 (1971).

[13] Prior to the 1973 Mexican Investment Law there was no maximum foreign ownership limitation in Mexican corporations, except for a few industries.

[14] We need to bear in mind that Mexico suffered several foreign interventions during the 19th century, including Spain, Great Britain, France and the United States. Some of these conflicts related to foreign investment. In part, the bad labor conditions and the low wages that some American companies paid to the Mexican laborers were one of the sparks that started the Mexican Revolution in 1910. In the Mexican psyche there was somehow a distrust toward foreign investment. This distrust has gradually lessened and currently the Mexican people are aware of the necessity of attracting foreign investment.

no consensus to approve greater access to foreign investment. At the time, the PRI had enough votes in order to pass any legislative attempt to liberalize foreign investment restrictions. Nevertheless, in order to avoid political problems inside and outside his party, Salinas issued only modifications to the 1973 Foreign Investment Law with the 1989 Regulations.[15]

Article 89, Paragraph I of the Mexican Constitution grants the President authority to enact regulations. Nevertheless, "the scope of the regulations is necessarily limited to the underlying law. Separation of powers, a governing concept fundamental to the Constitution, requires that the President carry out acts that provide for the exact observance of the law issued by the legislative branch."[16] A regulation issued on the contrary could be declared unconstitutional by the Supreme Court of Justice.

The 1989 Regulations to the FIL was issued to promote foreign investment and to avoid some legal limitations contained in the FIL. It accords foreigners broad investment opportunities. "A cornerstone provision, article five of the FIL Regulation, grants the foreign investor the right to establish a 100 percent foreign owned enterprise in Mexico, without first obtaining prior approval from the NFIC. The 100 percent ownership clause, along with other provisions of the Regulation contradict the FIL and other laws enacted by the legislature. However, because the FIL and other laws were approved and enacted by the legislature, they are superior to the FIL Regulation. Therefore, the FIL Regulation's provisions which contradict the FIL and other laws enacted by Congress appear to be technically illegal and unconstitutional."[17]

In order to obtain the benefits granted by Article 5 of the 1989 Regulations to the FIL any foreign investment should fulfill seven critical requirements. First, investments must be made in fixed assets used to conduct the company's economic activities in an amount up to that periodically established by the Trade Secretariat (in 1992 this amount was 100 million American Dollars). Second, the investment is made with financial resources obtained from abroad. Third, the minimum amount of paid-in capital stock must be equivalent to 20 percent of the total investment in fixed assets at the end of the pre-operational period. Fourth, the company so incorporated locates the industrial establishments outside of geographical zones of greatest industrial concentration and subject to

---

[15] Reglamento de la Ley para Promover la Inversión Mexicana y Regular la Inversión Extranjera [Regulations of the Law to Promote Mexican Investment and Regulate Foreign Investment], D.O. May 16, 1989 (Mexico).

[16] Ignacio Gomez-Palacio, The New Regulation on Foreign Investment in Mexico: A Difficult Task. 12 Hous. J. Int'l L. 253, 259 (1990).

[17] Id. at 253.

controlled growth, specifically the Metropolitan areas of Mexico City, Guadalajara and Monterrey.

Fifth, the company so incorporated maintains, as minimum results during the first three years of its operations, a position of equilibrium in its balance of foreign currency. Sixth, the company so incorporated will generate permanent jobs and establish sustained programs of training, qualification and personal development for its employees. Seventh, the company so incorporated shall make use of adequate technology and to comply with all environmental laws.[18]

If the investment did not comply with the aforementioned requirements it required approval by the Foreign Investment Commission. The process of review and approval was expedited. The Ministry of Foreign Relations had to decide upon an application within forty-five business days following the date of filing. Upon the lapse of the said term without the Ministry having resolved the application, it shall be deemed to have granted the authorization applied for.[19] This is known in Mexico as a "positiva ficta".

The 1989 Regulations did not develop and complement the law, it clearly contradicted the FIL and its validity could have been challenged in the Mexican Supreme Court.

A foreign investor looks for legal security for his investment and this contradiction had been considered in the developed countries as a risk factor against investing in Mexico. Besides, although the 1989 Regulation's aim was promoting foreign investment, it did not grant incentives. The only benefit was deregulation.

(v) The Execution of Treaties Law. International arbitration is an important tool for international commercial transactions. It offers flexibility and speed in dispute settlements. However, the Mexican legal system did not permit that mechanism for the settlement of disputes.

In order to change that situation the Mexican legislature enacted on January 2, 1992, very important legislation, the Execution of Treaties Law.[20] Although this legislation has been widely ignored by American legal researchers, it is a critical achievement in the Mexican legal system. This legislation regulates the celebration and execution of treaties and agreements.

---

[18] See Ogarrio and Pereznieto Castro, Mexico-United States Relations: Economic Integration and Foreign Investment. 12 Hous. J. Int'l L. 223 (1990).

[19] FIL Reg. Art. 2.

[20] Ley sobre la Celebración de Tratados [Execution of Treaties Law], D.O., Jan. 2, 1992 (Mexico).

Latin American nations were historically exposed to abuses of diplomatic protection. The Calvo Doctrine "emerged as a response to the institution of diplomatic protection in these countries. The Doctrine, which was named after a nineteenth-century law professor, denied that foreign nationals were entitled to diplomatic protection. It provided that investment disputes between foreign nationals and host countries had to be settled under domestic law in the local court system. Under the Calvo Doctrine, the intervention of foreign States in investment disputes was deemed a violation of the territorial jurisdiction of the host State."[21]

According to the Calvo Doctrine "there should be equality of treatment between nationals and foreigners and state intervention in the affairs of another state should not be permitted. As a result diplomatic protection by foreign states of their nationals in Latin-America in respect of business transactions should be excluded."[22]

Article 27 of the Mexican federal constitution contains a Calvo clause. This article provides that foreign investments in Mexico are not entitled to diplomatic protection. This clause has been narrowly construed to require that aliens submit disputes arising in Mexico to Mexican local courts. Also, Mexican federal courts have interpreted Article 104[23] of the federal constitution to prohibit the recourse to international arbitration in Mexico. Although the Mexican Constitution does not expressly prohibit international arbitration, if the Mexican Supreme Court maintains the narrow interpretation of Article 104 the Execution of Treaties Law could be declared unconstitutional.

The Execution of Treaties Law authorizes the Mexican government to enter into treaties or international agreements that contain international settlement of legal disputes mechanisms. Most modern international business contracts contain arbitration, forum of law, and choice of law clauses. The "Latin-American states show an increasing trend in favor of international commercial arbitration."[24] Mexico has followed that trend and the conclusion of the

---

[21] Political Risk Insurance: OPIC's Use of a 'Fiduciary Agent' to Facilitate Resolution of Subrogation Claims. 23 Int'l Law 271, 276 (1989).

[22] A.H.A. Soons, ed., International Arbitration: Past and Prospects: a Symposium to Commemorate the Centenary of the Birth of Professor J.H.W. Verzijl, 113 (1990).

[23] "Article 104. The Federal courts shall hear: I. All civil or criminal disputes originated from the compliance and application of federal laws or international treaties celebrated by the Mexican government." Mex. Const. Art. 104. The Supreme Court has held that since ALL the civil and criminal controversies resulting from the application and compliance of federal laws or international treaties must be tried by the federal courts, hence, international arbitration is not allowed.

[24] R. David, Arbitration in International Trade, 23-25 (1985).

Execution of Treaties Law removed investors from the restrictions of the Calvo Doctrine.

Article 8 of the Execution of Treaties Law[25] expressly permits international arbitration in Mexico. This law enabled the Mexican negotiators to accept arbitration and other dispute settlement mechanisms negotiated in NAFTA. Since, after all, NAFTA offers national treatment, a guarantee of due process, the fair exercise of defenses, and that decision organs are impartial.

2. 1993 FOREIGN INVESTMENT LAW

The Mexican legislature enacted on December 27, 1993 a new Foreign Investment Law (hereafter 1993 FIL).[26] The 1993 FIL is a very short statute[27] that deregulates and eliminates many of the protectionist measures that interfered with foreign investment in the Mexican Republic. The liberalized approach of this new law can be inferred not only from its text[28] but also from its name. The former foreign investment law's official denomination was: Law To Promote Mexican Investment and To Regulate Foreign Investment. On the contrary, the 1993 FIL's denomination is simply "Foreign Investment Law". This law changed the Mexican regulation of foreign investment in order to comply with the provisions contained in chapter eleven of the North American Free Trade Agreement.

The purposes of the 1993 FIL are essentially two-fold. First, the law establishes clear channels for the participation of foreign investment. Second, the legislation promotes national development.[29] The 1993 FIL defines foreign investment as participation of foreign investors in Mexican corporations, directly or indirectly, or in activities or acts covered by the Law.

[25] Ley sobre la Celebración de Tratados. D.O., Jan. 2, 1992.

[26] Ley de Inversión Extranjera [Foreign Investment Law], D.O. December 27, 1993 (Mexico).

[27] The new Foreign Investment Law only contains 39 articles (NFIL).

[28] NFIL Art. 1 states that the purpose of this law is to determine the rules to attract foreign investment and to assure that it contributes to the national development.

[29] NFIL Art. 1.

2.1   GENERAL RULE

Under the 1993 FIL foreign investors are authorized to participate in any proportion in the capital of Mexican companies, acquire fixed assets, enter into new fields of economic activity, or manufacture new product lines, open and operate establishments, and expand or relocate existing establishments, except as otherwise provided in the law.[30] "There are, however, a number of express provisions that limit foreign investment. Foreign investment in the financial sector is subject to the specific laws governing said sector, but article 7 summarizes the considerable latitude allowed participation by foreign investment in this sector, including up to 30% in the commercial banking and securities field, and up to 49% in a number of auxiliary credit businesses."[31]

2.2   RESTRICTED ACTIVITIES

Article 5 contains 14 restricted activities and reserves these strategic areas exclusively to the Mexican State.[32] The 1993 FIL maintains the same reserved activities contained in the repealed 1973 Investment Law. Nevertheless, while railroad activity is reserved to the State, Article 7 (IV) (s) permits participation of foreign investment in certain services related to railroads up to 49%.

The 1993 FIL reserves certain activities to Mexican persons or Mexican corporations, with an exclusion-of-foreigners clause.[33] These activities are: domestic land transportation of passengers, tourism and freight; gasoline sale at retail and gas distribution; wireless communications; credit unions; development banks and supply of professional and technical services pursuant to express provision of law.

Another exception to the general rule set forth in Article 4 is contained in

---

[30]   NFIL Art. 4.

[31]   Bryan, Gonzalez Vargas y Gonzales, Mexican Federation Enacts New Foreign Investment Law, 16 Int'l L. 6, 7 (1994).

[32]   "Article 5.- The functions determined by the corresponding laws are reserved exclusively to the State in the following strategic areas: I. Oil and other hydrocarbons; II. Basic petrochemicals; III.- Electricity; IV.- Generation of nuclear energy; V.- Radioactive minerals; VI.- Communications via satellite; VII.- Telegraphic communications; VIII.- Radiotelegraphy; IX.- Mail service; X.- Railroads; XI.- Circulation of bills; XII.- Minting of coins; XIII.- Control, supervision and policing of ports, airports, and heliports; and XIV.- Other activities established in specific laws."

[33]   NFIL Art. 6.

Article 8. This article enumerates the activities in which foreign investors may only participate in up to 49%.[34] Nevertheless, the same article authorizes the participation of foreign investors in excess of that limit when prior approval is granted by the Foreign Investment Commission.

One important innovation contained in the 1993 FIL is the provision that authorizes the participation of foreign investment in the important Mexican oil industry.[35] From 1938[36] to December 27, 1993, the date when 1993 FIL was enacted, the Mexican government did not permit the participation of foreign investors in the oil industry. Under NAFTA, the Mexican government accepted that it must permit foreign investment in the construction of ducts for the transportation of oil and its derivatives[37] as well as the perforation of oil and gas wells.[38] This change is a key innovation as it destroys the flat prohibition against foreign participation in the oil industry. It is important to remember that the "Mexicanization" of this industry was used for several decades as a political banner. Moreover, Lázaro Cárdenas, the President that ordered the nationalization of the Mexican oil industry, is still considered one of the greatest political heros of Mexico. Consequently, the Salinas Administration faced many political obstacles and sometimes clear opposition from some sectors of the PRI. Nevertheless, the Salinas Administration overcame all the obstacles and achieved the aforementioned change.

2.3 NEUTRAL INVESTMENT

"In addition to investment participation in Mexican companies and projects that involve full corporate rights, the concept of neutral investment –essentially a non-participatory financial investment tool– has been expanded under this new

---

[34] These activities are: port services; shipping companies; management of airports; private elementary, secondary, preparatory, and superior education; legal services; credit reporting; insurance agents; cellular telephony; construction of ducts for the transportation of oil and its derivatives; oil and gas wells drilling. NFIL Art. 8 (I-XI).

[35] NFIL Art. 8.

[36] In 1938 the Union of workers of "Companía Petrolera el Aguila" and the Union of workers of "Mexican-British Petroleum Company" sued their employers for an increase in wages and for better working conditions. The Supreme Court held in favor of the unions but the foreign employers defiantly decided not to obey the ruling. In those circumstances the President, Lázaro Cárdenas, was forced to declare on March 18, 1938, the nationalization of the oil industry.

[37] NFIL Art. 8 (X).

[38] NFIL Art. 8 (XI).

Law."[39] Article 18 defines neutral investment as the investment in Mexican corporations or through a trust that is not included in determining foreign investment participation.

The 1989 Regulations permitted neutral investment only through a trust in public corporations' stock.[40] The 1993 FIL extends neutral investment to: (a) investment through a trust in Mexican corporations not quoted on the Mexican Stock Market;[41] (b) investment in special stock series with limited corporate rights, upon prior authorization by the Secretariat of Commerce and, if the stock is quoted on the stock market, by the National Securities Commission;[42] (c) to neutral investment in holding companies of financial groups, commercial banks and brokerage houses through trust and prior authorization by the Secretariat of Commerce. Under this type of investment the Secretariat of Commerce must take a decision only after hearing the opinion of the Secretariat of Finance and Public Credit and the National Securities Commission;[43] (d) investment by international development organizations.[44]

2.4   REAL ESTATE

Article 27 of the Mexican Constitution expressly prohibits foreigners and Mexican corporations with a foreign-inclusion clause from acquiring direct dominion over land or water located within 100 kilometers of the national borders or within 50 kilometers of the coast.[45]

In contrast, the 1993 FIL allows Mexican corporations with a foreigners-inclusion clause to own real estate in Mexico if the land is to be used for non-residential activities as long as they record the acquisition with the Secretariat of Foreign Affairs.[46] If the land is to be used for residential purposes, it can be acquired only through a bank trust.

This new provision is very convenient for foreign investors. "Access to

---

[39]   Bryan, Gonzalez Vargas y Gonzalez, Mexican Federation Enacts New Foreign Investment Law, *supra* at 7.
[40]   1989 Regulations. Art. 13.
[41]   NFIL. Art. 19.
[42]   NFIL. Art. 20.
[43]   NFIL. Art. 21.
[44]   NFIL. Art. 22.
[45]   Constitución Política de los Estados Unidos Mexicanos [Mex. Const.] Art. 27 (Mexico).
[46]   NFIL Art. 10 (1).

direct title to real estate in the restricted zones by companies with foreign investment engaged in non-residential activities removes a significant barrier to major investment in those zones by bestowing ownership rather than simply renewable beneficial rights."[47] However, 1993 FIL Article 10 clearly contradicts the Mexican Constitution and it could be declared unconstitutional by the Mexican Supreme Court of Justice. Article 27 of the Mexican Constitution contains a flat prohibition,[48] it does not exempt acquisition for non-residential purposes from the constitutional prohibition.

For Mexican counsel this problem is quite serious. On the one hand, the 1993 FIL expressly permits the acquisition of land in the restricted zones for non-residential purposes. On the other hand, there is a risk that the 1993 FIL could be declared unconstitutional and the acquisitions under the new provisions held void. In order to be on the safe side, the acquisition of land through a trust remains probably the safest procedure until Article 27 of the Constitution is amended or the Mexican Supreme Court determines that the 1993 FIL is not unconstitutional.

Under the 1993 FIL foreign investors may acquire property rights through a trust and control real estate within the restricted zones without violating the Mexican Constitution. The beneficiaries of these trusts may be Mexican corporations with an admission-of-foreigners clause and even foreign persons and corporations, subject to compliance with the requirement of obtaining a permit from the Secretariat of Foreign Affairs.[49] There is no longer a need to incorporate a company in Mexico in order to be able to acquire land in restricted zones by means of a trust.

The trust must be constituted with the participation of a Mexican credit institution that has been granted authorization to acquire through a trust the title to real estate intended for industrial and tourist activities in the Restricted Zone for a period not to exceed fifty years. This period may be renewed if a request for extension is made.[50]

A foreign investor should bear in mind that property deeds in Mexico must be granted before a notary public. In Mexico, the notary public is a highly regarded specialized lawyer with a broad knowledge of civil, commerce, tax,

---

[47] Bryan, Gonzalez Vargas y Gonzalez, Mexican Federation Enacts New Foreign Investment Law, *supra* at 6, 9 (1994).

[48] "Within a distance of 100 kilometers from the borders and fifty from the beaches, without any exception, foreigners shall not be able to acquire the direct dominion over land and waters". Mex. Const. Art. 27 (I).

[49] NFIL Art. 11.

[50] NFIL Art. 13.

corporations, and investment law. The notary public is invested with "public faith" and his acts and the documents and deeds granted before him are presumed to be truthful. One of the notary public's duties is to help the Mexican government to enforce the Constitutional limitations of the restricted zones. For example, if the notary authorizes a foreign acquisition of "direct dominion" over land or water located within the restricted zones he would be liable to a fine and he would lose his job.

Outside the restricted zone there are no legal limitations and foreigners can acquire "direct dominion" over land and water. The only requirement needed is the attainment of an authorization granted by the Secretariat of Foreign Affairs.

2.5 SANCTIONS

The National Foreign Investment Commission will be empowered to levy penalties when there is a violation to the provisions of the 1993 FIL.[51] The penalties range from fines of thirty days to five thousand days of the general minimum wage in effect in Mexico City. The five-thousand-day-fine is assessed in cases where there is a failure to seek approval from the National Foreign Investments Commission when this is required.[52]

The most severe penalty is contained in Article 38 (V): in case of fraudulent acts or misrepresentation intended to obtain use and enjoyment of real estate in the restricted zones, the violator can be fined up to the amount of the value of the operation. Under the new liberal provisions of the NFIL the existence of a case in which the latter penalty could be assessed will be very unusual. There are many legal possibilities that can be used in order to obtain the use and enjoyment of real estate in the restricted zones, (e.g. trust, direct acquisition for nonresidential purposes). Hence, it is neither logical nor convenient to circumvent the law.

2.6 TRANSITORY ARTICLES

Important reservations and provisions are contained in the 11 transitory articles. Of critical significance is Article 2 which repeals the 1973 Foreign Investment

---

[51] NFIL. Art. 38.
[52] NFIL. Art. 38 (I).

Law among other regulations and decrees. Article 4 provides that until new regulations are issued by the executive branch, the former 1989 Regulations will remain in effect as long as they do not contradict the new investment law.[53] Article 6 gradually phases out the reservation applicable to Mexicans for supplying international services for land transportation of passengers, tourists and freight within Mexico, allowing 100% foreign investment in those activities by January 1, 2004. Article 7 provides that foreign investment will be possible in the automotive parts and accessories industry up to 49% and that by January 1, 1999 foreign participation in those sectors may be up to 100%. Finally, Article 9 permits the participation of foreign investment in the construction industry up to 100%, with the prior authorization of the Foreign Investment Commission. This requirement will be eliminated by 1999.

3. THE NORTH AMERICAN FREE TRADE AGREEMENT

Among NAFTA's goals are to gradually eliminate tariff and non-tariff barriers to trade in goods and services as well as to promote investment. This agreement creates "a comprehensive structure for trade and investment among the United States, Mexico and Canada. Once NAFTA is fully implemented, the agreement will encourage further economic integration in North America."[54]

NAFTA's investment provisions are contained in chapter eleven. The coverage of these provisions include all forms of ownership and interests in a business. "More specifically, NAFTA regulates minority as well as majority interest in business and other types of investment such as bonds, real estate and stocks. NAFTA significantly reduces the need for approval of investments by foreign governments."[55] The agreement flatly prohibits the imposition of the most important performance requirements and gives all North American and Canadian investors national treatment. Also the Agreement minimizes the review of new foreign investments and contains a detailed mechanism for the settlement of investment disputes.

Legal uncertainty felt by investors has long been considered the greatest barrier to long-term investment in Mexico. This uncertainty "which stems from the changes that occur in foreign-investment restrictions from one six-year

---

[53]   NFIL transitory Art. 4.

[54]   Dean C. Alexander, The North American Free Trade Agreement: An Overview. 11 Int'l Tax & Bus. Law 48 (1993).

[55]   Id. at 55.

presidential term to another"[56] has been regarded with distrust by the foreign investor.[57] For Mexican counsel, the unpredictability of the actual application of the FIL constituted a serious problem. Although the law was very restrictive, it was possible to try to negotiate a better deal with the Foreign Investment Commission.[58] Hence, Mexican lawyers could not advise their clients as to the exact restrictions that were going to be imposed on their investment until the project was reviewed by the National Foreign Investment Committee.

In addition to fostering greater certainty, the NAFTA will inject more transparency into the rules that govern foreign investment in Mexico. Rather than having to rely solely on liberal regulations that can be easily changed, or the discretion of government officials to apply the law in a liberal fashion, "the NAFTA essentially requires the parties (except for the defined exceptions) to permit foreign investment in their respective countries based on economic decisions made by investors."[59]

According to Article 133 of the Mexican Constitution, treaties, once approved are, other than the Constitution, the supreme law of the Republic and supersede previously enacted legislation. The NAFTA was recently ratified by the Mexican Congress.[60] Hence, it is superior in the Mexican legal system to the 1993 FIL.

In sum, NAFTA will promote and facilitate investment in Mexico, it "removes significant investment barriers, ensures basic protection for NAFTA investors and provides a mechanism for the settlement of disputes."[61]

---

[56] Foreign Investment in Mexico from the Perspective of the Foreign Investor. 24 St. Mary's L.J. 775, 787 (1993).

[57] This distrust has been partially groundless. Even though every new Mexican president can practically modify at will the Regulations and even the laws, since 1982 the Mexican government has followed a trend toward the gradual elimination of the protectionist provisions of the FIL.

[58] FIL Art. 5 states that the National Commission on Foreign Investment may decide on the increase or reduction of the maximum foreign ownership percentage permitted when, in its judgement, it is in the interest of the Mexican economy, and it may establish the conditions under which such investment may be received.

[59] Foreign Investment in Mexico from the Perspective of the Foreign Investor, *supra*.

[60] The North American Free Trade Agreement was ratified by the Mexican Senate on November 22, 1993.

[61] Description of the Proposed North American Free Trade Agreement.

3.1 NATIONAL TREATMENT

Article 1102 of NAFTA states that each Party shall accord to investors and to investments of investors of another Party treatment no less favorable than that it accords, in like circumstances, to its own investors or to investments of its own investors with respect to the establishment, acquisition, expansion, management, conduct, operation, and sale or other disposition of investments.[62] This provision is quintessential as it signifies for the North American and Canadian investors the end of the Mexican national investment preferred status.

In contrast, Article 6 of the 1993 FIL reserves exclusively for Mexicans or for Mexican companies with an exclusion-of-foreigners clause the following activities: (1) national cargo and passenger land transportation; (2) gasoline sale at retail and gas distribution; (3) wireless communications; (4) credit unions; (5) development banks and (6) certain professional and technical services.

At first glance, there is an apparent contradiction between the NAFTA and the 1993 FIL. Does the former supersede the latter? No, it does not. Rather, Mexico made the corresponding reservations in the agreement.

With respect to state, provincial or local government legislation or regulation, national treatment means "treatment no less favorable than the most favorable treatment accorded, in like circumstances, by that state or province to investors and to investments of investors, of the Party of which it forms a part."[63] In addition, each country must provide investments of NAFTA investors treatment in accordance with international law, including fair and equitable treatment and full protection and security.[64]

3.2 MOST-FAVORED-NATION TREATMENT

NAFTA not only accords to investors national treatment, but it also provides to investors of another party treatment no less favorable than it provides in similar circumstances to investors and investments of investors of any other Party or of a non-party with respect to the establishment, acquisition, expansion, management, operation, and sale or other disposition of investments. The most-favored-nation treatment is accorded to investors of another party by Article

[62] North American Free Trade Agreement, Aug. 12, 1992.
[63] NAFTA, Chapter 11, Art. 1102 (3).
[64] Id.

1103(1) and 1103(2).

Article 1103 positions the signing parties in a most-favored-nation treatment status and it extends any existing benefit accorded to a non-Party by any NAFTA Party to the other NAFTA Parties. Therefore, this provision in Mexico extends any benefit accorded to a non-Party in any international agreement ratified by the Mexican Senate to American and Canadian investors.[65]

In order to specify the standard of treatment that shall be accorded to an investment Article 1104 requires that "[e]ach Party shall accord to investors of another Party and to investments of investors of another Party the better of the treatment required by Articles 1102 and 1103".[66]

3.3 FOREIGN OWNERSHIP

The restrictive 1973 FIL limited equity ownership in Mexican corporations. The general rule was that the foreign investor could not own or control more than 49 percent of the equity of the enterprises.[67] However, the National Commission on Foreign Investment was granted the discretionary power to "decide on the increase or reduction of the percentage of foreign ownership when, in its judgement, it is in the interest of the country's economy, and it may establish the conditions under which foreign investment may be received in specific cases."[68]

The 1989 Regulations liberalized the ownership restriction. It allowed foreign investors to own stocks of companies in any proportion at the time of their incorporation. The foreign investor did not require authorization from the National Commission on Foreign Investment as long as his investment attained the conditions set forth in Article 5 of the 1989 Regulations.[69]

Under the 1993 FIL, foreign investors can own 100% of the equity of a

---

[65] Mexico has negotiated and ratified free trade agreements with Chile and Costa Rica. Also, Mexico intends to enter into a free trade pact with Venezuela and Colombia by June 1994. G-3 Talks Finalized, El Financiero, International Edition, May 16-22, 1994, at 3.

[66] Id.

[67] FIL Art. 5. "In cases where legal provisions or regulations do not specify a given percentage, foreign investment may hold no more than 49 percent of the capital of business enterprises, provided it is not empowered, by any title to determine the management of the business enterprise."

[68] Id. Art. 5.

[69] See Ogarrio and Pereznieto Castro, Mexico-United States Relations: Economic Integration and Foreign Investment. 12 Hous. J. Int'l L. 223 (1990).

Mexican corporation in an unrestricted sector, acquire any assets, establish new product lines, open and operate commercial establishments and enlarge or relocate existing enterprises, with certain exceptions provided in 1993 FIL and NAFTA annexes.[70]

Generally, NAFTA allows a 100% foreign ownership and forbids any compulsory sale or disposal of an investment by reasons of nationality. Article 1102 prohibits the imposition on an investor of another Party a requirement that a minimum level of equity in an enterprise in the territory of the Party be held by its nationals, with the exception of nominal qualifying shares for directors or incorporators of corporations. Also, NAFTA prohibits the requirement that an investor of another Party, by reason of its nationality, should sell or dispose of an investment in the territory of the Party.

Annex I establishes an exception to Article 1102 of NAFTA with respect to foreign acquisition of more than a 49%-ownership interest in a Mexican enterprise located in an unrestricted area. The Foreign Investment Commission will review direct or indirect acquisitions by an investor of another Party of more than 49 percent of the ownership interest in a Mexican enterprise in an unrestricted sector if the value of the gross assets of the Mexican enterprise is more than the applicable thresholds. These monetary thresholds are: twenty-five million dollars for the first three years; fifty million dollars for the next three-year period; seventy-five millions dollars for the following three years and one hundred-fifty million dollars during the tenth year that the agreement is in force.[71]

This same exception is contained in the text of 1993 FIL Article 9. The text of both provisions are almost identical. The only difference is that 1993 FIL Article 9's threshold will be determined annually by the Foreign Investment Commission. 1993 FIL transitory Article 10 determines the applicable threshold to be 85 millions new pesos, equivalent approximately to 25 million dollars, the threshold for the first three years of NAFTA.

Despite the liberalization created by NAFTA, the Mexican government will keep some activities restricted from foreign investment. More specifically, under Annex I, the National Foreign Investment Commission will have the power to evaluate applications for the acquisition or establishment of an investment in restricted activities, considering "(a) effects on employment and training; (b) its technological contribution; and (c) in general its contribution to increase the

---

[70] NFIL Art. 4.
[71] NAFTA Annex I-M-4.

Mexican industrial production and competitiveness".[72] This provision of the Annex also allows the Foreign Investment Commission to impose performance requirements that are not prohibited by Article 1106 of NAFTA.

Also, Annexes I, III, and IV set out a list of limitations that will either delay the liberalizing impact of the NAFTA on foreign investments or indefinitely exempt from the NAFTA certain activities in Mexico.

3.4   PERFORMANCE REQUIREMENTS

The 1973 Foreign Investment Law and the 1989 Regulations contained a burdensome list of performance requirements. These requirements have been considered by the foreign investors as "a major barrier to foreign investment in Mexico."[73] Article 1106 of NAFTA eliminates such barriers, enumerating these requirements and expressly prohibiting a party from imposing or enforcing them in connection with the establishment, acquisition, expansion, management, conduct or operation of an investment of an investor of a Party or of a non-Party in its territory.[74] This article was expressly aimed at eliminating the numerous specific performance requirements that the Mexican FIL and its Regulations used to impose on foreign investments.

In addition to prohibiting such requirements, Article 1106(3) of NAFTA conditions the receipt or continued receipt of an advantage, in connection with an investment in its territory by a foreign investor of a Party or of a non-Party, by requiring the investor

> (a) to achieve a given level or percentage of domestic content; (b) to purchase, use or accord a preference to goods produced in its territory, or to purchase goods from

---

[72]   NAFTA Annex I, I-M-4.

[73]   Foreign Investment in Mexico from the Perspective of the Foreign Investor, *supra* at 787.

[74]   The prohibited performance requirements are: (a) to export a given level or percentage of goods or services; (b) to achieve a given level or percentage of domestic content; (c) to purchase, use or accord a preference to goods produced or services provided in its territory; (d) to relate in any way the volume or value of imports to the volume or value of exports or to the amount of foreign exchange inflows associated with such investment; (e) to restrict sales of goods or services in its territory that such investment produces or provides by relating such sales in any way to the volume or value of its exports or foreign exchange earnings; (f) to transfer technology, a production process or other proprietary knowledge to a person in its territory, except when the requirement is imposed or enforced by a court, administrative tribunal or competent authority to remedy an alleged violation of competition laws and (g) to act as the exclusive supplier of the goods it produces or services it provides to a specific region or world market.

producers in its territory; (c) to relate in any way the volume or value of imports to the volume or value of exports or to the amount of foreign exchange inflows associated with such investment; or (d) to restrict sales of goods or services in its territory that such investment produces or provides by relating such sales in any way to the volume or value of its exports or foreign exchange earnings.

It is noteworthy that Article 1106 of NAFTA does not provide relief from all performance requirements. The liberation from performance requirements is not applicable to any requirement not listed in paragraphs (1) and (3) of Article 1106. As a result, the 1993 FIL eliminates all the specific performance requirements prohibited by NAFTA but does not contain a general prohibition of any kind on specific performance requirements. Moreover, 1993 FIL Article 29 provides that in cases when review by the National Foreign Investment Commission is required, the Commission "may only impose requirements that do not distort international trade." Hence, the Commission may impose a very limited scope of requirements, those not prohibited by NAFTA and which do not distort international trade.[75]

Among those permitted requirements are measures that prescribe formalities or require an investor of another Party to provide routine information concerning that investment for informational or statistical purposes. The host government can adopt or maintain a measure that "prescribes special formalities in connection with the establishment of investments by investors of another Party, such as a requirement that investors be residents of the Party or that investments be legally constituted under the laws or regulations of the Party, provided that such formalities do not materially impair the protection afforded by a Party to investors of another Party and investments of investors of another Party pursuant to this chapter."[76]

However, what about the requirements contained in the 1989 Regulations? As long as they do not contradict the text of the 1993 FIL and the new regulations are not issued by the Executive, they are still in effect. As a result, it appears that the prohibition not to locate a factory in a particular location in Mexico still remains in force.[77]

---

[75] NFIL does not contain a definition of what are the requirements that distort international trade and that concept will probably be defined by the FIC.

[76] NAFTA, Chapter 11, Art. 1111.

[77] Foreign investment in any business located within the metropolitan areas of the cities of Mexico, Guadalajara and Monterrey always requires review by the Foreign Investment Commission even if that investment does not exceed the monetary threshold set by the Commission. 1989 Regulation. Art. 5.

3.5 TRANSFERS

Each Party shall permit rapid and free transfers of investments of and the investor of another Party in the territory of the Party. Notwithstanding this provision,[78] a Party may prevent a transfer through the equitable, non-discriminatory and good faith application of its laws relating to: (a) bankruptcy, insolvency or the protection of the rights of creditors; (b) issuing, trading or dealing in securities; (c) criminal or penal offenses; (d) reports of transfers of currency or other monetary instruments; or (e) ensuring the satisfaction of judgements in adjudicatory proceedings.[79]

Yet, 1993 FIL does not mention the aforementioned prohibition. Nevertheless, Mexico no longer has exchange controls. Usually, transfers are made freely, without any inconvenience to the foreign investors. Article 1109 (1) of NAFTA reaffirms and codifies this practice.

3.6 INVESTMENT AND THE ENVIRONMENT

The NAFTA has been called the first "green" trade agreement. Although environmental issues have been raised in the context of free trade agreements before, NAFTA is the first trade agreement to explicitly address such issues within the terms of the agreement. While NAFTA's main focus relates to trade and investment, "[t]he debate over NAFTA, and the terms of the Agreement, however, have extended well beyond these traditional issues of trade in goods and services and have focused primarily on heretofore non-trade issues such as labor and the environment."[80]

A cornerstone of an environment-related investment issue is that the NAFTA "provides that no country should lower its environmental standards to attract an investment and that the countries will consult on the observance of this

---

[78] Such transfers include: (a) profits, dividends, interest, capital gains, royalty payments, management fees, technical assistance and other fees, returns in kind and other amounts derived from the investment; (b) proceeds from the sale of all or any part of the investment or from the partial or complete liquidation of the investment; (c) payments made under a contract entered into by the investor, or its investment, including payments made pursuant to a loan agreement; (d) payments made as compensation for expropriation or nationalization. NAFTA, Chapter 11, Art. 1109 (1).

[79] NAFTA, Chapter 11, Art. 1109 (a) (b) (c) (d) (e).

[80] Stanley M. Spracker, Environmental Protection and International Trade: NAFTA as a Means of Eliminating Environmental Contamination as a Competitive Advantage. 5 Geo. Int'l Envt'l. L. Rev. 669 (1993).

provision."[81] Since 1992 the Mexican government has improved the enforcement of Mexico's environmental regulations throughout the country and especially in the border areas. Also, there are in Mexico growing environmental organizations and even a "Green Party".[82] These factors are certainly going to promote a gradual increase in the Mexican environmental standards and will help Mexico comply with the NAFTA Supplemental agreement in environmental issues.

An important consequence of a more strict application of the Mexican environmental laws and the Supplemental Agreement of NAFTA in environmental issues will be the creation of opportunities for environmental equipment firms and services in the areas of solid waste disposal technology, hazardous and non-hazardous waste engineering consulting, sewage treatment, water treatment, environmental rehabilitation and specialized monitoring.[83] Environmental products and services will be needed by numerous Mexican industries. Currently, there are few Mexican firms who can provide such goods and services.

3.7   EXPROPRIATION AND COMPENSATION

NAFTA offers very good protection to investors against the risks of nationalization or expropriation.[84] Article 1110 of NAFTA limits the discretionary power of the Parties to nationalize or expropriate and requires specific remedies once a nationalization or expropriation occurs.

According to Article 1110 of NAFTA, no Party may directly or indirectly nationalize or expropriate an investment of an investor of another Party in its territory or to take a measure tantamount to nationalization or expropriation of such an investment, except: "(a) for a public purpose; (b) on a non-discriminatory basis; (c) in accordance with due process of law and Article 1105(1); and (d) on payment of compensation in accordance with paragraphs 2 through 6."

---

[81]   Description of the proposed North American Free Trade Agreement, at 74.

[82]   "Partido Ecologista Mexicano".

[83]   Dean C. Alexander, The North American Free Trade Agreement: An Overview. 11 Int'l Tax & Bus. Law 48, 62 (1993).

[84]   Currently, the risk of an expropriation or nationalization is quite remote. Indeed, the Salinas Administration has privatized numerous firms and the process of privatization still continues.

The compensation is to be paid without delay and shall be equivalent to the fair market value of the expropriated investment "immediately before the expropriation took place (date of expropriation), and shall not reflect any change in value occurring because the intended expropriation had become known earlier."[85] The utility of this provision is that it offers investors adequate, rather than symbolic compensation.

Under NAFTA, the compensation payment, if made in a G-7 currency, shall include interest at a commercially reasonable rate for that currency from the date of expropriation until the date of actual payment. In order to ensure that the valuation (in terms of currency) is appropriate for the expropriated or nationalized investment NAFTA provides that if the payment is made in a currency other than a G-7 currency, the amount paid on the date of payment, "if converted into a G-7 currency at the market rate of exchange prevailing on that date, shall be no less than if the amount of compensation owed on the date of expropriation had been converted into that G7 currency at the market rate of exchange prevailing on that date, and interest had accrued at a commercially reasonable rate for that G-7 currency from the date of expropriation until the date of payment."[86]

3.8 INVESTOR-STATE DISPUTE SETTLEMENT

NAFTA establishes a detailed mechanism for the settlement of investment disputes between a NAFTA country and an investor of another NAFTA country.

If the dispute involves a breach of the investment rules by the host country "a NAFTA investor, at its option, may seek either monetary damages through binding investor-state arbitration or the remedies that are available in the host country's domestic courts."[87]

An investor of a NAFTA country may on its own behalf, or on behalf of an enterprise that the investor owns or controls directly or indirectly, assert a claim that the investor or the enterprise has incurred loss or damage as a result of a breach by the host country of an obligation under the NAFTA.

NAFTA requires some conditions to occur prior to the submission of a claim to arbitration. First, investors and enterprises, may submit claims on their behalf only if they: "a. consent to arbitration in accordance with the procedures set out

---

[85] NAFTA, Art. 1110.

[86] NAFTA, Art. 1110 (5).

[87] Description of the proposed North American Free Trade Agreement, at 7.

in the NAFTA; and b. waive the right to initiate or continue before any administrative tribunal or court under the law of any NAFTA partner, or other dispute settlement procedures."[88] Furthermore, NAFTA requires that the consent and waiver shall be delivered to the host country in writing.

As a general rule the arbitration tribunal will "comprise three arbitrators, one appointed by each disputing party and the third (the presiding arbitrator) appointed by agreement of the disputing parties."[89] The governing law of the dispute will be NAFTA and international law. The place of arbitration, unless the parties agree otherwise, will be the territory of a NAFTA country that is a party to the New York Convention. An award by a tribunal will have no binding force except between the disputing parties. However, if the NAFTA host country "fails to abide by or comply with a final award, the NAFTA Commission, on the request of the home country of the investor, must establish an arbitral panel under Chapter 20."[90]

The Mexican judicial system is very slow. In contrast, the dispute settlement provisions in the NAFTA investment chapter should provide for the rapid and fair resolution of investment disputes. Thus, Canadian and United States investors would likely prefer to utilize international arbitration rather than Mexican courts.

4. CONCLUSION

Mexican investment laws have gradually evolved from the restrictive, anti-investor and protectionist 1973 Foreign Investment Law to the 1993 liberal new Foreign Investment Law. This gradual evolution is the result of a changing world, increased competition among countries for foreign investment, and the outcome of a change in Mexican attitudes towards foreign investment. Undoubtedly, this metamorphosis has also been hastened by the free-market policies supported by the Salinas Administration, by American influence in Mexico, and especially by the signature of the North American Free Trade Agreement.

The 1993 FIL was enacted in order to implement the commitments made in NAFTA.

[88] Kenneth P. Freiberg, Dispute Settlement Under the North American Free Trade Agreement. 653 PLI/Comm 381, 9 (1993).
[89] Id.
[90] Id. at 12.

NAFTA initiated the destruction of almost all the barriers that the Mexican government has erected to foreign investment. This agreement gives investors an invaluable asset: legal certainty. The legal certainty is for many investors a requirement sine qua non for investing in foreign countries and, with NAFTA, Mexico finally offers it.

Mexico has always been an strategic market with a great growth-potential, but its restrictive and burdensome foreign investment law has long deterred foreign investments. NAFTA and the new Foreign Investment Law are fortunately going to change that.

While some exceptions exist, NAFTA permits a 100% foreign equity-ownership and prohibits any Party from requiring investors of another Party to sell or dispose of an investment in its territory by reasons of nationality. Consequently, NAFTA and the 1993 FIL generally eliminated the 49% maximum foreign ownership and control provisions that were the hallmarks of previous Mexican investment law.

Under NAFTA, U.S. and Canadian investors will not only enjoy national treatment but also a most-favored-nation treatment. Except for a few exceptions, NAFTA provides that each party shall accord to investments of another Party fair and equitable treatment, with no limitations for transfers.

The former FIL and its Regulation imposed on foreign investors an impressive and burdensome list of performance requirements. With a few exceptions, NAFTA flatly prohibits the imposition of important performance requirements.

The enactment of NAFTA will not harm the environment of Mexico. On the contrary, NAFTA is the first trade agreement that protects the environment and provides that no Party should lower its environmental standards to attract or retain an investment.

The expropriation of an enterprise is a risk that every foreign investor must take into account when investing abroad. Fortunately, NAFTA shields the foreign investor in Mexico from any discriminatory or unfair nationalization or expropriation and grants the foreign investor the right to obtain fair market value compensation.

Also, for foreign investors it is important to have legal recourse against biased or unfair decisions by the host country. Under NAFTA, foreign investors will have a detailed mechanism for the settlement of investment disputes. NAFTA and the 1993 FIL radically changed Mexican investment rules and will make Mexico a far more attractive and safer place for foreign investors.

A CRITICAL ANALYSIS OF THE POST-1994 ELECTIONS: MEXICAN FOREIGN INVESTMENT REGULATORY SCHEME

by Dr. Jorge Witker & Rich Robins, Esq.[*]

1. INTRODUCTION

While Pacific Rim trade has grown rapidly, the European Union surpassed NAFTA's size with the inclusion of Austria, Finland and Sweden last winter, the North American Free Trade Agreement nevertheless creates one of the world's largest, richest free trade zones.[1] This is important to the U.S. which confronts the post-Cold War challenge of trying to compete in a rapidly expanding global marketplace.[2] All over the world, geographical neighbors are becoming increasingly important to countries' abilities to market and cooperatively produce globally-competitive goods and services. Indeed,

---

[*] Jorge Witker is a licensed attorney serving as a NAFTA arbitration panelist. He also serves on the law faculty at the National Autonomous University of Mexico's Instituto de Investigaciones Jurídicas in Mexico City. In addition, he is a permanent member of Mexico's national organization of Investigadores of the Secretary of Public Education. Dr. Witker is widely-recognized as one of Mexico's leading authorities on foreign investment law.

Rich Robins currently serves on the law faculty at the National Autonomous University of Mexico's Instituto de Investigaciones Jurídicas in Mexico City. He graduated from the University of Virginia School of Law, spent a semester on a fellowship with the law faculty at the University of Monterrey in Monterrey, Mexico before accepting his present one in Mexico City. Mr. Robins willingly assumes full responsibility and risk for any potentially controversial criticisms that might be expressed regarding this article.

[1] Juan J. Walte, Congress Tackles Free Trade Pact Today, USA Today, Sept. 8, 1992, at 8A.

[2] The White House, Office of the Press Secretary, Remarks by the President on the North American Free Trade Agreement, Aug. 12, 1992, at 1.

Northfield Laboratories President David Carter said that "by the year 2000, all business will be international business."[3]

Although this prediction's meaning is somewhat unclear, what is clear is that the U.S.'s ratifying NAFTA with its distinctly-different neighbor Mexico was a step in the right direction leading the U.S. on a visionary path to increased prosperity. Many obstacles lie along this path, however, at least as far as foreign investors in Mexico are concerned. This article addresses several of them. It does so in light of the August 1994 Mexican election results, NAFTA's investment guidelines, and Mexico's own new foreign investment legal framework.

This chapter analyzes the overall Mexican foreign investment regulatory scheme. It makes those criticisms more interesting by allocating space to relevant parts of Mexican history, the potential for American-Canadian-Mexican business culture clashes, and the political scene's direct and indirect impact on foreign investors. It also gives suggestions as to how foreign investors can succeed in Mexico despite, and at times because of, these and various other obstacles. This chapter concludes with a critical analysis of various sections of Mexico's laws on foreign investment.

2. MEXICO: AN EMERGING MARKET WITH ATTRACTIVE FEATURES FOR FOREIGN INVESTORS

Forecasts of balanced national budgets, and even a budget surplus by the end of 1992,[4] are among some of the many statistics that put Mexico into the world spotlight even before NAFTA was passed. While Mexico's national debt remains a large problem, other facts nevertheless look impressive too. Mexico's inflation is much lower than in the past, having dropped to about 8% for 1993.[5] There are forecasts of steady economic growth from now into the 21st Century.[6] Mexico's GDP is presently the thirteenth largest in the world. Its land mass of 764,000 square miles[7] ranks it the thirteenth largest country on Earth.

---

[3]   Michael S. Doyle et al., Exito Comercial viii (1991).

[4]   The Economist Intelligence Unit of Business International Limited, Mexico Country Report, No. 1, 1 (1992).

[5]   Bryan, Gonzalez Vargas & Gonzalez Baz, NAFTA Vadamecum 1 (1994).

[6]   Bryan, Gonzalez Vargas & Gonzalez Baz, NAFTA Vadamecum 1 (1994).

[7]   Charles T. DuMars, Liberalization of Foreign Investment Policies in Mexico: Legal Changes Encouraging New Direct Foreign Investment, 21 New Mex. L. Rev. 251, 273

Mexico produces many raw minerals, owns the world's fourth largest oil reserves,[8] and is the world's leading producer of silver.[9] Its population is presently the world's tenth largest.[10]

Mexico's growing and changing population shows why it has such great potential as an export market. By the year 2000, Mexico will have 100 million citizens,[11] up from its present population of around 85 million.[12] By comparison, the United States should have 275 million by the year 2000, up from its present population of a little over 250 million.[13] The majority of Mexico's population is quite young, with about seventy percent of the population under the age of 30. In contrast, in the U.S. less than fifty percent of its people are under 30. Moreover, the U.S. has nearly four times as many people over the age of 60 than Mexico.

Whereas the U.S., with its famous baby-boomer generation, will have a population with a growing number of retirees[14] and a government with an apparently growing national debt,[15] Mexico has a population with a growing number of workers and relatively little federal deficit. However, Mexico's national debt nevertheless merits the attention of foreign investors. The government's foreign debt stood at an all time high in July, 1994: 83.56 billion dollars.[16] In August, 1994, the public sector foreign debt was 22.4% of Mexico's GDP.[17] Nevertheless, Mexico had an impressive 1.6 billion dollar budget surplus for the first half of 1994, despite an 18% increase in public

(1991).

[8] Charles T. DuMars, Liberalization of Foreign Investment Policies in Mexico: Legal Changes Encouraging New Direct Foreign Investment, 21 New Mex. L. Rev. 251, 274 (1991).

[9] Charles T. DuMars, Liberalization of Foreign Investment Policies in Mexico: Legal Changes Encouraging New Direct Foreign Investment, 21 New Mex. L. Rev. 251, 274 (1991).

[10] Eugenio Salinas, Economic Counselor at the Trade Office of the Embassy of Mexico, and cousin of Mexico's President Salinas, Address to the Emerging Markets of Latin America Club at the University of Virginia Darden School of Business, December 7, 1992.

[11] The White House, Office of the Press Secretary, Press Briefing by U.S. Trade Representative Ambassador Carla Hills, Aug. 12, 1992, at 10.

[12] Statement by Ambassador Carla Hills, Hearings on NAFTA Before the House of Representatives Committee on Ways and Means, 102nd Cong., Sept. 9, 1992.

[13] Michael S. Doyle et al., Éxito Comercial 274 (1991).

[14] United States Government Printing Office, Economic Report of the President, 331 (1992).

[15] United States Government Printing Office, Economic Report of the President, 385 (1992).

[16] Patricia Nelson, How to Prepare Crow for Eating, The News, Aug. 28, 1994, at 16.

[17] Justin Bicknell, Government Issues Upbeat Statistics, El Financiero, International Edition, Aug. 22-28, 1994, at 3.

spending.[18]

Aside from the U.S. and Canada, Mexico has successfully negotiated free trade pacts with various other Latin American countries including Chile,[19] Costa Rica, Venezuela, Colombia, and most recently, Bolivia.[20] In 1986, Mexico joined the General Agreement on Tariffs and Trade.[21] In 1991, the European Economic Community granted Mexico most-favored-nation status.[22] Two years later, Mexico joined APEC, which has strengthened Mexico's economic ties with trading partners located in the Pacific Rim.

The U.S. is by far Mexico's largest trading partner.[23] Economists have predicted that due to NAFTA, the U.S. will probably add $10 billion a year to America's current trade surplus with Mexico.[24] In 1992 the top five states exporting to Mexico were: Texas ($15.5 billion), California ($5.5 billion), Michigan ($1.6 billion), Illinois ($1.1 billion) and Arizona ($991 million).[25] Even before NAFTA, all states exported goods or services to Mexico, although the values of total exports to Mexico varied from state to state, naturally.[26] The leading cities importing from Mexico were: New York City (72.8 thousand million dollars [as measured in Mexico]), Los Angeles (71.9 tmd), Detroit (42 tmd); San Francisco (33.2 tmd), Chicago (22.5 tmd), and Buffalo (21.2 tmd). The overall import total for the U.S. was 525 thousand million dollars.[27]

Mexico currently spends 70% of its trade dollars in the U.S.[28] Showing how

---

[18] Justin Bicknell, Government Issues Upbeat Statistics, El Financiero, International Edition, Aug. 22-28, 1994, at 3.

[19] Bryan, Gonzalez Vargas & Gonzalez Baz, NAFTA Vadamecum 4 (1994).

[20] Monica Gutschi Salazar, Mexico, Bolivia Conclude Talks on Trade Agreement, The News, Aug. 24, 1994, at 30.

[21] Bryan, Gonzalez Vargas & Gonzalez Baz, NAFTA Vadamecum 16 (1994).

[22] Bryan, Gonzalez Vargas & Gonzalez Baz, NAFTA Vadamecum 5 (1994).

[23] The Economist Intelligence Unit of Business International Limited, Mexico Country Report, No. 1, 1 (1992).

[24] USA Today Editor, Free-trade Agreement Can Be Net Gain for USA, USA Today, Aug. 14, 1992, at 14A.

[25] Jeff Wood et al., Head South, Young Graduate, The Wall Street Journal College Edition of the National Business Employment Weekly: Managing Your Career, Fall 1992, at 15.

[26] Eugenio Salinas: Economic Counselor at the Trade Office of the Embassy of Mexico, and cousin of Mexicos President Salinas, Address to the Emerging Markets of Latin America Club at the University of Virginia Darden School of Business, December 7, 1992.

[27] Ricardo Galan, Representa Sur de E.U. Mayor Potencial Comercial, El Norte, Jan. 4, 1994, at 18A.

[28] The White House, Office of the Press Secretary, Press Briefing by U.S. Trade Representative Ambassador Carla Hills, Aug. 12, 1992, at 8.

significant Mexico's commitment to U.S. goods and services already is, Mexico bought 35 percent more per capita from the U.S. than did the European Community.[29] The total value of Mexican imports per capita of U.S. goods is slightly higher than Japan's, and significantly higher than Germany's.[30] And even without a NAFTA, Mexico was clearly the U.S.'s fastest growing export market.[31] Encouragingly, the Mexican response to these developments has been relatively positive and friendly to the formerly-feared and mistrusted United States. A journalist for a daily Mexican newspaper captured Mexican sentiments when he recently wrote that "nothing has been able to contain, nor limit...the collective [Mexican] impulse to define ourselves, for the first time, as North Americans."[32]

Mexico's new economic policies have transformed it into one of the most open and receptive countries to foreign investment in the entire world.[33] On December 27, 1993, Mexico's new foreign investment law was passed. It created a general rule, with few exceptions, that every investment can be 100% foreign-owned. The new law's appendix lists those relatively few activities where only Mexicans can take ownership interests. It also addresses to what extent foreign ownership can participate both with, and without the National Foreign Investment Commission's approval.[34] NAFTA prompted this new law's existence and NAFTA's investment sections deal with essentially six areas: sectoral openings, treatment of investment, requisites for recovery, transparencies, expropriation, and conflict resolutions.[35]

In October, 1993, the five leading foreign investors in Mexico were: the U.S. (62.5%; 25.47 thousand million dollars); Great Britain (6.4%; 2.6 tmd); Germany (4.9%; 1.98 tmd); Switzerland (4.4%; 1.8 tmd); and Japan (4.1%;

[29] The White House, Office of the Press Secretary, Press Briefing by U.S. Trade Representative Ambassador Carla Hills, Aug. 12, 1992, at 7.

[30] Eugenio Salinas: Economic Counselor at the Trade Office of the Embassy of Mexico, and cousin of Mexicos President Salinas, Address to the Emerging Markets of Latin America Club at the University of Virginia Darden School of Business, December 7, 1992.

[31] The White House, Office of the Press Secretary, Remarks by the President on the North American Free Trade Agreement, Aug. 12, 1992, at 1.

[32] John Rice, Salinas Changes Mexico's Old Ways: Trade Pact Tops Leaders Successes, Washington Times, Oct. 8, 1992, at A1, A10.

[33] Slim Dumit, Marco Antonio, Inversión en Mexico y el Tratado de Libre Comercio. SEGUMEX-INBURSA. Grupo Financiero INBURSA 2 (1993).

[34] Bryan, Gonzalez Vargas & Gonzalez Baz, NAFTA Vadamecum 2 (1994).

[35] Jorge Witker, Practicas Restrictivas y Practicas Desleales, Collective Work addressing La Ley Federal de Competencia Económica, U.N.A.M.-Mexico (at press).

1.67 tmd).[36] Spain and Italy are also among the leading foreign investors in Mexico.[37] Recently, Mexico ranked third among all developing countries regarding the amount of foreign investment attracted by such a nation. Mexico received 8.2% of the foreign investment destined for a developing country, placing it behind only Singapore and the People's Republic of China.[38] Incidentally, this same study showed that the U.S. occupied the leading overall position, attracting 40.9% of the world's foreign investment. Canada occupied the ninth position overall, attracting 3.3%.[39]

Foreign investment in Mexico has recently reached nearly 50 billion dollars.[40] In August 1994, a SECOFI report found that direct foreign investment, not involving the stock and money markets, presently accounted for 55.4% of total foreign investment.[41] 160 projects tied to NAFTA came to Mexico during NAFTA's initial 8 months.[42] The most significant projects have been strategic alliances and direct exports. Additionally, around 60% of regularly-traded Mexican shares are held by foreigners, occupying about 13% of Mexico's GDP.[43] Reportedly, around 30% of Mexico's short-term government bonds are foreign-owned.[44] All of this is impressive for a developing nation that, as subsequent sections will show, used to greatly restrict foreign investment.

[36]   Carmen Alvarez, Negociar Mexico Acuerdos de Proteccióna Inversión, El Norte/Mexico, Oct. 7, 1993, at 19A.

[37]   Socorro Lopez Espinosa, Capital Forneo por 4 Mil Mdd en el Primer Bimestre: Secofi, El Financiero, Mar. 17, 1994, at 6.

[38]   Fernando Heftye Etienne, El Capítulo de Inversión del Tratado de Libre Comercio de Norteamerica. Revista de la Universidad Iberoamericana, Mexico 1993, No. 18, at 30.

[39]   Fernando Heftye Etienne, El Capítulo de Inversión del Tratado de Libre Comercio de Norteamerica. Revista de la Universidad Iberoamericana, Mexico 1993, No. 18, at 30.

[40]   Justin Bicknell, Government Issues Upbeat Statistics, El Financiero, International Edition, Aug. 22-28, 1994, at 3.

[41]   The News Staff, Analysts Skeptical of Second Quarter Growth Spurt, The News, Aug. 21, 1994, at 40.

[42]   CBI Casa de Bolsa, Bolsa Analytica News Service, The News, Aug. 28, 1994, at 36.

[43]   Caroline Allen, International Money Bets on Sunday PRI Victory, The News, Aug. 20, 1994, at 34.

[44]   Jaime Hernandez, Sopesan Aspectos Económicos y Financieros para Telefonia Lada, El Financiero, Aug. 22, 1994, at 35.

3. NAFTA: THE CATALYST FOR REFORM

NAFTA was the major catalyst for the apparently-improving legal climate foreign investors now enjoy in Mexico. As a bit of background, NAFTA is the most complex and thorough free trade agreement the U.S. has ever entered,[45] addressing roughly 9,000 tariff items and other subjects that constitute a major portion of goods and services presently exchanged or exchangeable between the U.S., Canada and Mexico. The tariffs on about 50% of these items vanished immediately in 1994;[46] and tariffs on about 15% more will be eliminated by 1999. There are also varying gradations running out between the years 2000 and 2009.[47] The resulting free trade zone has an annual economic output of over $6.4 trillion, containing over 360 million people.[48]

Critics in the U.S. fought NAFTA's passage by claiming, among other things, that the U.S.'s entry would prompt a rapid exporting of jobs and productivity to Mexico, popularly referred to as "that giant sucking sound to the South."[49] So far, however, this has not been the case. In fact, like a type of domestic Marshall Plan,[50] NAFTA is generating economic growth in all three countries.[51] During the first half of 1994, NAFTA's implementation resulted in the following: U.S. exports to Mexico grew by 17% while U.S. exports to Canada grew 10%. Meanwhile, during this period, Mexico's exports to the U.S. increased 21%, and Canada's to the U.S. augmented 10%.[52]

The U.S.'s success should come as no surprise. NAFTA has created tremendous export opportunities for the U.S. as its economy currently accounts

---

[45] The White House, Office of the Press Secretary, Press Briefing by U.S. Trade Representative Ambassador Carla Hills, Aug. 12, 1992, at 4, 5.

[46] The White House, Office of the Press Secretary, Press Briefing by U.S. Trade Representative Ambassador Carla Hills, Aug. 12, 1992, at 7.

[47] The White House, Office of the Press Secretary, Press Briefing by U.S. Trade Representative Ambassador Carla Hills, Aug. 12, 1992, at 7.

[48] The White House, Office of the Press Secretary, Text of a Letter From the President to the Speaker of the House of Representatives and the President of the Senate, Sept. 18, 1992, at 1.

[49] Ross Perot, Presidential Debate on NBC, Oct. 15, 1992.

[50] University of Virginia School of Law visiting faculty member Lane Kneedler, Legislative Drafting and Public Policy (Oct. 23, 1992).

[51] The White House, Office of the Press Secretary, The North American Free Trade Agreement Fact Sheet, Aug. 12, 1992, at 5 (quoting the United States International Trade Commission).

[52] The News Staff, Analysts Skeptical of Second Quarter Growth Spurt, The News, Aug. 21, 1994, at 40.

for 86% of the goods and services produced by the three member countries.[53] Additionally, before NAFTA was passed, the United States International Trade Commission did a survey of independent NAFTA studies and found "a surprising degree of unanimity" that its ratification would cause U.S. real GDP to increase by up to 0.5 percent annually upon full implementation.[54] U.S. employment would have an aggregate increase anywhere from under 0.1% to 2.5%[55] and real wages would increase from 0.1% to 0.3%.[56]

NAFTA certainly has made an impact on Mexico, which previously was far from warm to foreign investors. The following sections discuss some of NAFTA's foreign investment provisions, namely those addressing national treatment and dispute settlement.

3.1   NATIONAL TREATMENT

Foreign investors in Mexico must sign the famous, Constitutionally-recognized[57] Calvo clause,[58] which makes foreign investors legally consider themselves as nationals[59] and also waive their right to assert their foreign status as a defense to legal actions.[60] Some may argue that the Calvo Doctrine is

---

[53] Mark Memmott, Accords Benefits Will Come Gradually, USA Today, Aug. 13, 1992, at 9B.

[54] The White House, Office of the Press Secretary, The North American Free Trade Agreement Fact Sheet, Aug. 12, 1992, at 5.

[55] The White House, Office of the Press Secretary, The North American Free Trade Agreement Fact Sheet, Aug. 12, 1992, at 5.

[56] The White House, Office of the Press Secretary, The North American Free Trade Agreement Fact Sheet, Aug. 12, 1992, at 5.

[57] Constitución Política de los Estados Unidos Mexicanos, Art. 27, para. I (as amended January 6, 1960); Charles T. DuMars, Liberalization of Foreign Investment Policies in Mexico: Legal Changes Encouraging New Direct Foreign Investment, 21 New Mex. L. Rev. 251, 259 (1991).

[58] This doctrine, as stated by the Argentine jurist Carlos Calvo, holds that "[A] government is not bound to indemnify aliens for losses or injuries sustained by them in consequence of domestic disturbances or civil war, where the state is not at fault, and that therefore foreign states are not justified in intervening, by force or otherwise, to secure the settlement of claims of their citizens on account of such losses or injuries. Such intervention, Calvo says, is not in accordance with the practice of European States towards one another, and is contrary to the principle of state sovereignty." Black's Law Dictionary 205 (6th Ed. 1991).

[59] Ignacio Gomez Palacio, The New Regulation on Foreign Investment in Mexico: A Difficult Task, 12 Hous. J.Int'l L. 253, 256 (1990).

[60] Charles T. DuMars, Liberalization of Foreign Investment Policies in Mexico: Legal Changes Encouraging New Direct Foreign Investment, 21 New Mex. L. Rev. 251, 259

consistent with NAFTA's Chapter 11, Article 1102, which merely requires that member nations offer foreign investors "national treatment."[61]

The national treatment provision does not protect against the Calvo Doctrine's stern application to foreign investors. If a country's government changes hands and the new regime decides to fan xenophobic sentiments by expropriating foreign assets, the Calvo Doctrine permits the expropriation as long as the new regime treats domestic elites just as harshly as foreigners.[62] Fortunately, NAFTA's Chapter 11, Article 1110, now prohibits expropriation unless the following are met: a) it is done for a public purpose; b) in accordance with due process of law; c) on a non-discriminatory basis and d) upon payment of prompt, adequate and effective compensation at fair market value.[63]

Thanks to the Calvo Doctrine requirement in Mexico, it is conceivable that Mexicans get better treatment in the U.S. than U.S. citizens investing in Mexico, which seems unfair. Although not investment related, one should realize, however, that Mexicans dealing with the U.S. occasionally experience similar inequitable treatment vis-à-vis their U.S. counterparts who are dealing with Mexico. The most interesting example pertains to lawyers. A U.S. lawyer can go through rather extensive hurdles in Mexico to become a licensed Mexican attorney and thereby practice throughout the entire country. A Mexican lawyer, on the other hand, can only practice in those U.S. states for which he has qualified, because that is how the U.S. treats its own lawyers.

Even if foreign investors realize that in Mexico they will receive nothing more than mere national treatment, there remains the problem of determining just what national treatment actually means in Mexico. Currently, even clear-cut rules can be applied unfairly by some judges who depend on nepotistic members of the executive power not only for nomination, but also, for the right to remain in power. Consequently, one of President Ernesto Zedillo's most prominent campaign promises was to make the judicial branch more independent from the executive branch. Nevertheless, for now it is widely claimed that Mexico's judicial system "has always been inefficient and unjust."[64] One prominent columnist has written that "Justice in Mexico continues to favor the highest

(1991).

[61] NAFTA, Chapter 11, section 1102.

[62] Paul B. Stephan, III et al., International Business and Economics: Law an Policy 474 (1993).

[63] Paul B. Stephan, III et al., International Business and Economics: Law and Policy 474 (1993).

[64] Sergio Sarmiento, Zedillos Mandate, El Financiero, International Edition, Aug. 29-Sept. 4, 1994, at 6.

bidder and every class of crime is being committed with increasing impunity."[65] If Mexican nationals must endure the obvious ramifications of these sad facts, then NAFTA's offering mere national treatment to foreign investors should not be particularly comforting.

4. NO COUNTRY IS A PERFECT PLACE FOR FOREIGN INVESTORS, WHILE MEXICO IS NO EXCEPTION, IT STILL HAS MUCH TO OFFER

4.1 "CHEAP LABOR"

Mexico has relatively cheap labor that U.S., Canadian and other foreign firms can tap into. Yet, this tactic is not recommended for everyone. Before discussing the risks involved, it is worth noting that NAFTA bestowed the same competitive edge on U.S. firms that regional trade ties already had given Japanese and European companies.[66] Nearly 35% of Japan's exports are created under production-sharing schemes, whereas before NAFTA only about 5% of U.S. exports were similarly created.[67] Even before NAFTA brought the removal of barriers, General Electric stated that for each Mexican it employed in Mexico, it saved enough money to support and maintain three jobs in the U.S.[68] Yet, GE is already realizing the difficulties that can arise for it in Mexico, as a Juarez-based labor dispute has recently demonstrated.[69]

Consultants do their clients a major disservice by merely offering them impressive investment-related statistics and superficial legal advice regarding the potential advantages derived from tapping into Mexico's relatively cheap manual labor resources. Mediocre consultants will let their clients make potentially devastating decisions in light of such potential benefits without preparing them for the surprises they will encounter once it is practically too late to reconsider their investment decision. While Mexican laborers purportedly cost only a small fraction of their U.S. counterparts, the relatively hidden labor costs in Mexico

[65] Sergio Sarmiento, Zedillos Mandate, El Financiero, International Edition, Aug. 29-Sept. 4, 1994, at 6.
[66] Carla Hills, Sept. 9, 1992, at 6.
[67] Eugenio Salinas, Economic Counselor at the Trade Office of the Embassy of Mexico, and cousin of Mexico's President Salinas, Address to the Emerging Markets of Latin America Club at the University of Virginia Darden School of Business, December 7, 1992.
[68] Jim Hoagland, The Sticky Subject of Trade, Washington Post, Oct. 8, 1992, at A21.
[69] Jorge Banales, Juarez Workers First to Test NAFTA Treaty, The News, Sept. 10, 1994, at 1, 38.

leave many foreign investors scratching their heads as to why profit margins are much lower than expected. While the daily minimum salary is merely 15.27 new pesos[70] or about $4.70 a day, various "workers' well-being" tax contributions[71] required by the traditionally labor-friendly government greatly inflate labor costs to about $1.90 per hour.[72]

Compounding matters, Article 123 of Mexico's Constitution formally acknowledges extensive rights for workers.[73] Also, Mexico's labor law greatly restricts employers' freedom to discharge workers, or even contract employees on a temporary basis[74] like one can freely do in the U.S.[75] It is even difficult just to base Mexican laborers' salaries on productivity.[76] Nearly half of the Mexican workers belong to unions,[77] even though white collar workers may not join.[78] Moreover, while NAFTA gives tariff-free treatment to factories throughout Mexico where previously only maquiladora factories near the U.S. border got it, it is not necessarily wise for foreign factories to move to southern Mexico to capitalize on cheaper labor. In some southern regions of Mexico, Spanish is not even spoken, and reportedly the work ethic is not as strong as it is in the North.[79]

Additionally, illiteracy in Mexico is a truly significant problem. The average Mexican has around a fifth grade education.[80] In 1990, Mexico's illiteracy rate was 26%. According to the same source, the United States' illiteracy rate was

---

[70] Bryan, Gonzalez Vargas & Gonzalez Baz, NAFTA Vadamecum 6 (1994).

[71] Bryan, Gonzalez Vargas & Gonzalez Baz, NAFTA Vadamecum 4 (1994).

[72] Bryan, Gonzalez Vargas & Gonzalez Baz, NAFTA Vadamecum 4 (1994).

[73] Charles T. DuMars, Liberalization of Foreign Investment Policies in Mexico: Legal Changes Encouraging New Direct Foreign Investment, 21 New Mex. L. Rev. 251, 259 (1991).

[74] Charles T. DuMars, Liberalization of Foreign Investment Policies in Mexico: Legal Changes Encouraging New Direct Foreign Investment, 21 New Mex. L. Rev. 251, 259 (1991).

[75] Stanley D. Henderson et al., Contracts-Cases and Comment 307-313 (1987).

[76] Ivan Soza, Modernización Laboral Pendiente, El Financiero, Sept. 5, 1994, at 1.

[77] Charles T. DuMars, Liberalization of Foreign Investment Policies in Mexico: Legal Changes Encouraging New Direct Foreign Investment, 21 New Mex. L. Rev. 251, 259 (1991).

[78] Charles T. DuMars, Liberalization of Foreign Investment Policies in Mexico: Legal Changes Encouraging New Direct Foreign Investment, 21 New Mex. L. Rev. 251, 259 (1991).

[79] Interview with Licensiado Carlos Robles, TELMEX sales official in Monterrey, Mexico (Oct. 1993).

[80] David Shields, The Only Solution to Mass Unemployment, The News, Aug. 28, 1994 at 37.

a mere 1%.[81] Unfortunately, however, inexperienced, timid, or image-conscious consultants will shy away from really making sure their clients have grasped what they are getting themselves into when trying to accomplish important tasks with such relatively unskilled labor. Those employers used to training and motivating people in the United States will face difficulties in training workers in developing nations, such as Mexico. Hiring foreign laborers in Mexico is difficult as a minimum of 90% of the non-executive work-force must be Mexican.[82] Additionally, while the Mexican government may not require that a foreign corporation's senior management members be of any particular nationality, it may require that a majority of the board of directors or any committee thereof be of a particular nationality, subject to the vague and probably difficult to enforce caveat that the requirement "does not materially impair" the investors ability to control its investment.[83]

The full story on those Mexican workers foreign investors seek to employ begins with the statistic that in Latin America, separation between the rich and poor is the largest in the entire world[84] and nearly half [forty million] of Mexico's population lives at or below the poverty level.[85] In 1988, Mexico's per capita income was $2,116 compared with $19,646 in the U.S.[86] Not everybody even begins primary school, but out of every 1000 who do, only 6 go on to get a college degree.[87] Essentially less than 1% of the Mexican population is college-educated.[88] The prestigious Monterrey Technological Institute has estimated that Mexican unemployment is at around 25%.[89]

---

[81]   See Michael S. Doyle et al., Éxito Comercial 36, 274 (1991).

[82]   Bryan, Gonzalez Vargas & Gonzalez Baz, NAFTA Vadamecum 7 (1994).

[83]   NAFTA, Chapter 11, section 1107; Baker & McKenzie, 1993 Guide to Foreign Investors in Mexico, 29-30 (1994).

[84]   John Naisbitt, Global Paradox 227-275 (1994).

[85]   PAN Political Brochure, July 1994.

[86]   Charles T. DuMars, Liberalization of Foreign Investment Policies in Mexico: Legal Changes Encouraging New Direct Foreign Investment, 21 New Mex. L. Rev. 251, 274 n.128 (1991).

[87]   PAN Political Brochure, July 1994.

[88]   Interview with Dr. Roberto Rios, Dean of the law faculty at the University of Monterrey, Neuvo Leon, Mexico. Sept. 25, 1993. Dr. Rios was citing World Bank statistics.

[89]   Rick Wills, Analysts Question Unemployment Data, The News, Aug. 20, 1994, at 31, 39.

4.2   BEWARE OF THE LACK OF RELIABLE DATA

Those who might know most of the story regarding the manual labor situation in Mexico might shy away from it but nevertheless seek to market products there. It seems, after all, like an attractive place to sell highly-coveted U.S. goods considering how the government's disclosed unemployment rate in Mexico is an impressive 3.2%.[90] Mexico actually has a very low domestic demand.[91] It is important to note that such a figure is a statistic derived by INEGI, the National Institute of Geographic and Informative Statistics. This government-funded source of national data computes the unemployment rate only in the largest 37 urban areas, and then only considers people unemployed if they work less than one hour weekly.[92] INEGI then somehow dilutes the unemployment rate's severity even further by scaling everything according to a relatively less prosperous 1990 base year.[93] Again, the prestigious Monterrey Technological Institute has estimated that Mexican unemployment is actually around 25%.[94] GDP data gets massaged as well, according to analysts at Goldman, Sachs investment bankers in New York, and the Small Business Chamber.[95]

With the high cost of telecommunications and skilled labor in Mexico, competing sources of information are simply not that available there. The prevalence of a statistic like the 3.2% figure in the Mexican media is misleading to U.S. investors. As the Mexican Academy of Human Rights has stated, the Mexican media has paid a disproportionate amount of attention to the ruling party PRI's candidates and ideologies.[96] A panel of experts at the Autonomous Technological Institute of Mexico (ITAM) also complained of strong media bias, with one expert from the U.S. calling it "grotesque".[97] The television (virtual)

[90]   Rick Wills, Analysts Question Unemployment Data, The News, Aug. 20, 1994, at 31, 39.
[91]   Patricia Nelson, How to Prepare Crow for Eating, The News, Aug. 28, 1994 at 16.
[92]   Rick Wills, Analysts Question Unemployment Data, The News, Aug. 20, 1994, at 31, 39.
[93]   See Generally INEGIs Cuaderno de Información Oportuna, Number 255, June (1994).
[94]   Rick Wills, Analysts Question Unemployment Data, The News, Aug. 20, 1994, at 31, 39.
[95]   The News Staff, Analysts Skeptical of Second Quarter Growth Spurt, The News, Aug.21, 1994, at 40.
[96]   Media Coverage Returns to Old Vices, El Financiero, International Edition, Aug. 22-28, 1994, at 2.
[97]   Mike Esterl, Forum: Fair Elections So Close, Yet So Far, The News, Aug. 27, 1994, at 4.

monopoly Televisa reportedly blatantly favored the ruling party during its pre-election coverage,[98] and subsequently received "extremely favorable" debt-renegotiation concessions from the recently-privatized largest Mexican bank Banamex.[99] Indeed, the Mexican media treats the ruling party's ideologies, and especially the President, with "solemn reverence".[100]

These are just a few examples of how large U.S. law firms sporting big-named clients but inexperienced or timid, image-conscious attorneys can create catastrophes for clients. More of the few very well-informed U.S. lawyers dealing with Mexico should place client interests over their own personal ones and not be afraid to tell the full story even if it runs contrary to the image prominent Mexican national contacts are trying to exude. Otherwise, client mismatches will continue happening to various U.S. foreign investors and further contribute to the interesting structural changes we have observed in the U.S. economy since globalization became more prominent: in 1970, the Fortune 500 companies accounted for over a fifth of the U.S.'s gross domestic product but today they account for less than a tenth of it.[101]

Occasional Mexican consultants are so used to things the way they are in Mexico that they do not think it is important to make foreign executives aware of that which appears like common sense to them. As some say, "nadie es profeta en su tierra" meaning that nobody is a prophet in their own land. Even those Mexican consultants who are truly gifted and who have the experience living abroad that is necessary to their becoming better prophets, still sometimes do not suffice. After all, foreign investment is highly-coveted in Mexico and there are not too many domestic consultants who want the reputation of having discouraged badly-needed foreign capital flows. If one doubts the existence of such pressures, one can ascertain how concerned the government is about whether or not it at least appears authoritarian. Article 33 of the Mexican Constitution states that

"The Executive of the Union holds the exclusive authority to force the exit from national territory, immediately and without previous trial, with regard to any foreigner whose stay it may deem inconvenient."[102]

---

[98] Mike Esterl, Forum: Fair Elections So Close, Yet So Far, The News, Aug. 27, 1994, at 4.
[99] Televisa Awarded Billion-Dollar Loan, El Financiero, International Edition, Aug. 22-28, 1994.
[100] Ignacio Gomez Palacio, The New Regulation on Foreign Investment in Mexico: A Difficult Task 12 Houston J.I.L. 253, 263 n.44 (1990).
[101] John Naisbitt, Global Paradox 13 (1994).
[102] Ignacio Gomez Palacio, The New Regulation on Foreign Investment in Mexico: A

It is fairly clear why Mexico is hardly becoming the "giant sucking sound from the South"[103] that NAFTA critics claimed wuld rob the U.S. of jobs and productivity. The cost of labor is only one of many factors businesses consider when contemplating relocation to Mexico. As Ambassador Carla Hills said, "If wages were the only factor, many less-developed countries would be economic superpowers." Other significant factors businesses consider are: worker productivity, availability of capital, interest rates, quality of infrastructure and education of the work force. The U.S. Trade Representative's Office has stated that when we consider all of these factors, U.S. workers are, on average, at least 5 times more productive than their Mexican counterparts.[104] U.S. agricultural labor productivity is actually 25 times that of its Mexican counterparts, partly due to the greater availability of arable land and water.[105]

These productivity measures even take into account the fact that Mexican wages (presumably excluding tax contributions) are merely a tenth of what they are in the U.S.[106] Furthermore, Mexican wages may not always be as low, as Mexico's improving business standing is apparently driving Mexican wages up. Additional support for the assertion that U.S. workers or robots can out-compete their Mexican counterparts is the fact that just before NAFTA's passage, the U.S. had a large and growing trade surplus with Mexico despite Mexico's tariffs being, on average, higher than the U.S. Additionally, imports from Mexico took up less than 1/2 of 1% of the U.S. GDP.[107]

The quality of Mexican products continues to leave something to be desired.[108] If Mexican workers are even as productive as U.S. workers or automized factories, it would seem that Mexican imports would occupy a greater portion of the U.S. GDP. Recalling how Mexican labor laws require that Mexicans comprise at least 90% of the non-executive labor force[109] should make it clear that foreign investors should think long and hard before choosing to tap into Mexico's "less expensive" manual labor force.

Nevertheless, Mexico's position as a geographical neighbor of the U.S. helps

---

Difficult Task 12 Houston J.I.L. 253, 256 n.13 (1990).

[103] Ross Perot, Presidential Debate on NBC, Oct. 15th, 1992.

[104] Carla Hills, Committee on Agriculture, Sept. 9, 1992, at 6.

[105] Carla Hills, Committee on Agriculture, Sept. 9, 1992, at 6.

[106] John P. Cregan, NAFTA is a Loser, USA Today, Aug. 14, 1992, at 14A.

[107] Carla Hills, Committee on Agriculture, Sept. 9, 1992, at 6.

[108] Ashley Maxwell, Quality Expert Contends Learning Key to Success, Sept. 10, 1994, at 27.

[109] Tod Robberson, Firms Reshape Workplace in Face of North American Pact, Washington Post, Oct. 27, 1992, at D1, D12.

make tapping into its developing nation labor relatively attractive.[110] Additionally, U.S. labor costs are high while, generally speaking, Mexican living standards still are not.[111] Also, the monetary exchange rate between Mexico and the U.S. favors the U.S., thereby making Mexican labor even cheaper for U.S. businesses.[112]

The maquiladoras in the north of Mexico provide the country with its second leading source of foreign exchange.[113] Maquiladora employment has grown 4.7% in the first 5 months of NAFTA over the same period in the previous year.[114] Nevertheless, many ranking officials, including Mexico State Governmental Diputado Manuel Arciniega, believe maquiladoras have less future than one might think. Tariff eliminations and the removal of duty drawbacks should be part of the attractiveness of maquiladoras. Also, due to the labor strikes companies like Ford have contended with recently, along with Mexico's heavily protective labor laws, automated plants will often replace what people had thought were cheap, productive workers. Mexico will advance, instead, in the exportation of primary minerals.[115]

The facts seem to support this. In 1993, for instance, revenues from Mexico's mining of minerals grew over 1%, which was more than twice Mexico's overall 1993 economic growth of 0.4 percent.[116] While the Mexican government offers no statistics on the bankruptcy rates, bits and pieces of the overall picture nevertheless support this forecast too. In the Northern industrial capital Monterrey, overall furniture sales have fallen 40% and 500 related businesses disappeared from the market during 1992-93.[117] Meanwhile,

---

[110] Sandra F. Maviglia, Mexicos Guidelines For Foreign Investment: The Selective Promotion of Necessary Industries, 80 Am. J. Int. L. 281, 301 (1986).

[111] Charles T. DuMars, Liberalization of Foreign Investment Policies in Mexico: Legal Changes Encouraging New Direct Foreign Investment, 21 New Mex. L. Rev. 251, 263 (1991).

[112] Charles T. DuMars, Liberalization of Foreign Investment Policies in Mexico: Legal Changes Encouraging New Direct Foreign Investment, 21 New Mex. L. Rev. 251, 263 (1991).

[113] Charles T. DuMars, Liberalization of Foreign Investment Policies in Mexico: Legal Changes Encouraging New Direct Foreign Investment, 21 New Mex. L. Rev. 251, 274 (1991).

[114] The News Staff, Maquiladora Employment, The News, Aug. 28, 1994, at 35.

[115] Interview with Mexico State Governmental Diputado Manuel Arciniega, in Mexico City, Mexico (Sept. 4, 1994); M.G.G. Pillai, The World Paper, Aug. 1994, at 2.

[116] Arturo Gomez Salgado, Reputar la Inversión Extranjera Para el Sector Energetico, El Financiero, March 13, 1994, at 11.

[117] Armando Torres, Industria Mueblería, en Franca Recesión; Caen 40% las Ventas, El Financiero, Sept. 2, 1994, at 15.

Mexico's leading source of foreign exchange remains a precious mineral, petroleum.[118] Thus, while cheap labor seems like part of Mexico's appeal to foreign investors, such investors would do well to invest their time into deliberating over whether relocation to Mexico for that sole reason is wise.

4.3 POTENTIALLY LESS-STRINGENT ENVIRONMENTALISM

Foreign investors may choose to relocate their factories to Mexico in order to save on the expenses they would otherwise incur elsewhere due to the new wave of environmentalism. After all, in Mexico there was practically no enforcement of the Mexican environmental laws before 1988.[119] Mexico City still holds the dubious distinction of being the most polluted city in the entire world,[120] largely due to the lingering lack of enforcement of the impressive new environmental laws drafted before NAFTA's ratification. In August 1994 it was reported that still only 25% of the Mexico City clean-up projects planned two years before had actually been completed, or even began.[121] Mexico City has millions of motor vehicles and over 100,000 local industries. Reportedly, there are already over six million tons of toxins floating around for people there to breathe.[122] With lax enforcements being a probability even in a post-NAFTA world, Mexico just might seem like an attractive location for relocation.

In response, even if this aspect of the foreign investment regulatory scheme favors foreign investors significantly, one should remember that for most U.S. industries, the cost of complying with U.S. environmental standards is supposedly less than 2% of total costs.[123] Thus, even if Mexico will continue having lax environmental policies, it is not necessarily wise to relocate there. Besides, productivity sacrifices could counter any savings one has from not

---

[118] Charles T. DuMars, Liberalization of Foreign Investment Policies in Mexico: Legal Changes Encouraging New Direct Foreign Investment, 21 New Mex. L. Rev. 251, 274 (1991).

[119] Bryan, Gonzalez Vargas & Gonzalez Baz, NAFTA Vadamecum 8 (1994).

[120] Telephone interview with Greg Block, Attorney at the Mexican Environmental Law Center, in Mexico City, Mexico (Aug. 13, 1994).

[121] Michael Kleinberg, Legislators Blame DDF for Failures of Promised Environmental Programs, The News, Aug. 18, 1994, at 1, 39.

[122] Charles T. DuMars, Liberalization of Foreign Investment Policies in Mexico: Legal Changes Encouraging New Direct Foreign Investment, 21 New Mex. L. Rev. 251, 267 (1991).

[123] Report of the Administration of the NAFTA and Actions Taken in Fulfillment of the Agreement, May 1, 1991 Commitments, Sept. 18, 1992, at 4-5.

having to comply with U.S. environmental regulations.

Additionally, one should not completely forget about NAFTA which requires, among many other things, that no member nation may lower its health, safety or environmental standards to attract investment.[124] Article 5, Section 3 of the NAFTA supplementary agreements[125] provides for the imposition of sanctions if Mexico does not adequately comply with its NAFTA obligations. Admittedly, Mexican Constitutional issues of sovereignty greatly limited the potential effectiveness of these side agreements, but the prospect of Mexico possibly suffering from economic sanctions just might prompt the government to compel foreign investors' businesses to comply with the written environmental regulations after all.

5. NOT ENOUGH APERTURE

Many foreign investment attorneys criticize Mexico's modern regulatory scheme as still not creating enough aperture for foreign investors. The aforementioned sections give one a general framework with which to assess the validity of such criticisms. In many ways Mexico's foreign investment scheme is one of the most receptive to foreign investment in the world, but there are certain areas which trade negotiators excluded from the otherwise broad-sweeping liberalization.

Mexicans care a great deal about maintaining their national sovereignty. Mexico's Constitution embodies these concerns. Article 33 regulates foreign land ownership and Article 27 regulates foreign exploitation of Mexico's petroleum resources. The 1993 foreign investment law also reflects some Mexicans' concerns for preserving national autonomy which the Constitution does not strongly recognize, such as the restrictions upon foreigners' rights to engage in transportation activities within Mexico.[126] If the foreign investment regulatory scheme does not expressly restrict foreign investor involvement in an activity, foreigners may acquire any percentage[127] interest in that non-restricted activity as long as that interest's total value does not exceed

---

[124] U.S. Trade Representative, Description of the Proposed North American Free Trade Agreement, Aug. 12, 1992, at 44.

[125] Paul B. Stephan, III et al., International Business and Economics 1994 Supplement, 438 (1994).

[126] Baker & McKenzie, 1993 Guide to Foreign Investors in Mexico, 14 (1994).

[127] Baker & McKenzie, 1993 Guide to Foreign Investors in Mexico, 3 (1994).

roughly 30 million U.S. dollars.[128] Additionally, even in areas where the amount of foreign investment allowed is greatly restricted, Article 20 of the new foreign investment law permits ownership in excess of the permissible percentages if it is neutral investment (i.e. if it is ownership of shares which lack voting rights or which have limited corporate rights).[129]

5.1 LAND OWNERSHIP

Foreigners may acquire land in Mexico as long as it is not located in the restricted zone (i.e. within 100 kilometers of the border or 50 kilometers of the coasts). If the desired land is located within the restricted zone, foreign investors may still acquire title for non-residential purposes if they record the acquisition with the Secretariat of Foreign Affairs. Otherwise, title can only be acquired through a trust.[130] Yet, various technicalities permit rule-bending in certain cases, though.[131]

Regarding criticisms of the restrictions on land ownership, some additional historical background information is highly relevant. The U.S. now possesses what was formerly half of Mexico's territory, namely the states of Texas, New Mexico, Arizona, and part of California.[132] While many dispute that there were enough Mexicans in these states over a century ago to justify Mexico's claim to that subsequently-lost territory, the U.S. certainly would not permit foreigners to usurp Alaska on similar grounds.

While some criticize these restrictions as unnecessary, the counter-argument is that bans on most forms of foreign ownership within several kilometers of the border or coastline exist, at least in part, for national security reasons. With Mexico's relatively small economy, it lacks the U.S.'s luxury of policing zones with costly military establishments so the practical approach is to minimize foreign involvement in these strategic zones. An additional point is that as the law presently stands, critics contend it violates Article 27 of the Mexican Constitution by granting foreigners the liberty to, nevertheless, invest in the

---

[128] Bryan, Gonzalez Vargas & Gonzalez Baz, NAFTA Vadamecum 128 (1994).

[129] Baker & McKenzie, 1993 Guide to Foreign Investors in Mexico, 18-19 (1994); Bryan, Gonzalez Vargas & Gonzalez Baz, NAFTA Vadamecum 112 (1994).

[130] Bryan, Gonzalez Vargas & Gonzalez Baz, NAFTA Vadamecum 5 (1994); Baker & McKenzie, 1993 Guide to Foreign Investors in Mexico 3 (1994).

[131] Bryan, Gonzalez Vargas & Gonzalez Baz, NAFTA Vadamecum 6 (1994).

[132] Mary Lee Bretz et al., Pasajes 259 (1987).

restricted zones.[133] Defenders could make the plausible argument that one cannot fairly assert that a law is overly-restrictive against foreigners when it favors foreigners over the supreme law of the land.

Of course, one could rebut that by claiming that the Constitutional standard, itself, should be relaxed so that land ownership is more greatly permitted in these otherwise restricted areas. Additionally, by permitting foreign interests to own land throughout the republic, Mexico would create incentives for foreigners to better care for and develop that land. Countering this rebuttal involves referring back to Mexico's history once more, as well as looking across the globe for related examples of how other governments addressed similar issues.

Land ownership by foreigners in Mexico has been a sensitive issue for years and at least some restrictions on it seem reasonable. One of the major causes of Mexico's largest 20th Century revolution was the Diaz government's permitting unlimited foreign ownership of real property. Such permissiveness resulted in the removal of farm-dwellers from the lands they had traditionally farmed, leading to tremendous civil disturbances.[134] The resulting Mexican Constitition subsequently created restricted zones, but essentially only near the borders and seacoasts.[135]

In spanning the globe for related examples of how other governments deal with similar situations, Austria restricts land ownership by its neighbor Germany for both national security as well as economic protection reasons.[136] Defenders could assert that countries which fail to protect their own interests soon cease being countries, and Mexico fought hard for its independence.

There is also the argument that such laws merely discriminate against foreigners in order to keep prices down and thereby promote local ownership in the more valuable territories. Defenders could counter by stating that there are some areas in Mexico that even Mexican nationals cannot individually own. Territory within 50 meters from whatever frontier is federal property, and not even Mexicans can buy it. This would seemingly call into question any economic protectionism criticism of the restricted zones.

---

[133] Julieta Medina, Aprueban Ley de Inversiones, El Norte/Mexico, Dec. 12, 1993, at A1.

[134] Charles T. DuMars, Liberalization of Foreign Investment Policies in Mexico: Legal Changes Encouraging New Direct Foreign Investment, 21 New Mex. L. Rev. 251, 259 (1991).

[135] Charles T. DuMars, Liberalization of Foreign Investment Policies in Mexico: Legal Changes Encouraging New Direct Foreign Investment, 21 New Mex. L. Rev. 251, 259 (1991).

[136] Paul B. Stephan, III et al., International Business and Economics: Law and Policy 484 (1993).

6. PETROLEUM

Even under the modern foreign investment regulatory scheme, the petroleum monopoly Pemex retains exclusive control of Mexico's vast petroleum distributorships.[137] Those who are from countries where competition in the gas distributorship realm abounds but who now live and drive in Mexico know this restriction's significance. Low grade, often lead-ridden and certainly polluting gas will continue to be nearly all that is readily available in the near future, and for at least $U.S.10 per tankful more than its competition-ridden U.S. counterparts.

In rebuttal, nationalists will undoubtedly refer to the foreign exploitation of Mexico's petroleum resources which led President Lázaro Cárdenas to nationalize related foreign establishments in 1938.[138] They will further assert that it is better to endure some of the side-effects of lacking significant foreign competition than to risk future exploitation which deprives Mexico of its precious mineral resources, purportedly without fair compensation. Petroleum is the leading source of Mexico's foreign exchange[139] as well as a source of economic stability as Mexico possesses the world's fourth largest oil reserves.[140] Thus, Article 27 of the Mexican Constitution protects this vital resource, and justifiably so.

In response, one can point out how the U.S. produces 90% of the world's computer software[141] but still permits healthy competition in the realm of this vital source of revenues. In other words, the U.S. government does not have a monopoly over software production. Sure, exploitation has occurred and will continue to occur until computer piracy is more under control, but that does not prompt the U.S. to monopolize the industry. Healthy competition is good for the economy and for the consumer.

One could rebut, claiming the U.S. has many other sources of foreign

---

[137] Bryan, Gonzalez Vargas & Gonzalez Baz, NAFTA Vadamecum 39 (1994); Baker & McKenzie, 1993 Guide to Foreign Investors in Mexico, 37-40 (1994).

[138] Charles T. DuMars, Liberalization of Foreign Investment Policies in Mexico: Legal Changes Encouraging New Direct Foreign Investment, 21 New Mex. L. Rev. 251, 260 (1991).

[139] Charles T. DuMars, Liberalization of Foreign Investment Policies in Mexico: Legal Changes Encouraging New Direct Foreign Investment, 21 New Mex. L. Rev. 251, 263 (1991).

[140] Charles T. DuMars, Liberalization of Foreign Investment Policies in Mexico: Legal Changes Encouraging New Direct Foreign Investment, 21 New Mex. L. Rev. 251, 274 (1991).

[141] John Naisbitt, Global Paradox 32 (1994).

currency so constitutional protection of some proposed governmental software monopoly is not as necessary. Mexico's 1917 Constitution gave the federal government the domineering role in managing the economy, on the other hand, because Mexico is not as wealthy and must have strong overseers protect its well-being.

In response, however, one can use history to show that the age of Pemex's monopoly is over. After 1917, the number of federally-owned or controlled business entities began to grow tremendously. The ones particulary susceptible to government annexation were: those designated as strategically important on constitutional grounds; those where takeover was deemed essential to preserve employment or to continue the supply of items deemed necessary for the economy; or those entities which were on the verge of bankruptcy. During the oil boom of the 1970s there were only 391 parastatal entities but by the December 1982 devaluation crisis, the Mexican government owned or controlled 1,155 such entities, responsible for nearly a fifth of Mexico's GDP.[142] Essentially, privatization and competition help an economy which is why so many governments around the world, including Mexico, are adopting privatization programs. Mexico realizes this which is why in 1991, there remained only 269 of these parastatal entities.[143]

Furthermore, making consumers pay the added costs of a lack of competition detrimentally impacts the economy. As Ambassador Michael Cook noted, Australian living standards declined immensely after Australia adopted protectionist barriers in the last century. The barriers forced consumers to pay higher prices and their resulting reduction of discretionary income limited the other goods they could buy. Manufacturers and service providers witnessed their markets shrink. This, in turn, led to greater unemployment as well as a decreased standard of living from which Australia has struggled to recover.[144]

It is not as if the merit of competition is new to the Mexican government, either. Article 28 of the same Constitution protecting Pemex's monopoly ironically shows a tendency to disfavor monopolies. In light of Mexico's relatively limited domestic market, it is peculiar that this legally-sanctioned monopoly remains. Newsweek magazine offers a potential clue. Just before the

---

[142] United States International Trade Commission, Review of Trade and Investment Liberalization Measures By Mexico and Prospects for Future United States-Mexican Relations: Investigation No. 332-282, 39 (1990).

[143] Hope H. Camp, Jr. et al., Foreign Investment in Mexico From the Perspective of the Foreign Investor, 24 St. Mary's L. Rev. 775, 787 (1993).

[144] Ambassador Michael Cook, Address to the J.B. Moore Society of International Law at the University of Virginia School of Law (Oct. 6, 1992).

recent elections, Newsweek reported how oil workers in petroleum-rich Tamaulipas alleged union leaders had threatened them with discharge and bodily harm if they did not vote for the ruling party, which has maintained Pemex's monopoly for decades.[145]

Fortunately, at least some forms of competition are coming to Mexico's petroleum industry under NAFTA. Mexico's state-owned oil monopoly (Pemex) and its state-owned electricity monopoly (CFE) must enable entities from other NAFTA members to procure as much as 50% of their companies immediately. Over the subsequent eight years, this figure expands to 70%. By the tenth year, there will be no limit to the percentage of such service-providers that U.S. firms can procure. NAFTA permits procurers as well as suppliers of natural gas and basic petrochemicals to deal directly with Mexican customers, better enabling the U.S. to market what is the best petrochemical technology in the world.[146] In the past, U.S. gas and electricity industries have sold services and goods into Mexico but could not enjoy such a freedom.[147] Despite this relative progress, however, more liberalization is due and the Mexican Constitution should evolve with the times to promote the badly-needed welfare of the Mexican citizenry.

As an additional criticism, NAFTA protects Mexico's freedom to prompt other member nations to become dependent on Mexican energy imports and subsequently reduce supplies drastically. Under NAFTA, Mexico is not required to maintain any particular levels of energy supply to the U.S. or Canada. The U.S. and Canada do, however, have such a security of supply agreement with each other.[148] This seemingly justifies at least moderate fears that Mexico could encourage fuel-dependencies and then drastically cut supplies, causing energy prices and Mexican profits to soar.

Former United States Trade Representative Carla Hills explained that Mexico is exempt from the security of supply requirement because of Mexican constitutional restraints as well as its having dramatically opened up procurement and related opportunities in its energy and electricity markets.[149] Unfortunately, however, under NAFTA, U.S. interests cannot own more than

---

[145] Tim Padgett, Moment of Truth, Newsweek (International Edition), Aug. 8, 1994, at 16.

[146] The White House, Office of the Press Secretary, Press Briefing by U.S. Trade Representative Ambassador Carla Hills, Aug. 12, 1992, at 7.

[147] The White House, Office of the Press Secretary, Press Briefing by U.S. Trade Representative Ambassador Carla Hills, Aug. 12, 1992, at 4.

[148] The White House, Office of the Press Secretary, Press Briefing by U.S. Trade Representative Ambassador Carla Hills, Aug. 12, 1992, at 5.

[149] The White House, Office of the Press Secretary, Press Briefing by U.S. Trade Representative Ambassador Carla Hills, Aug. 12, 1992, at 5.

50% of energy subsidiaries in Mexico until the year 2002. Thus, even if procurement offered such U.S. firms much control of Pemex's decisions, it is not as if U.S. firms can very effectively prevent Mexican suppliers from creating dependencies and then cutting off supplies sharply before 2002. In response to this criticism it seems fair to say that free trade makes Mexico vulnerable in several similar ways and its having this one basic strength hopefully gives other countries' corporations more incentives to deal humanely with Mexico.

7. TRANSPORTATION BREAKTHROUGHS

NAFTA makes breakthroughs in transportation which have far-reaching implications. U.S. trucking and bus companies will eventually have open roads for carrying international cargo to all of Mexico.[150] Before NAFTA, U.S. truckers could not carry cargo beyond the border or set up trucking subsidiaries in Mexico even though over 90% of U.S./Mexican trade was by land.[151] NAFTA eradicates such inefficiencies by permitting, for example, U.S. companies to carry cargo to the Mexican borderline states by 1995, and to all of Mexico by the end of 1999.[152] Similarly, U.S. railroads and land-side port service providers will have the opportunity to invest heavily and operate in Mexico.[153]

Such developments in Mexico's transportation laws will eventually lead to a more efficient intermodal transport system throughout the entire North American continent. Having an effective transportation system available will benefit nearly all business sectors. Nevertheless, as many complain, the law remains too restrictive. No foreign investment in domestic cargo transportation from one Mexican location to another is permissible at any time during NAFTA.[154] Foreign investors cannot take a majority interest in international land transportation until 2001, and ownership limitations in this area do not

---

[150] The White House, Office of the Press Secretary, Press Briefing by U.S. Trade Representative Ambassador Carla Hills, Aug. 12, 1992, at 2.

[151] The White House, Office of the Press Secretary, The North American Free Trade Agreement Fact Sheet, Aug. 12, 1992, at 4.

[152] The White House, Office of the Press Secretary, The North American Free Trade Agreement Fact Sheet, Aug. 12, 1992, at 4.

[153] The White House, Office of the Press Secretary, The North American Free Trade Agreement Fact Sheet, Aug. 12, 1992, at 4.

[154] Bryan, Gonzalez Vargas & Gonzalez Baz, NAFTA Vadamecum 63 (1994).

vanish until 2003.[155]

Limiting foreign access to ownership of shares in a company might seem like a prudent way of preventing economic annexation[156] by the U.S., or of avoiding harmful speculation or disastrous panic by investors who take Mexico's well being away whenever they divest their funds.[157] But, there certainly are counter-arguments. To begin, it is useful to consider the example of Federal Express carrier service. It is so much better than the competition[158] in terms of actually guaranteeing delivery in half the time while charging less, and it consequently benefits international commerce. It has the freedom to provide such services in Mexico and the consumer wins as a result.

Because of the aforementioned land transportation restrictions, however, the consumer loses. Perishable goods like U.S.-produced milk often do not get down to southern Mexico, not even Mexico City, soon enough. This seems to defeat the purpose of NAFTA, which otherwise is supposed to remove the obstacles such products must overcome to enter the Mexican market successfully. In the future, Mexican investment regulators should keep in mind that the more trade barriers vanish, the more choices are available to consumers and the lower their cost.[159]

There is an additional justification for accelerated liberalization. As the private sector finally gets greater opportunities and incentives to invest in Mexican roadways, railways and ports, and as the Mexican and U.S. governments see fit to upgrade cross-border access, resulting borderline infrastructure improvements should ease traffic tensions immensely. Drug inspections will subsequently become less burdensome to innocent travelers at otherwise highly-congested areas like the crossway between Tijuana and San Diego. Less congestion will make it more likely that customs officials can become more effective at reducing drug flows.

A counter-argument could be that with Mexico's many uneducated and impoverished people, protectionism such as this might seem necessary to give this emerging economic force a fair chance at succeeding in the competitive capitalistic arena. But the aforementioned example of Australia's economic decline purportedly resulting from its becoming protectionist suggests that

---

[155] Baker & McKenzie, 1993 Guide to Foreign Investors in Mexico, 14 (1994).

[156] Federal Senator Jose Conchello, El TLC: Un Callejon Sin Salida 25 (1992).

[157] Federal Senator Jose Conchello, El TLC: Un Callejon Sin Salida 24 (1992).

[158] Including Estafeta, Mexpost and D.H.L.

[159] The White House, Office of the Press Secretary, Press Briefing by U.S. Trade Representative Ambassador Carla Hills, Aug. 12, 1992, at 8.

protecting this sector of the economy is not ideal for the citizenry. Sure, permitting greater foreign investment might conjure up bad memories of foreign exploitation such as that which occurred during the Diaz regime. But one must also take another historical fact into consideration. In 1880, Mexico only had 700 miles of railroad track.[160] Thanks to the Diaz regime's openness to foreign investment, by 1910, Mexico had over 12,000 miles of railroad track. Mexico, as well as the U.S. must weigh the merits of protectionism in various sectors [such as mail delivery] against the need to progress and adapt for the challenges of the emerging global marketplace.

8. TELECOMMUNICATIONS

Discussing Mexico's telecommunications system provides a great opportunity to further emphasize how both consumers, and the economy, usually lose when competition is discouraged. NAFTA's Chapter 13 does not liberalize basic services such as telephone, cable or broadcast distribution of radio or television programming.[161] In fact, only Mexicans and Mexican companies can successfully apply for concessions or permits.[162]

Nevertheless, NAFTA does at least give U.S. and Canadian entrepreneurs access to various areas of Mexico's $6 billion telecommunications market.[163] The Mexican telecommunications market still has enormous growth potential, especially regarding the cellular telephone industry, rural areas networking, satellite communications, integrated services digital networks, and value-added services such as voice-mail.[164] NAFTA makes certain areas of Mexico's telecommunications market immediately open itself to over 80% of current U.S. telecommunications exports to Mexico.[165] These areas are set to completely

---

[160] Hope H. Camp, Jr. et al., Foreign Investment in Mexico From the Perspective of the Foreign Investor, 24 St. Mary's L. Rev. 775, 781 (1993).

[161] Bryan, Gonzalez Vargas & Gonzalez Baz, NAFTA Vadamecum 64 (1994); Baker & McKenzie, 1993 Guide to Foreign Investors in Mexico, 23 (1994).

[162] Bryan, Gonzalez Vargas & Gonzalez Baz, NAFTA Vadamecum 66 (1994).

[163] The White House, Office of the Press Secretary, Press Briefing by U.S. Trade Representative Ambassador Carla Hills, Aug. 12, 1992, at 2.

[164] Eugenio Salinas: Economic Counselor at the Trade Office of the Embassy of Mexico, and cousin of Mexicos President Salinas, Address to the Emerging Markets of Latin America Club at the University of Virginia Darden School of Business (December 7, 1992).

[165] Carla Hills, Sept. 9, 1992, at 4.

open to U.S. exports by mid-1995.[166]

It will be some time before foreign competition for long distance calls comes to Mexico. This is distressing because calling the U.S.A. from Mexico currently costs $2 per minute and one must sometimes wait at least several months to get a phone installed, a service which costs over $600. Mere local phone call service is metered and typically costs around $50 each month. When is the magic date? By January 1, 1997, Mexico will be completely open to enhanced phone services competition including E-mail, specialized network services, and voice mail. These are among the fastest growing sectors of the telecommunications industry,[167] and yet one must wait years before significant foreign competition can enter.

A fascinating book provides a great vehicle for further discussing the telecommunications situation in Mexico. In John Naisbitt's interesting and informative work *Global Paradox*, this author of *Megatrends 2000* examines current business trends and forecasts what appears to be happening to businesses in the emerging global marketplace of the 21st Century. Unlike ever before, smaller corporations are succeeding in developed countries as telecommunications advances are enabling such corporations to compete where they previously could not. In the U.S., for instance, it no longer costs a fortune to have instantaneous access to huge banks of data or large groups of potential customers, thanks to the development of inexpensive electronic mail. Small corporations can use progressive developments like improved satellite technology to connect with business allies across the globe and thereby create alliances which have already greatly threatened the bulkier, bureaucratic and slower multinational corporations.

It is probably no coincidence that whereas the Fortune 500 used to comprise a fifth of the U.S.'s GDP in 1970, it now composes around a tenth of it.[168] Telecommunications advances have unleashed the potential of entrepreneurs in quantities the world has never seen.[169]

Naisbitt's analysis is highly relevant to Mexico, largely because of its protectionist stance in the telecommunications realm. Mexico is not presently suited to experience such a business evolution due to the extremely high cost of

---

[166] The White House, Office of the Press Secretary, The North American Free Trade Agreement Fact Sheet, Aug. 12, 1992, at 3.

[167] Thomas M. Shoesmith, Telecom Opportunities Abound, El Financiero, International Edition, Aug. 29-Sept. 4, 1994, at 7.

[168] John Naisbitt, Global Paradox 13 (1994).

[169] See generally, John Naisbitt, Global Paradox, Ch. 1 (1994).

telecommunications the public must incur as it competes with formidable foreign corporations. Whereas electronic mail in the U.S. generally costs less than $100 monthly,[170] Mexican businesses must endure these trying times that are relatively devoid of competition, and pay roughly $20,000 each month.[171] If this is not bad enough, in Mexico there are only 8.7 phone lines for every 100 Mexicans.[172] One in every thousand people in Mexico has access to a computer compared to one in every hundred in the U.S.[173]

It probably comes as no surprise to see the comparative effects. In the U.S., and Germany, 50 percent of each nation's exports are created by companies with 19 or fewer employees. Only 7% of U.S. exports are created by companies with 500 or more employees.[174] Smaller manufacturers created virtually all of the new U.S. jobs during the 1980s.[175] In Mexico, data is difficult to come by but the following nevertheless gets the point across. 1.9% (2,350 of 122,169 companies) of the Mexican industrial corporations contribute 56% of the total industrial realm's contribution to Mexico's GDP. These large corporations occupy half of the industrial jobs in Mexico, and 95% of all of Mexico's industrial exports.[176] It is probably not surprising that Mexico's economy is 5% of the U.S.'s,[177] and that the Monterrey Technological Institute has estimated that Mexican unemployment is around 25%. While even Western Europe needs to liberalize foreign investment in telecommunications more than it has or else risk lagging behind in the global marketplace,[178] it is hard to imagine the Europeans have it nearly as bad as the Mexicans who currently must wait until 1997 before things start significantly improving.

The counter-argument might be that Telmex needs protection from foreign competition so it can improve its services. After all, upon foreign competition's

---

[170] Philip Elmer-Dewitt, Battle for the Soul of the Internet, Time Magazine, Jul. 25, 1994, at 50-56.

[171] Maria Carlino, User Friendlier, El Financiero, International Edition, Aug. 22-29, 1994, at 8.

[172] Dario Celis Estrada, Telmex y su Papel Histórico Durante los Comicios, El Financiero, Aug. 22, 1994, at 40.

[173] Maria Carlino, User Friendlier, El Financiero, International Edition, Aug. 22-29, 1994, at 8.

[174] John Naisbitt, Global Paradox 13 (1994).

[175] John P. Cregan, NAFTA Is A Loser, USA Today, Aug. 14, 1992, at 14A.

[176] Salvador Esquivel, El Rol de las Empresas Grandes en las Exportaciones Mexicanas, El Financiero, Aug. 22, 1994, at 38A.

[177] The Economist Intelligence Unit of Business International Limited, Mexico Country Report, No. 1, 3 (1992).

[178] Frank Bajak, Continent Could Be Technologically Inferior, Sept. 10, 1994, at 28.

entry, the Mexican telephone monopoly Telmex is expected to immediately lose between 500 and 1000 "millones de dolares."[179] But one must weigh the losses of Telmex with the losses of the country, which appear grave according to data in this article. As University of Virginia international business law Professor Paul Stephan writes, monopolies as a necessary means of modernizing a country's telecommunications system are more or less a thing of the past. This is because of new technological advances whereby various types of telecommunications services can now inexpensively enter the competitive arena via new and less expensive technology such as microwaves, fiber optics cables, or satellites. Additionally, unlike the pre-1980s world, there are now all types of competitors waiting to enter and compete in other countries. Governments should adequately justify blocking out competition before actually doing so. Perhaps sufficient justifications involve promoting low cost access, the fostering of civic values, or the development of national technologies.[180] These potential justifications do not appear to justify Telmex's monopoly, although that topic is a bit beyond this chapter's scope.

9. INTELLECTUAL PROPERTY

While on the topic of the goal of preserving civic values or cultural identity,[181] it is appropriate to discuss the legal regime by which foreign investors can make money off their intellectual property in Mexico. Intellectual property receives better protection under NAFTA than under any previous agreement, including the pre-Uruguay Round of GATT which did not cover intellectual property rights. Patents, copyrights and trademarks on U.S. high technology and entertainment products realize substantial protections[182] due to NAFTA, which solidifies Mexico's June 1991 intellectual property legal reforms.[183]

Under NAFTA, trademarks receive protection for 10 years, as opposed to

---

[179] Ivan Sosa, Nociva Para Telmex la Total Apertura en Telefonoa, Dice Hernndez Juarez, El Financiero, Sept. 5, 1994, at 14.

[180] See generally, Paul B. Stephan, III et al., International Business and Economics: Law and Policy 792 (1993).

[181] Senador Jose Conchello, El TLC: Un Callejon Sin Salida, 26 (3rd ed. 1992).

[182] The White House: Office of the Press Secretary, The North American Free Trade Agreement Fact Sheet, 4, Aug. 12, 1992.

[183] Eduardo Montiel Ducker, Contexto Jurídico Internaciónal del Contrato de Franquicias. Bachelor's degree thesis, UNAM-Mexico, 1994, at 29.

just 5 years under the previous law.[184] U.S. film makers and videocassette producers have previously suffered from unfair "pirating" [copying] which discourages them from many otherwise profitable endeavors,[185] but this is improving.[186] This is especially significant considering how the U.S. copyright industry is presently the country's second largest exporter.[187] Some of the many other major beneficiaries under NAFTA are high technology producers such as agricultural chemical makers, "Silicon Valley" computer accessory producers,[188] and pharmaceutical companies.

Just as there are distinct legal systems in the U.S., with its common law tradition, and Latin America, with its Civil Code one, there is also a great variety throughout the hemisphere regarding technology transfer. Legal variation exists in the realm of, for instance, contracts of know how, licensing, franchises or joint ventures. Thanks to NAFTA and particularly Chapter 17 of the Agreement, North America has harmonized many of the regulations regarding intellectual property which were previously regulated by the World Intellectual Property Organization. Nevertheless, one must be careful when maneuvering in future NAFTA members throughout the remainder of Latin America as conflicting systems regarding intellectual property rights still exist, and confusion and frustration may occur.

An additional point worth noting is that the provider of licensed knowledge nearly always has the upper hand over the recipients from less technologically-advanced countries. This is not only because the provider knows the licensed-knowledge better than the recipient, but also because he has more familiarity with the legal terminology involved with the contracting, such as performance bonds and indemnification for damages. Parties from less advanced countries such as Mexico are not as aware of potential problems that U.S. investors are used to seeing surface. While care should be taken that contracts are thoroughly explained to all signing parties, it nevertheless remains inevitable that the road will be a bumpy one as a relatively less-advanced nation seeks to catch up.

---

[184] Bryan, Gonzalez Vargas & Gonzalez Baz, NAFTA Vadamecum 13 (1994).

[185] University of Virginia School of Law Professor Paul Stephan, International Business Transactions (Mar. 11, 1992).

[186] Mexico continues to be what the Washington, D.C.-based International Intellectual Property Alliance ranks as the the largest pirate market of U.S. audio cassettes in the entire world.

[187] International Intellectual Property Alliance, China robs over $842 million, Feb. 13, 1994, at 5.

[188] Ambassador Carla Hills addresses the Committee on Agriculture, Sept. 16, 1992, at 3.

10. FINANCIAL INDUSTRY BREAKTHROUGHS, SO TO SPEAK

Due to NAFTA, for the first time since the early 1930s, U.S. securities firms and banks may establish entirely American-owned Mexican subsidiaries[189] which must be treated the same as local firms.[190] Remaining transitional restrictions will completely vanish by the year 2000.[191] The U.S. competes very successfully in Mexico's capital goods market. From 1986 to 1991, for instance, U.S. capital goods exports to Mexico more than doubled to total $11.3 billion.[192] Growth potential remains as the actual size of Mexico's financial services market is presently $330 billion.[193] It should be even greater in the near future. As the Wall Street Journal observed "developing countries are likely to be larger importers of private capital during the 1990s than during any decade since before the First World War...As a result of the fall of communism and the spread of liberal economic ideas to the Third World, over three billion people are now poised to re-enter the global marketplace for goods and capital after periods of absence ranging from 40 to 80 years."[194]

Nevertheless, even by the year 2008 foreign banks, on the aggregate, can only occupy a mere fifteen percent of the total Mexican market. The Mexican government may loosen the requirement thereafter, if it so chooses.[195] An increased aperture would directly benefit the U.S. capital goods sector, and would also indirectly benefit other Mexican sectors seeking to modernize and compete. Capital's increasing availability in Mexico should strengthen that trading partner and promote further trade increases.

A counter-argument is that banks were only privatized very recently, back in 1990[196] after the Lopez Portillo government nationalized them and imposed exchange controls in 1982.[197] Not giving the Mexican banks a grace period

---

[189] Carla Hills addresses the Committee on Agriculture, 3, Sept. 16, 1992.

[190] The White House: Office of the Press Secretary, Press Briefing by U.S. Trade Representative Ambassador Carla Hills, Aug. 12, 1992, at 2.

[191] Carla Hills, Sept. 9, 1992, at 4.

[192] The White House, Office of the Press Secretary, The North American Free Trade Agreement Fact Sheet, Aug. 12, 1992, at 3.

[193] Carla Hills addresses the Committee on Agriculture, Sept. 16, 1993, at 3.

[194] Michael R. Sesit, Your Stock Portfolio in the Year 2000 May be Loaded with Asian, Latin Shares, Wall St. J., Oct. 29, 1992, at C1, C11.

[195] Bryan, Gonzalez Vargas & Gonzalez Baz, NAFTA Vadamecum 69 (1994).

[196] Bryan, Gonzalez Vargas & Gonzalez Baz, NAFTA Vadamecum 70 (1994).

[197] Charles T. DuMars, Liberalization of Foreign Investment Policies in Mexico: Legal Changes Encouraging New Direct Foreign Investment, 21 Nev. Mex. L. Rev. 251, 253

relatively free of extensive foreign competition in order to improve its services would leave Mexico's economic destiny in the hands of foreigners.[198]

An additional counter-argument might be that Mexican inflation could increase if more money was available. Actually, though, peso devaluations intended to attract capital flows into Mexico would be less necessary and inflation would therefore be less likely.

Another counter-argument pertains to how foreign banks can potentially defraud Mexican customers. The fewer there are, the easier it is to regulate them and thereby protect the Mexican citizenry.[199]

Yet, it is helpful to note that Mexico's cost of capital is quite exhorbitant. Mexico will not advance rapidly enough to compete if capital does not become more readily available. Once it is more available, Mexico's extremely young population can learn all sorts of important tasks such as how to know when to avoid a business transaction that appears "too good to be true".

Mexico's inability to modernize quickly enough could diminish if capital was more available. But presently U.S. companies seeking to co-produce with Mexico for selling around the world must put up with all sorts of unnecessary inefficiencies and U.S. vendors must try to sell to impoverished Mexican masses. This state of affairs is hardly conducive to the regional integration NAFTA negotiators sought.

11.   INSURANCE

Regarding Mexico's $3.5 billion insurance market,[200] NAFTA requires that U.S. firms with current joint ventures may obtain 100% ownership by 1996. New entrants to the Mexican market may obtain a majority share of their Mexican branches by 1998. The entire Mexican insurance market will completely open to U.S. insurers by 2000.[201] This market is sure to grow because the more entrepreneurial endeavors there are in Mexico, the greater the demand for insurance.

(1991).

[198] Micronotas: Peligran Bancos Nacionales Ante los Extranjeros: UNAM, El Financiero, Sept. 4, 1994, at 6.

[199] Senator Jose Conchello, El TLC: Un Callejon Sin Salida, 22-22 (3rd ed. 1992).

[200] The White House, Office of the Press Secretary, Press Briefing by U.S. Trade Representative Ambassador Carla Hills, Aug. 12, 1992, at 2.

[201] Carla Hills, Sept. 9, 1992, at 4.

While delaying a greater opening and thereby giving Mexican insurers the opportunity to make their services competitive with those of the U.S. seems like a worthwhile goal, one must at least consider the trade-offs. Once U.S. insurers can compete more effectively in Mexico, still more businesses will be able to afford to spring up there. This will result in badly-needed foreign investment and economic growth. Mexico's laws gradually permit this influx of foreign insurers but in light of the trying economic circumstances which Mexico presently endures, there seems like no better time than the present to increase the aperture for them. Foreign insurers' competitive advantages in terms of having greater access to capital and more advanced actuarial science will possibly be more than outweighed by their inevitable difficulty of finding out the best way to dispute claims when Mexico's legal system and the means of conducting investigations are relatively less reliable.

12.   AUTOMOTIVE GOODS

Mexico is now our second largest market for manufactured goods.[202] In addressing automotive goods, it is particularly significant to the U.S. that NAFTA created greater access for Mexico to open to U.S. cars, light trucks, and auto parts.[203] Mexico has the fastest growing major auto market in the world.[204] With NAFTA, half of the tariffs in this sector will immediately vanish in 1994 and within the first five years, 75% of the duties on U.S. auto parts exports to Mexico will disappear.[205] As of January 1999, foreign investors may own up to 100% of the Mexican automotive manufacture and assembly entities.[206] Mexican local content requirements and trade balancing will phase out over 10 years[207] and Mexico will continue pre-NAFTA restraints on foreign investment in this realm until the start of 2004.[208]

---

[202] Ambassador Carla Hills, Sept. 9, 1992, at 3.

[203] The White House, Office of the Press Secretary, Press Briefing by U.S. Trade Representative Ambassador Carla Hills, Aug. 12, 1992, at 2.

[204] The White House, Office of the Press Secretary, The North American Free Trade Agreement Fact Sheet, Aug. 12, 1992, at 2.

[205] The White House, Office of the Press Secretary, The North American Free Trade Agreement Fact Sheet, Aug. 12, 1992, at 3.

[206] Bryan, Gonzalez Vargas & Gonzalez Baz, NAFTA Vadamecum 124 (1994).

[207] The White House, Office of the Press Secretary, The North American Free Trade Agreement Fact Sheet, Aug. 12, 1992, at 3.

[208] Baker & McKenzie, 1993 Guide to Foreign Investors in Mexico, 36 (1994).

In response, an accelerated liberalization in this realm would help reduce the number of polluting cars in Mexico which lack catalytic converters and pollute the atmosphere. It would also benefit consumers who otherwise cannot afford Mexican car dealers' exhorbitant prices. The major criticism of this realm of NAFTA, however, is significantly different. It pertains to this sector's rule of origin requirements which require various products to have minimum percentages of components made in a NAFTA country for the products to warrant reduced-tariff or tariff-free treatment. This has been criticized as a form of protectionism against non-NAFTA members. This criticism is very misleading, however. NAFTA is not really a form of protectionism because it does not raise tariffs or impose restrictive quotas on non-member nations. It simply does not, on its own, lower tariffs or abolish quotas to the outside world.[209]

Admittedly, non-NAFTA component manufacturers will have a comparative disadvantage as a result of this pro-member favoritism. Indeed, American companies are already experiencing increased sales to, for example, Japanese subsidiaries in Mexico which used to buy from Japanese firms.[210] Besides, a major justification for having this rule of origin requirement is to enhance North American global competitiveness.[211] However, this is not the same as saying that NAFTA's rule of origin requirements are protectionist. They are not a means of increasing local competitiveness by restricting access to the outside world. They are more of a means of ensuring that the benefits negotiated within the NAFTA region are, indeed, for that region.

There is some fear that NAFTA's implementation will prompt retaliation from non-member nations. This is certainly a worthwhile concern because the last thing the U.S. or the world needs is more protectionist trade barriers. Furthermore, the potential for such repercussions exists because, for example, Mexico's trade with the European Union has fallen close to 25% since NAFTA's enactment.[212] Perhaps Australian Ambassador Cook was correct when he proposed that in the near future the world might have three fairly divided centers: the Pacific Rim, the European Coalition and the North

---

[209] The White House, Office of the Press Secretary, Press Briefing by U.S. Trade Representative Ambassador Carla Hills, Aug. 12, 1992, at 5.

[210] Matt Moffett, U.S. Manufacturers Already are Adapting to Mexican Free Trade, Wall St. J., Oct. 29, 1992, at A1, A7.

[211] The White House, Office of the Press Secretary, Press Briefing by U.S. Trade Representative Ambassador Carla Hills, Aug. 12, 1992, at 6.

[212] The News Staff, NAFTA Cuts EU Trade, The News, Aug. 27, 1994, at 29.

American Free Trade Alliance.[213] While this is not an altogether desirable state of affairs, it is probably much more desirable than what we had a few years ago: a world abounding with nations divided by protectionist barriers. Hopefully, the GATT Uruguay Round will succeed in alleviating many potential trade tensions between these various economic centers. The current presence of such tensions still does not justify abandoning the rule of origin requirements, however, as they appear to be a necessary evil in the world's progression towards a harmonized global marketplace.

13. CONCLUSION

In conclusion, NAFTA presents foreign investors with a way of capitalizing upon future opportunities in Mexico and consequently competing better in the emerging brave new world order. Thanks to NAFTA, North Americans will get to enjoy more of what members of GATT's previous successful rounds sought: increased standards of living; virtually full employment; a large and steadily growing real income and effective demand; a full development and use of at least some of the world's resources; and an expanded production and exchange of goods.[214] Even foreign investors from non-NAFTA nations will have increased opportunities due to the liberalized foreign investment regulatory scheme which NAFTA prompted. Nevertheless, as this chapter asserts, succeeding in Mexico as a foreign investor is not as easy as it might seem at first glance. But there is a saying that few things that are worth having come easily. With the right legal consultants, success in Mexico may be both attainable and well worth seeking.

---

[213] Australian Ambassador Michael Cook, Speech to the University of Virginia School of Laws J.B. Moore Society of International Law (Oct. 6, 1992).

[214] Paul B. Stephan, III et al., International Business and Economics: Law and Policy - Statutory Supplement 52 (1993).

THE LIKELY IMPACT OF NAFTA ON INVESTMENT IN SELECTED GOODS AND SERVICES SECTORS IN MEXICO, CANADA, AND THE U.S.

by Dean C. Alexander[*]

1. INTRODUCTION

This article provides an overview of the probable impact of NAFTA on investment in particular goods and service sectors in Mexico, Canada, and the U.S. More specifically, the article outlines the findings of one of the leading studies to date on this subject. Initially, a review of the likely impact on specific goods will take place, including the: agricultural sector [alcoholic beverages, citrus products, cotton, cut flowers, dairy products, fish, grains/oilseeds, livestock/meat, other fruit (fresh/processed), peanuts, poultry, sugar, sugar containing products, and vegetables]; automotive products; bearings; ceramic floors/wall tiles; chemicals; computers/electronics; electricity transmission; energy; flat glass; household appliances; household glassware; industrial machinery; pharmaceuticals; primary petrochemicals; steel mill products; and textiles/apparel. Subsequently, a discussion of the perceived impact on specified service sectors will occur: banking, construction/engineering, insurance, tele-communications, transportation, petrochemicals, natural gas, related services.

[*] Director, The NAFTA Research Institute, Washington, D.C. Mr. Alexander would like to thank Daphne Taylor for her assistance in preparing the article.

148   *Dean C. Alexander*

2. GOODS

2.1 AGRICULTURAL SECTOR

(i) Alcoholic Beverages: NAFTA's reductions in barriers to investment are likely to encourage a modest expansion of U.S. investment as U.S. firms attempt to establish themselves in the Mexican industry. Short-term investment will likely focus on joint ventures regarding marketing and distribution. Long-term investment may expand to include production as well. Currently, however, there is little direct U.S. investment in the Mexican beer and wine industries with the exception of distilled spirits. The sale of imports in each country is done through agreements with domestic firms to promote and distribute within the importing country.[1]

(ii) Citrus Products: Investment in Mexico's citrus sector is expected to be modest at first and increase considerably in the long-term. U.S. investors, trying to provide year-round alternative juice sources at low prices, invest primarily in the processing plants for export since most groves are Mexican owned. Limits to such capital intensive investment may include infrastructure problems, particularly power shortages, and transportation availability.[2]

(iii) Cotton: NAFTA is unlikely to affect foreign investment in Mexico or the U.S. Water shortages, problems with environmental contamination from chemicals and greater profits from production and processing of food crops rather than cash crops, make further investment in Mexico unlikely.[3]

(iv) Cut Flowers: NAFTA is expected to have a minor, negative impact on investment in the cut flower industry except in the segment producing fresh cut roses. Investment there is expected to decline modestly in both the short- and long-term. No new investment will likely be undertaken until the information on import trends and the level of duty free imports from Colombia and Bolivia under ATPA becomes more clear following NAFTA's implementation. Most of the cut flower production is family owned, therefore no significant cross-border investment is expected. The majority of investment will come from Mexican

---

[1] Potential Impact on the U.S. Economy and Selected Industries of the North American Free-Trade Agreement, USITC Publication 2596, January 1993, at 31-2.
[2] *Id.* at 25-3.
[3] *Id.* at 37-2.

growers, in cooperation with their government, to develop the infrastructure to produce and market high quality flowers and roses in the U.S. market.[4]

(v) Dairy Products: NAFTA is expected to yield virtually no U.S. investment in Mexico's dairy sector in both the short- and long-term. Factors affecting the lack of investment include: the surplus U.S. production; Mexico's lack of climatic conditions similar to the U.S. for producing sufficient food supplies; the use of existing and new U.S. exports of feedgrains to feed not dairy herds but pork and poultry; the lack of infrastructure for handling and transporting milk and state-of-the-art techniques for manufacturing and distributing; and the fact that Mexicans traditionally do not consume large amounts of dairy products. Mexican domestic investment is also expected to be nil in the face of tough U.S. competition and surplus production.[5]

(vi) Fish: Currently there is little cross-border investment between the U.S. and Mexico. But, under NAFTA, a minor increase is expected in the short-term while modest growth is expected in the long-term. Specifically, most investment is expected to concentrate on the maquiladora processing plants which process shrimp for re-export to the U.S. because: U.S. distributors seek to take advantage of Mexico's low labor costs; and they have the quality control knowledge and other experience many Mexican firms lack. Some investment outside of the maquiladoras is likely in shrimp, mackerel and tuna, both unprocessed and canned, destined for export to the U.S.[6]

(vii) Grains/Oilseeds: Reduced Mexican tariffs are expected to yield considerable U.S. investment in grain and oilseed processing particularly grain elevators and facilities necessary for bulk transportation. Little investment is expected to go toward farming. Lack of investment in infrastructure will seriously limit Mexico's expanding volume of trade.[7]

(viii) Livestock/Meat: Most U.S. livestock imports already enter duty free, therefore little impact is expected on imports or investment because edible offals are low-value by-products of the livestock and meat sectors. U.S. exports of live swine and pork products likely will increase by 4 percent in the short- and 35-

---

[4] *Id.* at 30-2 to 30-3.
[5] *Id.* at 35-2 to 35-3.
[6] *Id.* at 29-2.
[7] *Id.* at 23-2 to 23-3.

40 percent in the long-term. However, it will lead to little new investment as existing facilities would be expanded to meet demand.[8]

(ix) Lumber/Wood Products: Currently little direct U.S. investment has been made in Mexico's timberland and primary production. This situation is unlikely to change under NAFTA. There has been, however, substantial U.S. investment in Mexico's remanufacturing industry with U.S. affiliates producing primarily for the U.S. market. NAFTA may lead to a minor amount of new investment here as firms begin to produce for the Mexican market, especially the building construction industry.[9]

(x) Other Fruit (Fresh/Processed): New U.S. investment in Mexican fruit production is likely to be limited as U.S. food brokers/shippers normally enter into an agreement with Mexican growers to purchase their production at a pre-arranged price in exchange for providing capital, technical assistance, machinery and other support services.[10]

(xi) Peanuts: No significant investment is expected in any of the three countries' peanut industries. Peanut production is capital intensive and would fail to benefit from Mexico's low labor costs. Also, large quantities of water are needed in peanut production. Meanwhile, in Mexico, there is tough competition from other higher value crops for water. In addition, peanuts do not fit well into multi-crop rotations due to their long maturity. NAFTA will have no effect on existing U.S. investment by peanut product producers in Canada.[11]

(xii) Poultry: U.S. investment is likely to increase in Mexico as restrictions on foreign ownership and repatriation of profits are liberalized. An industry restructuring is also likely to encourage smaller Mexican producers to seek foreign investment. Constraints to investment include: a general lack of familiarity in the Mexican market; the animal disease and plant inspection system situation; and uncertainty regarding Mexican import liberalization of feedgrains.[12]

---

[8]   *Id.* at 27-2.
[9]   *Id.* at 32-2.
[10] *Id.* at 26-2.
[11] *Id.* at 36-2.
[12] *Id.* at 28-2 to 28-3.

(xiii) Sugar: Although Mexico is currently a net sugar importer, the potential for expanded production exists through an expansion of sugarcane acreage, improvements in milling and refining efficiencies, and the introduction of new sugarcane varieties. Currently, no U.S. investment is pending despite active attempts by Mexico to seek such investment. Investment in Mexican sugar and corn wet milling to produce high fructose corn syrup (HFCS) will depend upon: Mexican domestic prices on sugar and sugar production costs; the support prices of corn; and the volume of duty free corn imports. The Mexican government's present policy of subsidizing sugar producers and consumers has meant profit margins too small for the newly privatized sugar processing operations to modernize and therefore has hurt production efficiency. Switching to HFCS in the Mexican soft drink industry may be the spur to increase investment in HFCS. However, HFCS must have a lower price than sugar for that to happen. Such investment is made even more unlikely due to the cost of transferring either corn or HFCS in the switch from sugar to HFCS.[13]

(xiv) Sugar Containing Products: Short-term U.S. investment in Mexican sugar containing products is likely to service the Mexican market as current distribution channels are inadequate for U.S. exports. Since sugar containing product industries are capital intensive, increases in Mexico's wholesale sugar prices to the U.S. level could minimize savings in labor costs and make investment less likely. A decrease in the wholesale price would favor investment but raise the profit sugar producers could make by selling in the U.S. market thereby increasing sugar costs to sugar containing product producers in Mexico.[14]

(xv) Vegetables: Currently there is little U.S. investment in Mexican land or equipment, only in the production of commodities not produced in the U.S. or those that can be shipped during periods of little domestic production. Resulting from NAFTA will be a shift to investment in joint production of vegetables for sale in the Mexican market. Investment in new vegetable freezing operations will be limited as multinational firms merely improve their existing Mexican facilities.[15]

---

[13]   *Id*. at 33-2 to 33-3.

[14]   *Id*. at 34-4 to 34-5.

[15]   *Id*. at 24-5 to 24-5.

2.2   AUTOMOTIVE PRODUCTS

NAFTA's short-term impact on Mexico's automobile and auto parts sector is expected to be both minor and positive. Long-term projections for Mexico include a considerable increase in investment accompanied by a restructuring of the industry. Long-term projections for the U.S. automotive industry show little significant investment. The impetus for the restructuring of Mexico's automotive and auto parts industries is the desire of U.S. automakers: to fully integrate their Mexican assembly plants into their North American production system; reduce the number of models produced; and produce those auto parts in Mexico which are more labor intensive and thereby greatly increase Mexican assembly plant output and efficiency. Mexico's value-added and trade-balancing requirements, untouched under NAFTA, will limit the extent of the restructing by U.S. automakers. The Mexican government currently regulates trade and foreign investment, limiting the extent of the integration between the Mexican, U.S. and Canadian auto industries.[16]

2.3   BEARINGS

Due to excess U.S. and Canadian production capacity, NAFTA is expected to yield little short-term change in U.S. or other investment in the bearing sector and only a modest long-term increase. The U.S. and Mexico are expected to be the primary beneficiaries of any increased investment with most of it going to the U.S. because of the capital intensive nature of the industry. Some U.S. manufacturers see the benefits split if labor intensive bearings and those for just-in-time delivery are produced in Mexico and the capital intensive types in the U.S.[17]

2.4   CERAMIC FLOORS/WALL TILES

No significant short- or long-term investment is expected due to sagging U.S. residential and commercial construction markets and an expansion in the U.S. production capacity. Some long-term investment in Mexico may result from joint ventures and increased foreign investment by Italy and Asia, attracted by

---

[16] *Id.* at 4-8 to 4-9.
[17] *Id.* at 7-3.

the lower costs of production and the proximity to the U.S. market. Such investment will likely center upon production of basic, lower cost (i.e., unglazed, non-mosaic) tiles as opposed to the more expensive tiles produced in Italy, Spain and Japan. Thus, there is expected to be little impact on North American trading patterns.[18]

2.5   CHEMICALS

NAFTA is expected to have a minor but positive effect on U.S. investment in Mexico in the short-term but more significant growth in the chemical industry in the long-term. In all three countries, a major share of new investment will be used to meet the requirements of environmental regulations.[19]

2.6   COMPUTERS/ELECTRONICS

NAFTA is expected to lead to a modest increase in U.S. investment in Mexico's electronics industry in the short-term and considerably in the long-term. This is in addition to the already increased U.S. investment following Mexico's 1990 liberalization of its investment and trade policies in the electronics sector. The increased long-term investment will, in part, result from NAFTA's investment chapter, the elimination of tariffs for goods produced in North America, and the rules of origin and drawback provisions designed to increase North American production. Rather than cause disinvestment in the U.S., NAFTA is expected to divert U.S. investment from other low-wage countries toward Mexico. Mexico also stands to benefit from its close proximity and lower transportation costs.[20]

2.7   ELECTRICITY TRANSMISSION

Both Canada and Mexico need substantial investments in electricity generating facilities to meet domestic demand. For Mexico, however, due to the inadequate

---

[18]   *Id.* at 13-2 to 13-3.

[19]   *Id.* at 14-2.

[20]   *Id.* at 5-3, 5-5.

infrastructure and the provisions of NAFTA, foreign investment is likely to be concentrated only in the construction of independent power projects and co-generation units in Mexico's industrial areas. Such investments would allow foreign operation and consumption of the electricity produced with any excess being sold to CFE.[21]

2.8   ENERGY

Chapter 11 of NAFTA assures national treatment and MFN status for U.S. investments in Mexico and Canada. NAFTA, which enables the generally unrestricted U.S. investment is, however, subject to several exceptions. For instance, Mexico and Canada can require government approval for takeovers of existing businesses above specified monetary thresholds and Mexico's right to reserve certain "strategic activities" and investment in these activities to the state.[22]

2.9   FLAT GLASS

NAFTA's long-term equalization of duty rates between the U.S. and Mexico is expected to yield only slight investment increases. The existence of excess capacity for production and Mexico's 1989 liberalization of foreign ownership restrictions for flat glass and glass fabrication facilities that allows 100 percent foreign ownership will fail to increase North American investments because of the access to Mexico's competitive advantages in raw materials, labor costs and fuel already held by foreign firms.[23]

2.10   HOUSEHOLD APPLIANCES

NAFTA's equal annual staging to eliminate tariffs on household appliances in the U.S. and Mexican markets as well as the rules of origin will likely encourage the production of specific parts in North American plants.

---

[21]   *Id*. at 20-2.
[22]   *Id*. at 17-2.
[23]   *Id*. at 11-2.

Furthermore, these factors should result in the use of these parts in the construction of such appliances and increase U.S. short-term investment in Mexico. Since Mexico liberalized its trade laws in the mid-1980s, U.S. investment has already increased in capital equipment for increased plant productivity and Mexican producers have acquired product technology and marketing expertise from their U.S. partners in the anticipation of NAFTA. Short-term investment in Mexico under NAFTA will be impeded by: high tariffs on U.S. exports in the early stages; the limited size of the Mexican market; low personal income levels; and a weak infrastructure that makes distribution difficult. Over the long-term with development of the infrastructure and higher income levels, U.S. investment should increase considerably. NAFTA's provisions for companies to operate wholly-owned subsidiaries will further increase U.S. investment and ownership. Non-NAFTA investment by Brazil, Japan and Korea is also expected to rise as Mexican demand and market size grows.[24]

2.11 HOUSEHOLD GLASSWARE

The staged elimination of duty rates, 15 years for the U.S. and 10 for Mexico, on household glass products under NAFTA is not expected to yield any impact on short- or long-term investment in the U.S. market. This prediction is based on: the high cost of building a greenfield plant; the intense competition in the market; and the relatively low growth expected in this mature market. Investment in the Mexican market is limited by Vitro's, a major Mexican producer, domination of 75 percent of the Mexican market. To date, the only U.S. investment in the Mexican market will come under a joint venture between Corning and Vitro.[25]

2.12 INDUSTRIAL MACHINERY

NAFTA's liberalization of Mexico's investment regulations and tariffs is expected to provide a minor boost in the short- and long-term to U.S. investments in industrial machinery production facilities in Mexico and the U.S. Low labor costs will not be sufficient to shift investment funds due to the state

---

[24] *Id*. at 16-2 to 16-3.
[25] *Id*. at 12-2.

of the Mexican economy and infrastructure. Emphasis is likely to be in servicing the Mexican economy by shipments from U.S. plants with excess production capacity and by increasing the distribution and warehousing facilities that provide spare parts in servicing existing equipment. NAFTA's opening of the government procurement market will yield more opportunity in oilfield machinery and refrigeration equipment.[26]

2.13 PHARMACEUTICALS

NAFTA is expected to yield modest investment in response to increased IPR protection created by the 1991 Mexican reforms. Disinvestment in the U.S. R&D is unlikely due to several factors. First, the U.S. is a world center of pharmaceutical R&D. Second, the U.S. has the largest market for pharmaceuticals in the world. Third, the U.S. has the necessary infrastructure and tough regulatory standards.[27]

2.14 PRIMARY PETROCHEMICALS

NAFTA includes provisions to end the 40 percent limitation on foreign investment in "secondary" petrochemicals and no limit on foreign investment in other petrochemical classifications. Under NAFTA, investment in primary petrochemicals will be limited as "basic" petrochemicals are reserved for the state. Moreover, the cost of establishing a petrochemical plant, its dependence upon PEMEX for the bulk of its feedstock, and uncertainties regarding the Mexican government and PEMEX policies make it unclear to what extent U.S. firms will take advantage of opportunities in "secondary" petrochemical industries.[28]

---

[26] *Id.* at 15-3.
[27] *Id.* at 9-3 to 9-4.
[28] *Id.* at 19-2.

2.15   STEEL MILL PRODUCTS

Only modest increases in investment by U.S. firms in warehousing and distribution and almost no new investment in the major steel making operations is expected. This prediction exists despite Mexico's 1989 revision of investment regulations to allow 100 percent participation by foreign interests in steel manufacturing. Capital restraints and the difficulty of getting approval for steel operations near some of the major cities also is hampering new investment. Investment in distribution and warehousing would expand under NAFTA's procurement rules as would servicing PEMEX oil fields with items needed for daily operations.[29]

2.16   TEXTILES/APPAREL

NAFTA is expected to yield only minor short- and long-term increases in investment in the Mexican textiles sector and a big increase in the Mexican apparel industry. Already investment in Mexico's textile, apparel and leather industries has reached nearly $100 million during 1989-91. Textile investment will be limited due to the size and efficiency of the U.S. textile industry as well as its capacity to meet any short-term increase in demand. The large capital investments required, Mexico's underdeveloped infrastructure, quotas and TPLs under NAFTA that will allow non-NAFTA producers to continue supplying to Mexican firms producing for the U.S. market, make significant investment in Mexican textiles unlikely. In contrast, the apparel industry is expecting increased U.S. investment by firms where labor costs are crucial and who expect increased Mexican demand for their goods. In addition, U.S. firms will shift from East Asia to Mexico where proximity allows for: monitoring of production and quality; development of quick response programs; and faster transportation that is free of duties and quotas. Yet, such investment by U.S. firms probably will be limited to only large companies with experience producing abroad.[30]

---

[29]   *Id.* at 10-3.
[30]   *Id.* at 8-3 to 8-4.

3. SERVICES

3.1 BANKING

NAFTA is likely to increase U.S. investment by a modest figure in the short-term as the agreement focuses primarily on direct foreign investment by U.S. and Canadian banks. Trade in banking services between Mexico and Canada is currently very limited and is likely to remain so despite NAFTA. NAFTA's attempt to spur U.S. and Canadian retail (small customer) banking operations in Mexico is established in Article 1403 which provides that foreign banks must establish themselves as separately capitalized subsidiaries. Yet, such a move will limit opportunities to extend lucrative capital loans in corporate banking -- which currently constitutes the majority of U.S. loans in Mexico. The long-term benefit to Mexico is expected to be modest, particularly as U.S. and Japanese banks are attracted to Mexico's universal banking system in which they can operate commercial banking, investment banking, insurance, leasing and factoring businesses simultaneously. Regulations in the U.S. and Japan currently separate commercial from investment banking. New investment by Mexican banks, long allowed to operate in the U.S., is not expected in the short- or long-term.[31]

3.2 CONSTRUCTION/ENGINEERING

Although NAFTA allows for wholly owned U.S. construction and engineering subsidiaries in Mexico, U.S. firms are expected to continue with their current joint venture agreements with Mexican firms. Short- and long-term investment is expected to be minor due to the ease of exporting relatively mobile, personnel-based construction and engineering services with the exception of heavy construction firms.[32]

---

[31] *Id*. at 42-3.
[32] *Id*. at 41-2.

3.3   INSURANCE

NAFTA's liberalized investment rules are expected to significantly increase investment by U.S. and Canadian insurers. Especially attractive to foreign investors is Mexico's commitment to permit foreign insurers actual control over their Mexican insurance investments. Furthermore, Mexico's largely underdeveloped insurance market has great potential for growth while the U.S. and Canadian markets are largely saturated.[33]

3.4   TELECOMMUNICATIONS SERVICES

No short-term impact is expected in telecommunications investment in Mexico due to the need for further modernization of the telecommunications infrastructure. Meanwhile, long-term investment will depend upon the pace of that modernization and the demand for information services that is expected to grow as business activity and the economy grow in Mexico. NAFTA allows U.S. service providers the option of offering services through direct foreign investment or from U.S. based facilities. It is foreseeable that U.S. firms will establish facilities in Mexico in order to take advantage of lower labor costs in areas such as data entry. Seeking to further the likelihood of U.S. investment are NAFTA provisions regarding intellectual property rights protection that are expected to reduce the risk of unauthorized use of copyrighted software.[34]

3.5   TRANSPORTATION

NAFTA is expected to yield modest short-term and considerable long-term investment by U.S. firms. The majority of long-term investment is expected to come from U.S. firms already in joint venture agreements who are seeking more active participation in the Mexican transportation market, particularly trucking. Such investment may, however, be limited due to the lack of equal investment opportunities as U.S. owned carriers in Mexico can only transport international freight. In contrast, Mexican owned U.S. carriers can both transport and distribute freight. Mexico's developing infrastructure will also limit investments by U.S. trucking and bus service firms. Mexican investment, expected to be

---

[33]   *Id.* at 43-2 to 43-3.
[34]   *Id.* at 39-2 to 39-3.

minor despite the 7-year head start under NAFTA for trucking and bus firms, will focus largely on small- to medium-size trucking and bus service firms in U.S. border states. No large-scale Mexican investment in railroads is expected as U.S. rail companies are already building customs and freight centers inside Mexico.[35]

3.6   PETROLEUM/NATURAL GAS/RELATED SERVICES

NAFTA is unlikely to have any significant impact on investment in the petroleum and natural gas industries, including oilfield services and pipelines, in the short- and long-term. Under NAFTA, no restrictions apply to foreign investment in these industries in the U.S. and Canada while Mexico's constitutional provision prohibiting foreign investment in these industries remains untouched.[36]

[35]   *Id.* at 40-4.
[36]   *Id.* at 18-3.

THE ROLE OF THE MULTILATERAL INVESTMENT GUARANTEE AGENCY (MIGA) IN ATTRACTING FOREIGN INVESTMENTS TO LATIN AMERICA

by Luis Dodero[*]

1. INTRODUCTION

There is little room for argument today against the fact that foreign investment constitutes an important vehicle for expanding the economies of developing countries. Although certain doubts are still promulgated, especially by defendants of obsolete concepts such as the Calvo Doctrine,[1] the trend is clearly in favor of opening borders to foreign investment as evidenced by the increased activity in Argentina, and the recent conclusion of the North American Free Trade Agreement (NAFTA) by the United States, Canada, and Mexico.

The debt crisis of the 1970s and 1980s certainly contributed to this new trend. During these two decades, international trade focused mainly on sales. Industrialized countries provided export incentives utilizing all types of instruments available for this purpose, such as subsidized financing and export credit insurance. Developing countries profited greatly from these facilities and borrowed vast amounts of money to pay for imported goods and services. In

---

[*] Vice President and General Counsel of the Multilateral Investment Guarantee Agency, the World Bank Group in Washington, D.C.
[1] A doctrine by Argentine jurist Carlos Calvo which declares that foreign investors shall be granted no fewer or greater rights or privileges than those available to nationals, and shall be treated as nationals in the State courts, which have exclusive jurisdiction. There are many ramifications of the doctrine. For example, alien investors may not seek international arbitration. In addition, they may not invoke diplomatic protection. Calvo Clauses have found their way into the foreign investment laws and Constitutions of a number of Latin American States.

many cases they were not needed, but the exporting companies managed to sell them utilizing marketing techniques that in some instances were, to say the least, rather unorthodox.

While import-export operations will continue to be the core of international trade, there is a clear trend towards the transformation of traditional export operations through certain new forms of investment, especially in the construction and industrial sectors.

Practically all Latin American countries have realized the importance of foreign investment. The debt crisis of the past decades certainly played a catalytic role in changing the negative perception, sometimes justified, that existed in many Latin American countries towards foreign investment. Perhaps the debt-to-equity swaps programs pioneered by Chile, Mexico, Brazil and other countries have contributed to this renewed awareness of the importance of foreign investment.[2]

The liberalization of the admission of foreign investment has been impressive, although it was unthinkable a few years ago. For the first time in their history many Latin American countries are concluding bilateral investment treaties, granting national and most favored treatment to foreign companies, and submitting disputes to international arbitration. New foreign investment laws have been and are being enacted. Also, the general attitude towards foreign companies is much more positive today than in the past.

The newly liberal approach and the dramatic improvement in most Latin American countries' foreign investment climate are commendable, though insufficient, elements to attract foreign investment. The wave of expropriations and nationalizations that took place in the region from the early 1900s through the 1980s, and the fragility and lack of stability of many of the democratic governments in the area remain in the mind of prospective investors. These factors gave rise to the awareness of the so-called political risks (expropriation, war and civil disturbance, currency inconvertibility, breach of contract, and denial of justice) over which the investor had no control. Yet, the investor still struggles with these perceptions. The likelihood of these risks materializing in the medium- or short-term simply cannot be calculated or estimated. This fact

---

[2]   "All countries implementing debt to equity conversion programs hope to achieve two objectives, regardless of the mechanics involved in particular cases. First, reduce external indebtedness to serviceable levels. Second, promote new foreign investment. It should be emphasized that promoting foreign investment is just as important to the health of debtor nations' economies as reducing external debt." (Fernao Carlos Botelho Bracherand Antonio Mendes, "Latin American Sovereign Debt Management", Inter-American Development Bank, 1990, pp. 173-174.)

constitutes a major deterrent to foreign companies investing in developing countries. As medium- and long-term investments are the types of transactions that contribute the most to the enhancement of the economies of recipient countries, it is important that countries desiring to attract foreign investment provide prospective investors with adequate instruments to minimize or eliminate the negative impact that political risks may have in the minds of those target investors.[3]

More importantly, not only are investors worried about political risks. Banks that finance investments in developing countries may be satisfied with the commercial feasibility studies made by the investors. But the uncertainties concerning the occurrence of political risks may jeopardize their participation in an investment project. The regulations of many central banks in industrialized countries mandate that commercial banks allocate a percentage of the amount of the financing to country risk. Sometimes the obligation to honor this provision makes financing too expensive. When that occurs the investor simply cannot go forward with the project.

Investors can diminish their political risks through insurance. However, very few private insurance companies in the world are willing to cover these risks. Coverage for more than three years is impossible to obtain from such sources. War risk is never covered and inconvertibility is accepted in these private markets only in exceptional circumstances. The reason for this situation is that actuarial calculations are simply not applicable to medium- and long-term coverage of political risks. Therefore, industrialized countries that want to motivate their national companies to invest abroad have created investment insurance schemes with Treasury backing that do provide medium- and long-term coverage against all types of political risks. With the exception of the Overseas Private Investment Corporation (OPIC) of the USA and TREUARBEIT in Germany, which only provide investment insurance, these schemes form part of national export credit insurance programs. Naturally the purpose of these official insurance institutions is to help and protect their nationals. However, they contribute indirectly to the developmental efforts of the host countries.

The initiative to create a multilateral scheme that could directly serve the developmental purposes of countries by providing insurance against non-

---

[3] "Perceptions of foreign investors about the non-commercial risks they are likely to face in developing countries have to be dramatically dissipated before substantial increases in the volume of foreign investment flowing to these countries can materialize." (Ibrahim F.I. Shihata, *MIGA and Foreign Investment*, M. Nijhoff Publishers, Dordrecht, the Netherlands, 1988, p. 7.)

commercial or political risks was a logical solution to some of the setbacks suffered by the private and official insurance institutions. Although the concept dates back to 1948, it did not materialize until April 1988, when the Convention Establishing the Multilateral Investment Guarantee Agency (the MIGA Convention) came into force. Earlier, in April 1974, a regional scheme, the Inter-Arab Investment Guarantee Corporation, was created. While its aim was the same as that of the Multilateral Investment Guarantee Agency (MIGA), it was limited to Arab countries.

This chapter describes MIGA's role in promoting foreign investment in developing countries. Also, it discusses the way in which the Latin American member countries may profit from the activities of the Agency.

2. COVERAGE OF POLITICAL RISKS THROUGH MIGA

2.1   MIGA As Insurer

MIGA is a member of the World Bank Group, which also comprises the International Bank for Reconstruction and Development (IBRD), the International Development Association (IDA), the International Finance Corporation (IFC), and the Centre for the Settlement of Investment Disputes (ICSID). As of March 15, 1994, MIGA has 119 member countries, of which 19 are industrialized or Category One countries and 100 are classified as developing or Category Two countries. An additional 27 developing countries are in the process of completing their membership requirements.

Membership in the Agency is open to all countries that are members of IBRD. Countries willing to become members of the Agency must sign and ratify the MIGA Convention. Also, such nations must subscribe and pay the number of shares allocated to them. The allocation takes into account the proportion of IBRD capital owned by each country.

In accordance with its Convention,[4] the aim of the Agency is to facilitate additional flows of investment into developing countries, ensuring that the investments contribute to the overall economic development of the recipient country. In order to comply with its mandate, MIGA carries out two distinct

---

[4]   Convention Establishing the Multilateral Investment Guarantee Agency (Convention) opened for signature by members of the World Bank and Switzerland on October 11, 1985 and entered into force on April 12, 1988.

programs. MIGA provides guarantees (or insurance)[5] against political risks to private investors. In addition, the institution offers advice to developing member countries on how to enhance their foreign investment climate.

2.2   GUARANTEE PROGRAM

MIGA offers long-term political risk insurance to eligible investors for qualified investments in developing member countries. Beyond insurance protection, MIGA's participation in a project enhances confidence that the investor's rights will be respected due to the voluntary association of developing and developed countries in the Agency. Since commencing operations in late 1989 through December 1993 MIGA has issued approximately US$978.8 million in guarantees of direct investments into developing member countries.

2.3   TYPES OF POLITICAL RISKS COVERED BY MIGA

MIGA covers four types of non-commercial or political risks. The institution issues guarantees or insures against the risks of direct or indirect expropriation, currency inconvertibility and transfer restriction, war and civil disturbance, and breach of contract. The investor has the choice of acquiring cover against one or any combination of these risks by paying a premium for each of the risks covered.

Expropriation. The guarantee against indirect or direct expropriation covers any expropriatory action attributable to the host government, including, *inter alia*: actions (or omissions) that deprive the guarantee holder of its title, rights or tangible assets; or prevent the guarantee holder from carrying out the investment project, as a consequence of which the guaranteed investor suffers a loss.

---

[5]   The Committee that prepared the draft of MIGA's Convention decided to use the term guarantee instead of insurance. There is no doubt that the Committee followed the advice of Mr. Ibrahim F.I. Shihata, Vice-President and General Counsel of the World Bank and the main architect of MIGA. In his book in Arabic, *The International Guarantee on Foreign Investments* (1971; Eng. Trans. from Arabic, ch. 2), Mr. Shihata advocates the use of the term "guarantee" since the coverage of investments against political risks cannot be provided by applying the technical principles of insurance.

Transfer restrictions and inconvertibility. This coverage protects the investor from losses attributable to actions or omissions of the host government that prevent the guarantee holder from converting and/or transferring the profits from an investment or proceeds from its liquidation outside the host country.

War and Civil Disturbance. This guarantee protects the investor against losses resulting from any military action or civil disturbance that partially or totally destroys or damages tangible assets of the project enterprise or interferes with its operations so that the investor is unable to carry out its operations in the investment project. The definition of civil disturbance extends to losses sustained through events such as international war, revolution, insurrection, *coup d'état*, sabotage, and, in certain cases, terrorism. These events must be politically motivated, (i.e., with the primary intent of achieving a political objective). Therefore, losses due to labor strikes or non-political violence are not included in this coverage.

Breach of Contract/Denial of Justice. This coverage protects a guarantee holder from any loss that is suffered due to a government's unilateral breach of an undertaking and a subsequent denial of justice. In order to obtain compensation from MIGA, the guarantee holder must prove its inability, due to acts imputable to the host government, to: (i) have recourse to a judicial or arbitral forum to determine the claim of repudiation or breach; (ii) obtain a decision from a competent court or arbitration tribunal due to interference by the host government for the period set forth in the contract of guarantee; or (iii) enforce a court decision or arbitration award recognizing the right of the investor to be compensated due to the breach of obligations by the host government.

2.4   TYPES OF INVESTMENT AND CRITERIA FOR ELIGIBILITY

Types of Investment. The Convention defines investment broadly in order to allow MIGA optimum flexibility to issue guarantees for the ever varying types of investments that may require coverage. The definition of investment is a substantial issue for MIGA since it is prevented from guaranteeing other types of transactions, for instance, export sales. The approach adopted by the Agency's Operational Regulations is to identify who bears the commercial risk: if it is born by the guarantee holder (i.e., its remuneration depends on the performance or revenues of the project), it is an investment; if it is borne by the enterprise in the host country (i.e., the remuneration consists of a fixed price that is payable irrespective of the performance of the project), it is an export transaction.

Forms of investment that can be covered may include equity, medium- and long-term shareholder loans, and loan guaranties issued by equity holders. Loans to unrelated borrowers can be guaranteed provided that other investment in the project is being insured concurrently. MIGA may also extend its guarantee program by covering non-equity forms of direct investment such as production sharing, profit sharing, management, turnkey contracts, and build, operate and transfer (BOT) projects, franchising, licensing, and operating/leasing agreements provided that the remuneration of the investor substantially depends on the production, revenues or profits of the investment project. Non-direct investments such as portfolio investments may also be covered by the Agency.

Criteria for Eligibility. An essential criterion for eligibility for coverage is that investments must be new ones. This requirement meets the Agency's goal of promoting additional flows of capital into developing countries. Reinvested earnings from already existing investments also qualify for guarantee if such earnings may otherwise be transferred outside the host country. There is no limit on the minimum amount of guarantee that may be purchased but there is a maximum limit--currently set at US$50 million per project.

Meeting Developmental Objectives. One very important aspect associated with MIGA's guarantee program is the necessity for investment projects to conform with the developmental needs of the host country. MIGA is obligated under its Convention and Operational Regulations to undertake a fairly detailed appraisal of the development merits of a project: its economic viability, contribution to the host country's development, consistency with the host government's declared development objectives and priorities, and compliance with the host country's laws and regulations.

In addition, MIGA reviews a project to determine whether it: (i) is financially, economically and environmentally sound; and (ii) will generate employment, technology transfer, foreign exchange, and exports. MIGA also assesses whether the particular investment would be likely to receive fair and equitable treatment and legal protection from the host country. In this exercise, MIGA relies to a great extent on the information resources and experience of its sister organizations in the World Bank Group.

2.5 ELIGIBLE INVESTORS

In order to be eligible to obtain guarantees from MIGA, a prospective investor must generally be a national of a member country other than the member country into which the investment is to be made. A company will qualify for coverage if it is incorporated and has its principal place of business in a member country, or if it is majority-owned by nationals of member countries. In the latter case, the company could be incorporated in a non-member country. State-owned corporations of member countries are also eligible for guarantees if they are constituted to operate on a commercial basis. An investor who is a national of a developing (Category Two) member country can invest in that country and obtain cover from MIGA if the investment funds in a freely usable currency are brought in from outside of the host country, as a way to attract flight capital. And, of course, an investor from a Category Two member country can also invest in another Category Two member country. In summary, only investments made in a Category Two member country can be guaranteed by the Agency; however, the investor may be a national of either a Category One or a Category Two member.

2.6 DURATION OF GUARANTEE

MIGA's standard term of coverage is 15 years, however, this may be increased to 20 years if MIGA finds that the extended term is justified by the nature of the project. Perhaps one of the most important features of MIGA's contract is that during the coverage period the guarantee holder may cancel the contract at any time after the first three years of its entry into force, but MIGA may not. This is precisely what the investor requires to overcome its fears about political risks: a long-term, non-cancelable guarantee. This can only be obtained from MIGA or a national investment insurance institution. As mentioned before, the private insurance market does not provide this type of cover.

2.7 APPLICATION FOR GUARANTEE

An investor seeking coverage from MIGA should submit a Preliminary Application for Guarantee before the investment is made or irrevocably committed, thereby ensuring that the investment qualifies as a new one. Currently, there is no fee for the submission of the Preliminary Application, and it does not commit the investor to purchase a guarantee. Once MIGA determines that the investment appears to qualify for a guarantee and the investor decides to buy the coverage, then the investor files a Definitive Application and the underwriting process begins.

2.8   UNDERWRITING

In consideration for issuing cover, MIGA charges appropriate premiums. Premiums have a direct correlation to the perceived risk and depend basically on the risk profile of the type of operation to be guaranteed more than on the host country (for instance, a mining project is more likely to be expropriated than other types of business). Annual premiums for each coverage generally fall in the range of 0.50-1.25 percent of the amount insured. It must be noted that MIGA, as is characteristic with many national insurance schemes, normally insures up to 90 percent of the investment contributions, plus up to 300 percent of the initial amount of guarantee to cover retained earnings attributable to the investment (in exceptional circumstances, these figures may range up to 95 percent and 500 percent, respectively). For loans and loan guarantees, MIGA normally insures 90 percent of the principal and the amount of interest that will accrue over the term of the loan. For technical assistance contracts and similar agreements, MIGA insures up to 90 percent of the total value of payments due under the agreement.

2.9   CLAIMS AND SUBROGATION

Claims Management. It is perhaps an encouraging sign that MIGA has not experienced a claim to date, but it is impossible to predict the number of claims that may be filed in the future. Given the fact that MIGA most frequently covers an investment for a period of 15 years, it is highly unlikely that the Agency will continue operations without facing a claim at some point in time. If, however, a claim is filed, MIGA's contract of guarantee facilitates payment within as reasonable a time as possible. If the guarantee holder is not satisfied with a decision by MIGA on a claim, there can be recourse to *ad hoc* arbitration either in accordance with MIGA's arbitration rules or, if preferred, by incorporating into the contract of guarantee a mutually acceptable form of *ad hoc* arbitration.

Subrogation. Once a claim is filed with MIGA by the guarantee holder and the claim has been established to the satisfaction of the Agency, it will compensate the guarantee holder when the period set forth in the contract of guarantee has elapsed, and succeed to the latter's rights inherent in any claim against the host country. The MIGA Board of Directors is responsible for all policy-making decisions that affect the Agency. If, in fact, the Agency incurs a loss due to the host country's non-compliance with the Agency's subrogation rights when such rights are asserted, the loss will be borne by the shareholders of the Agency. This will inevitably include the host country which has caused the loss in the first place. While pressures can be brought upon a host country to avoid causing a loss, if non-compliance continues, the Convention provides for negotiation, conciliation, and finally binding *ad hoc* international arbitration between the Agency and the concerned host country to resolve the dispute.

2.10 MIGA AND NATIONAL INSURANCE AGENCIES

A question that is often raised with reference to MIGA's guarantee program is how it is viewed in relation to national investment insurance schemes. Many developed countries, and even some developing countries, have their own schemes under which their national investors may obtain political risk coverage similar to the program offered by MIGA. MIGA is directed under its Convention to supplement and complement these national programs through coinsurance and reinsurance arrangements. These collaborative efforts often provide for increased guarantee capacity for projects with large capital and asset bases. MIGA has already executed these types of arrangements with OPIC, the Export Development Council (EDC) of Canada and the Ministry of International Trade and Industry (MITI) of Japan. Presently, MIGA is negotiating similar agreements with many other national schemes.

However, national programs have a number of inherent limitations. First, these programs can cover only investments by their own nationals. Second, these programs need to spread their risks by fixing exposure limits by countries and for this purpose the insurers have to take into account the claims paid as a consequence of their export credit insurance program, these claims being very numerous. Third, national programs may decline to cover or limit cover in particular countries due to political rather than technical considerations.

The limitations which are characteristic of national programs may not be relevant to MIGA's program. In this sense, the Agency fills a vital and important gap in political risk management. For example, MIGA can cover the assets of a joint venture investment made by investors of various nationalities. However, if joint coverage is requested, all investors must be nationals of MIGA member countries. Noteworthy, too, MIGA is least constrained by political considerations in its guarantee program since it assesses prospective projects on a purely technical basis. Yet, MIGA is always taking into account the developmental impact of the guaranteed project.

2.11 SPONSORSHIP TRUST FUND FACILITY

A supplemental mechanism for facilitating foreign investment flows is the establishment of a Sponsorship Trust Fund (the Fund). Through the Fund an investment may be sponsored for guarantee by any member or a group of members. The Fund would be administered by MIGA in accordance with the operational principles and policies that apply to its guarantee business, with some exceptions regarding risk as may be pertinent to the sponsored investments. The sponsors would contribute to the Fund either with money or guarantees and its assets would increase in value with premium income received on account of guarantees issued and interest accrued. Any losses would be paid out of Fund assets, without recourse to MIGA's capital and reserves. Appropriate administrative fees and costs incurred by MIGA would be charged to the Fund. MIGA would review and settle any claims of loss. Upon liquidation of the Fund, the balance remaining would be distributed pro rata to participants.

The Fund can be established by members that do not have a national insurance scheme, or it may be used as a risk diversification device for members that do have their own insurance scheme. The Fund could also be employed to greatly increase MIGA's guarantee capacity in those countries in which the Agency has reached its limit or in order to reserve its guarantee capacity for certain types of investments.

3. ADVISORY SERVICES

MIGA is also mandated under the Convention to advise host countries on ways to enhance their investment environments. While neither insulating investments against political risks nor the investment environment from political erosion, such advice tends, in at least the short run, to improve the investment climate and reduce inherent political risks. Once a country has taken steps to improve

its foreign investment climate, it must do its marketing among prospective
investors.

3.1   Policy and Advisory Services (PAS)

PAS has developed a number of programs, the most important of which is the
convening of conferences where potential investors interested in investing in a
given host country are brought together and informed of the investment
opportunities in that country. PAS conducts various activities, including:
executive development programs; foreign direct investment (FDI) policy
roundtables and workshops; and assists developing member countries in
preparing policies and institutions for investment promotion and strengthening
investor services; and image-building and investment generation activities. PAS
is in the process of establishing a new electronic network to exchange
information and experiences among the investment promotion agencies (IPAs)
of its member countries.

3.2   Other Advisory Services

Either directly, or in cooperation with the World Bank Group, MIGA provides
advice to developing member countries on how to enhance their foreign
investment infrastructure by, for example: assisting them in surveying their
investment environment in general; drafting foreign investment laws; preparing
regional investment codes; increasing bilateral investment treaty negotiating
skills; and pre-mediating investment disputes.

4. MIGA AND LATIN AMERICA

When MIGA's Convention came into force in April 1988, there was little hope
that the initiative would trigger enthusiasm among Latin American countries.
For the first several years, Ecuador and Chile, both of which joined the Agency
immediately, were the only countries in the region that decided to become
members of MIGA. Few other Latin American countries showed any interest
in joining. However, with the relaxation of the Calvo Doctrine, Argentina,
Bolivia, Brazil, Costa Rica, El Salvador, Guyana, Honduras, Nicaragua,
Paraguay, Peru, and Uruguay gradually joined the Agency. In addition, as of

March 15, 1994, Colombia and Guatemala have signed and are in the process of ratifying the Convention. Venezuela has signed and ratified the Convention. It is in the process of paying its capital subscription and is expected to become a full member before the end of March 1994. Only Mexico, Panama, and the Dominican Republic have not yet signed the Convention.

As of January 31, 1993, nearly 30 percent of the investments guaranteed by MIGA were in Latin America, and the number of applications received for investments in the Latin American region constitute 32 percent of all applications. The types of projects guaranteed in the area vary, from mining and manufacturing to financial services, investments guaranteed to nearly US$300 million and an additional US$200 million is in the pipeline. After only five years of operations and considering that many Latin American countries joined very recently, these figures are remarkable and demonstrate the interest that investors have in the region. Annex 1 lists the contracts of guarantee issued by MIGA for projects in Latin American countries. Annex 2 depicts the number of applications for guarantee received for projects in Latin America.

While it is true that a majority of investments in the region have been made without MIGA's guarantees, many of the investors have obtained insurance from their national insurers. The possibility of political risks materializing is still fresh in the minds of investors.

4.1   CASE OF MEXICO

Despite its record of nationalization of foreign investments, Mexico has recently managed to attract significant foreign investment, making it the exception to the general trend. Mexico has progressed from one of the most protected economies in the world to one of the most open. Mexico acceded to GATT in 1986, and recently signed free trade agreements with Chile and created NAFTA.

In addition, the admission of foreign investment has been highly regulated and restricted in a great many sectors. For example, foreign companies may not own the majority of the stock of a Mexican company in a number of sectors. Ownership of land by non-Mexicans was not allowed within certain restricted areas (a 100 kilometer strip along the Mexican border and a 50 kilometer strip along the Mexican coastline). Even the new Foreign Investment Law enacted on December 27, 1993, is quite restrictive. Mexico has yet to rescind its restrictive monetary policy. This policy is expected to aid in the attraction and retention of foreign capital.

Although Mexico is a member of the International Bank for Reconstruction and Development and the International Finance Corporation, it is neither a member of MIGA nor of the International Centre for Settlement of Investment Disputes. Also, Mexico has not signed an investment agreement with the U.S. Overseas Private Investment Corporation. While Mexico's new Foreign Investment Law has made many improvements in foreign investment regulations, it still falls short of being as liberal as the new laws on foreign investment of neighboring countries.

Albeit, Mexico's economy presents a more positive picture than a negative one. After six years of restructuring and stabilization, Mexico seems to be achieving political and economic viability. The nation has important resources and a mixed labor force of highly skilled workers and low-cost, unskilled trainable workers. In addition, Mexico's infrastructure is relatively developed. Yet, Mexico's highways and railroads need significant improvement. Despite this fact, its geographic situation is extraordinarily attractive.

However, with the recent assassination of favored presidential candidate Luis Donaldo Colosio, some investors may proceed with greater caution than before. Furthermore, while NAFTA provides investors with a more attractive climate for Mexican projects, the process is still very new and slow. In any case, although the assassination should not affect the security of foreign investors, nor even increase the risk, there may be a perception among some investors that it would be better to put their projects on hold for a period of time.

NAFTA, which entered into force in January 1994, will give rise to a dramatic increase in the flow of investment to Mexico from the other two parties to the treaty, at least as long as the labor costs remain lower in Mexico than they are in the United States or Canada. But NAFTA may trigger, among others, two significant adverse effects:

(i)   It may act, up to a point, as a deterrent to prospective investors from other countries, especially from Europe, that may feel discriminated against since Mexico has not concluded bilateral investment treaties with them. Thus, they cannot benefit from the most favored treatment granted by Mexico to the NAFTA signatories.

(ii)   It may increase the flow of investment from companies established in Mexico to third countries, especially to those in Central America where wages are lower still than in Mexico or the other adherents to NAFTA.

Both NAFTA and the new Foreign Investment Law are important elements in attracting new foreign investment to Mexico. Such funds should help to increase Mexico's level of international competitiveness. Nonetheless, Mexico's investment environment would be greatly enhanced if it were to join MIGA, especially if it wants to attract investments from non-NAFTA countries, or to protect foreign investors established in Mexico when investing abroad. Mexico's admission to MIGA would be particularly important to Mexican companies wanting to pursue new foreign markets for investment opportunities. As Mexico's economy continues to strengthen, its domestic enterprises grow and its investor base widens, the capacity for Mexican firms to have their investments secured through MIGA will grow in importance.

ANNEX 1

MIGA Contracts of Guarantee
Outstanding for Projects in Latin American Countries
As of January 31, 1994

Host Country	Date of MIGA Membership	Investor Country	Investor Name	Type of Project
Argentina	2/11/92	United States	Bank of Boston	Banking Services
		Spain	Banesto Banking Corp.	Banking Services
		Belgium	Generale Bank S.A.	Telecommunications
		Netherlands	Intl. Nederlanden Bank	Banking Services
		United States	Citibank N.A.	Banking Services
Brazil	1/07/93	Netherlands Antilles	Middenbank Curaçao N.V.	Local Financial Services
		United States (2 contracts)	F.N. Bank of Boston & Bank of Boston	Banking Services
Chile	4/12/88	United States	Mariculture	Agriculture
		Luxembourg	Millicom	Cellular Telephones
		United States	Motorola	Cellular Telephones
		United States	McDonald's	Restaurant Chain
		Canada	Rio Algom	Copper Mining
		Japan	Sumitomo Corporation	Copper Mining
		Switzerland	Credit Suisse	Copper Mining
El Salvador	12/20/91	Singapore	AVX	Manufacturing
		United States	AVX	Manufacturing

Peru	12/02/91	United States	Newmont Mining Corp.(2 contracts)	Gold Mining
		France (2 contracts)	Compagnie Miniere Intl. (2 contracts)	Gold Mining
		United States	Citibank N.A.	Pension Fund
		United States	Citibank Overseas Invest.	Pension Fund
		United States	Union Bank of Switzerland	Gold Mining

ANNEX 2

Applications for MIGA Guarantees
for Projects in Latin American Countries
As of February 28, 1994

Host Country	Date of MIGA Membership	Applications
Argentina	2/11/92	76
Belize	6/29/92	0
Brazil	1/07/92	41
Bolivia	10/03/91	7
Chile	4/12/88	56
Costa Rica	2/08/94	10
Ecuador	4/12/88	8
El Salvador	12/20/91	8
Guyana	1/18/89	14
Honduras	6/30/92	13
Nicaragua	6/12/92	7
Paraguay	6/30/92	3
Peru	12/02/91	49
Uruguay	3/01/93	5

THE INSTITUTIONAL BASES OF THE ECONOMIC MODEL AND THE TREATMENT OF FOREIGN INVESTMENT IN CHILE

by Roberto L. Mayorga[*]

1. INTRODUCTION

The legal treatment of foreign investment has its basis in the Chilean Constitution. The Constitution embodies the basic elements that shape our economy.

The importance of this, as you may know, is the great stability the norms have achieved. That stability is fostered by the fact that any change to the Constitution is subject to strict parliamentary procedures in both chambers of Congress and, in certain cases, to ratification by a plebiscite.

I will now explain, in more detail, these basic norms known as Public Economic Order. Basically, they include (i) the property regime, (ii) the enterprise regime, (iii) the state regime, (iv) the social market economy and (v) the constitutional entities.

2. THE PROPERTY REGIME

The right to property in Chile maintains one of the highest levels of protection which can be found in international comparative law. In effect, the Constitution

---

[*] Foreign legal consultant at the law firm Andrews & Kurth in Washington, D.C. and a partner at the Santiago, Chile law firm Urrutia & Co. Formerly, he served as Executive Vice President and General Counsel at the Foreign Investment Committee of Chile. He and Luis Montt co-authored the book *Foreign Investment in Chile* (1995, Martinus Nijhoff Publishers).

not only guarantees the ownership over all classes of corporeal and incorporeal property, but also over intellectual and industrial property. Recently, protection of industrial property has been strengthened: pharmaceutical products may now be patented. Furthermore, decisions by the Industrial Property Department, which deals with the granting of patents, can be appealed to the newly created Industrial Property Arbitration Tribunal with further review by the Supreme Court.

Perhaps the most outstanding feature of this legislation is that a person cannot be deprived of his or her property or any of the essential privileges of ownership, except by virtue of a law which authorizes expropriation and is duly qualified by the legislature. The expropriated party has the right to a legal review of the expropriation before the ordinary courts of justice, and always has the right to indemnification for the harm caused by the expropriation. The indemnification is established by mutual agreement or by a verdict of the courts, and is paid in cash. Material possession of the expropriated property will take place following total payment of the indemnification. In case of disagreement, the judge may suspend possession of the expropriated property.

As previously mentioned, the guarantee of ownership also includes incorporeal property rights. Consequently, both doctrine and jurisprudence developed the idea that the parties to a contract are owners of the rights established in that contract. As the next speaker will explain in more detail, the foreign investor enters into a contract with the state of Chile, known as contract law, and thereby becomes the owner of the rights conferred in that contract. Under the guarantees accorded by the Constitution, the contract cannot be modified unilaterally, even by a posterior law.

3. ENTERPRISE REGIME

In Chile, private enterprise is firmly established both with respect to the constitutional provisions guaranteeing it and in practice. The latter is demonstrated by the fact that 70% of the GDP is generated by the private sector.

The following principles outline the constitutional basis of private enterprise:

The right to free association, with equal treatment accorded to local and foreign investors in economic matters. This right permits the establishment of different kinds of companies. The established company would be known in our legal system as the "receiving company" of the foreign investment. The importance of this will be explained later in the seminar.

It is evident that private enterprise is also founded on the principles of private property protection, which were elaborated earlier. Essentially, one has the freedom to acquire all types of property, including productive entities. Furthermore, the Chilean legal system allows 100% foreign ownership.

It is also important to highlight the constitutional norm that promotes private initiative and economic freedom, acknowledging the right to develop any economic activities which are not contrary to public or moral order, national security, or the law. In Chile, no economic sectors are excluded from private enterprise, and the same treatment is accorded to local and foreign investors. It is relevant to mention the exception in the fishing sector, in which the principle of international reciprocity exists. In other words, the foreign investor has the same rights the Chilean investor would have in the foreign investor's country.

This economic freedom also extends to labor relations. This is established in the Constitution by the right to free employment and free selection of work. The rights of the labor force are codified in several statutes, intended to maintain a balance between labor's interests and the interests of the private enterprise. Some of the new features of this legislation include: the possibility to negotiate collectively through a union, provided the employer consents to it; the right to continue a strike indefinitely, with the provision that during the strike the employer cannot hire substitute workers, unless his last offer included full acceptance of the terms of the existing collective contract, as well as 100% inflation adjustment; and the power to terminate a labor contract due to the economic situation of the employer, or as a result of improper conduct of the employee. If, however, the worker contests his dismissal and the court finds in his favor, he will be entitled to compensation. Another new feature is the possibility to create a labor union federation without obtaining prior authorization. Finally, the law now regulates the system of social security, which was for some years basically private.

4. STATE REGIME

The State is at the service of the individual, and its goal is to promote the common welfare. To this end, it should contribute to the creation of the social conditions which will permit each and every member of the community to achieve the greatest possible spiritual and material fulfillment.

At the entrepreneurial level, the Constitution foresees private individuals as the main actors. It reserves a subsidiary role for the State, participating only in those entities for which there is not enough private interest.

The Constitution is not enthusiastic about state participation in enterprises, requiring authorization of such activities by law passed by a qualified quorum. Such activities are subject to the common legislation applicable to private individuals.

In Chile, the faculties of the State adhere to the principle of legality. Therefore, public institutions can act only by specific mandate laid down by the Constitution and the law, thereby preventing capricious or arbitrary actions.

The obligation of the State to provide an environment free from contamination should also be considered within the concept of promoting common welfare. Economic activities should be compatible with the preservation of nature, a topic which will be explained in detail later in the conference.

The Constitution also explicitly protects private enterprise from all arbitrary economic discrimination with respect to the State or its institutions. This protection is also expressed specifically in the foreign investment legislation, where it establishes equality between local and foreign entrepreneurs. The legislation also foresees independent judicial procedure for resolving any disagreement on this matter. This very important principle of non-discrimination is found in various parts of the Constitution, such as the provisions regarding taxation. In this area, the law assures equal levy proportional to income or in progression as the law may establish. It also prohibits all special duties that may be imposed disproportionately or unjustly.

Among the State's activities with regard to foreign investment, I would especially like to mention the great importance the State has shown by not only promoting and regulating, but also by creating a high level autonomous body: the Foreign Investment Committee. This committee consists of five Ministers and is responsible directly to the President.

5. SOCIAL MARKET ECONOMY

The legal regimes mentioned above set up the framework which enabled Chile to develop a social market economy.

Although the Constitution is formulated in a classic and not economic manner, and in fact does not refer to the economic market in any of its articles, the basis for a free market economy is firmly established. One finds the building blocks in the rules regarding freedom of individual initiative, and in those securing private property, economic freedom, and the subsidiary role played by the State in these matters.

In practice, the economic development of recent years has shown more than convincingly that a market economy is functioning in Chile. In effect, the traditional three economic questions: what to produce, how to produce it, and for whom (the allocation and reallocation of resources) are decided entirely by the market. Therefore, the authorities have shown much care in applying a strict and stable monetary policy in order to make price a real indicator in the market.

The free economic market is assisted, of course, by economic planning. This planning respects the independence of the private sector, acting toward it as incentive or disincentive for possible options or decisions. The authority in charge of these matters is the Ministry of Planification. The decisions taken by this Ministry are complied with by other authorities, but act in a subsidiary way with regard to the private sector.

It is important to emphasize that a free market economy coexists in Chile with political democracy. This political democracy has its foundation in those norms of the Constitution which relate to the structure and application of power, as well as the traditional guarantees of the individual, known as fundamental human rights. It is possible to ascertain that Chile is a country in which a free market economy and democracy are not empty provisions in a Constitution, but are actually part of the daily life of its inhabitants.

6. CONSTITUTIONAL ENTITIES

I would like to point out two entities which have economic attributes and constitutional significance: the Central Bank and the Office of the Comptroller General of the Republic (hereafter the Comptroller).

The Constitution grants autonomous status to the Central Bank. Because the Central Bank is not dependant on the government in office, and its directors are independent, decisions are made on a technical basis. The Constitution also explicitly prohibits the Central Bank from issuing new money or lending directly or indirectly to finance public spending.

The Central Bank is of utmost importance to the subject of this seminar because it is the institution which regulates all foreign exchange transactions. Moreover, it handles the Chilean foreign debt. For this reason, the Bank has been involved in the so-called debt equity swap program which, until last year, played a major role in reducing our foreign debt. This program has lost importance, as the Chilean debt at present is traded at 90 to 91% of face value. This is an outstanding, independent sign of the strength of the Chilean economy.

The Office of the Comptroller General of the Republic is another very important autonomous body. This office monitors the legality of acts of the Administration and controls revenues and investment of the funds of the National Treasury, the Municipalities, and other official bodies and services, as determined by law. It also handles the general accounting of the nation, and examines and controls the accounts of persons entrusted with assets of the public bodies enumerated above.

These entities, together with the ordinary courts of justice, guarantee the respect of the rights of private individuals, who have the faculty to appeal to them in case of contraventions.

Finally, I would like to comment that, apart from the aforementioned guarantees and rights, the Chilean Government has signed bilateral investment treaties with several countries. Essentially, these agreements have lifted the national investment legislation to an international level, and in this way contributed to the positive image which Chile has earned as a country where the foreign investor can feel confident.

SELECTED UNITED STATES-MEXICO-CANADA CROSS-BORDER INVESTMENT AND TRADE DEALS: 1992-1993

by Kent S. Foster* & Dean C. Alexander**

1. 1992 TRANSACTIONS[1]

* *Hitachi Home Electronics America*, a unit of *Hitachi Ltd.*, the large Japanese electronics concern, plans to close its Anaheim, California plant and shift some of its operations to Mexico and Malaysia.

* *Metalclad Corp.* reached an agreement with several Mexican business executives on a joint venture dubbed *Eco Administracion S.A. de C.V.* This venture plans to build a $25 million hazardous waste treatment plant in San Luis Potosi, Mexico.

* *Quebecor Printing Incorporated*, a unit of Montreal-based *Quebecor Incorporated*, acquired *Graficas Monte Alban SA* of Queretaro, Mexico from the French publishing and broadcasting firm *Hachette SA*.

* *Corning Incorporated* of Corning, New York and *Vitro SA* of Monterrey, Mexico completed their previously announced joint venture agreement which

* Of Counsel, Sharretts Blauvelt & Paley Carter and President of Global Communications Systems, Inc. in Washington, D.C.
** Director, The NAFTA Research Institute, Washington, D.C. The authors would like to thank Donna Eberly and Alexis Belladonna for their assistance in preparing this article.
[1] Preparation of this article was done through the use of various media and resource/research materials. The transactions have not been independently verified.

combined their consumer housewares businesses. The new Corning-Vitro company is known as *Corning Vitro Corporation* in the U.S. and as *Vitro Corning SA de CV* in Mexico.

* *Aetna International, Inc.*, a unit of the *Aetna Life and Casualty Co.*, formed a joint venture with *Valores de Monterrey*, a Mexican insurance company. Under this arrangement, Aetna paid $33 million for 10% interests in *Seguros Monterrey*, a Mexican multi-line insurer and *Fianzas Monterrey*, a Mexican bonding company. Both firms are subsidiaries of Valores de Monterrey.

* *Tyson Foods, Inc.* of Springdale, Arkansas, a poultry and food products concern, is entering into a joint venture with *Trasgo S.A. de C.V.* of Gomez Placio, Mexico, a Mexican poultry firm in an attempt to expand its operations.

* *The Fleming Companies* of Oklahoma City, Oklahoma, the largest distributor of wholesale foods in the U.S., entered into a joint venture in Mexico with Mexico City-based *Grupo Gigante S.A.* to develop retail stores stocked with groceries and consumer goods. Under this arrangement at least four stores, which will carry from 10,000 to 14,000 items, are expected to open.

* *Bank of America* gave Mexico's state-owned electric company a five-year, bank syndicated trade loan of $218 million. This move appears to be signalling a new openness among banks to offer long-term loans to Mexican businesses.

* *Banamex*, Mexico's largest bank, has joined with *American Express Co.*, to offer new financial services including an American Express Gold Card bearing the Banamex name.

* *Bank of Boston* plans to open an office in Mexico City by mid-1993.

* *Southern Pacific Railroad* plans to purchase a minority interest in *Ferropuertos SA de CV*, a Mexican venture aimed at developing distribution centers in Mexico.

* New Orleans-based *Lykes Brother's Steamship Co.* plans to begin the most comprehensive service to and from Mexico.

* *R.R. Donnelley & Sons Co.* purchased the Mexican printing company, *Laboratorio Lito Color SA de CV*, in order to produce promotional material and magazines for the Mexican publishing market.

* *Cadbury Schweppes PLC*, the British soft-drink and confectionary firm, purchased the mineral water division of *Valores Industriales SA de Mexico* for $325 million, and thereby increased its share of the Mexican soft-drink market from 2% to 6%. Around $145 million of the money needed for the purchase will be obtained by Cadbury issuing new shares. Mexico is the world's second largest consumer of soft-drinks due to its poor water supply.

* To further capitalize on its fast-growing international cargo-transportation business, *American President Lines,* an Oakland, California-based freight-transportation company formed a Mexican subsidiary.

* In an attempt to avoid stricter air pollution guidelines, *General Motors Corporation*, plans to relocate its 56-year-old Mexico City truck plant within five years. Currently, this plant employs 1,500 workers.

* New York-based *American Telephone and Telegraph Co.* bought 51% of Mexico's telecommunications distributor, *Informatica y Telecomunicaciones S.A.*

* *Sears, Roebuck and Co.* sold 25% of its Mexican retail operations for $120 million. *Sears de Mexico* operates 33 stores in 26 cities. Also, Sears holds a 62.6% interest in *Sears Canada, Inc.*, its Canadian subsidiary.

* The Mexican government will purchase electronic toll-collection systems from *Amtech*, a Dallas, Texas maker of electronic identification systems. Amtech will be assisted on the project by Mexico City-based *Integra Ingeniera SA de CV*.

* *Bombardier, Inc.*, a Montreal transportation equipment and aerospace firm, acquired the assets of *Constructora Nacional de Carros de Ferrocaril SA*, the Mexican government-owned rail car maker known as *Concarril*, for approximately $23.2 million.

* *Cadbury Schweppes P.L.C.*, the British soft-drink and confectionary firm, signed an agreement to purchase *Aguas Minerales S.A.*, Mexico's largest bottler and distributor of mineral water, from *Fomento Económico Mexicano S.A. de*

C.V. for $325 million. The transactions are subject to certain commercial and regulatory conditions.

* *Nabisco Foods Group*, a unit of *R.J.R. Nabisco, Inc.*, exchanged its almost one-third interest in *Grupo Gamesa* for five of Grupo Gamesa's consumer food and pet food companies. Nabisco will receive the pasta, confectionery, dry dessert mix, nuts and pet food businesses of this joint venture between Nabisco and *Pepsico Foods International*. Also, Nabisco will receive an undisclosed amount of cash while Pepsico will gain Nabisco's 32% in Grupo Gamesa, raising its total stake in the Mexican firm to 80%.

* In response to the explosions that ripped through the streets of Guadalajara on April 22, 1992, *PEMEX*, Mexico's national oil company, has employed San Francisco-based *Bechtel Group* to check the condition of its gas, oil, and gasoline lines.

* *Southwestern Bell Corporation* of St. Louis, Missouri and *Telcel* of Mexico, the cellular subsidiary of *Teléfonos de Mexico*, entered into a roaming telephone service agreement that will allow cellular phone users the ability to place and receive calls outside their home services areas.

* *Dell Computer de Mexico SA de CV* of Mexico City established a new subsidiary of *Dell Computer Corporation*.

* *Insteel Construction Systems Incorporated*, a unit of *Insteel Industries Incorporated*, has organized *Insteel Panel-MEX SA de CV* with associates to make 3-D panels in Mexicali, Baja California.

* *Burlington Northern Incorporated* and *Grupo Protexa SA* of Monterrey, Mexico entered into a joint venture with the Port of Galveston to provide port facilities for its rail-barge service to Mexico.

* *Cifra S.A.*, a leading Mexican retail concern, and *Wal-Mart Stores Inc.* of Bentonville, Arkansas, a unit of *Walton Enterprise, Inc.*, agreed to expand their joint venture retailing efforts in Mexico.

* Toronto-based *Cineplex Odeon Corporation* sold 57 of its Texas theaters to *Carmike Cinemas* of Columbus, Georgia.

* San Francisco-based *Shaklee Corporation*, a unit of *Yamanouchi Pharmaceutical Co.*, commenced its Mexican operations.

* *Browning-Ferris Industries* and *Domos Internacional S.A.* agreed to form a joint venture, *Browning-Ferris Industries de Mexico S.A.*, which will specialize in long-term waste management for municipalities throughout Mexico.

* *Teléfonos de Mexico* awarded *American Telephone and Telegraph* of Murray Hills, New Jersey a $28.9 million contract for digital switching equipment to upgrade Mexico's current communications system.

* *Miami Subs Corporation* signed its first international franchise agreement to expand its restaurant chain in Cancun, Mexico. The three new restaurants will be built by *B.R. Del Caribe* of Cancun.

* *Taco Bell*, a unit of Purchase, New York-based *Pepsico Inc.*, opened a food cart in Mexico City and plans to open two more in Mexico City and one in Tijuana. These food carts, which can be operated by two people, offer a limited menu including soft-shelled tacos, burritos, and Pepsi.

* The *Mexico City Water Authority* sent a $2.2 million order to *Ionics, Inc.*, of Watertown, Massassachusetts, for two Cloromat systems for the manufacture of bleach. This bleach will be utilized to disinfect water.

* *Burnham Pacific Properties, Inc.*, a real estate investment trust, disclosed that it purchased a factory-outlet center on the U.S./Mexican border from *Wohl/San Diego Partners* for $19.3 million.

* *Pepsico Foods International*, a division of *Pepsico Incorporated*, purchased 50% of the *Hostess Frito-Lay Company*, a Canadian-based snack food partnership, from *Kraft General Foods Canada Incorporated*, a unit of *Philip Morris*. The deal cost between $100 million to $200 million cash, while making Pepsico the sole owner of the leading snack food concern in Canada.

* *Mr. Gasket Company* announced that it will sell its *Cragar Wheel* division in Compton, California and its maquiladora facility in Mexicali, Mexico to an undisclosed investor group for between $20 million to $25 million.

* New Canaan, Connecticut-based *Smith Corona* plans to move its typewriter manufacturing operations somewhere in Mexico, probably to Tijuana. Smith Corona's much smaller engineering, distribution, and customer service divisions will remain in Cortland, New York. The move is expected to subtract 875 workers form the 1,300 now in the U.S. The cost of the move will be $15 million, which apparently will be made up in savings from lower wages and costs.

* The *Transco Energy Ventures Company*, a unit of *Transco Energy Company*, and *Duke Energy Corporation*, an affiliate of *Duke Power Company*, have entered a joint venture agreement to pursue the development of a proposed 700-megawatt power plant, the Samalayuca Project, to be built in Ciudad Juarez, Mexico.

* *Radio Shack de Mexico SA de CV* is the newly-formed joint venture between *Tandy Corporation* of Fort Worth, Texas and the Mexican retailing company, *Grupo Gigante SA de CV*. At least 50 new Radio Shack stores are expected to open in 1993.

* *Mattel Incorporated* announced that it was acquiring the remaining 60% of the Mexican toy marketer and distributor, *Auritel SA*. Thereby, making Mattel the sole owner of the Mexican firm.

* Milwaukee, Wisconsin-based *Allen-Bradley Co., Inc.*, an industrial automation products concern and a unit of *Rockwell International Corp.*, purchased *Controlmatic Allen-Bradley S.A.* of Mexico City.

* Troy, Michigan-based *Ziebart International*, a maker of automotive paint protection, signed a master franchise agreement with the *Praxis Corporation* of Monterrey, Mexico.

* The joint venture of *Perini Corporation* of Framingham, Massachusetts, *ICA Construction Corporation* of Mexico City, and *O&G Industries* of Torrington, Connecticut, has been awarded a $168 million contract to build tunnels, shafts, and connecting structures for the *Metropolitan Water Reclamation Project* in Chicago.

* The *Bank of Nova Scotia* acquired a 5% stake in *Grupo Financiero Inverlat SA* for $75 million. Grupo Financiero Inverlat includes brokerage and

commercial banking operations. This deal represents the first move by a Canadian or U.S. firm into the recently privatized Mexican banking industry.

* The last auto factory in Southern California, the *General Motors* Van Nuys plant, closed its doors on August 28, 1992 as GM planned to move manufacturing of these autos to Montreal, Canada, where manufacuring costs are lower than in the U.S.

* *Petroleos Mexicanos S.A.* (PEMEX) and Houston-based *Shell Oil Company* entered a joint venture to process Mexican oil into unleaded gasoline at a Deer Park, Texas refinery. PEMEX plans to buy half of the refining operation and supply crude oil. The refinery will return 45,000 barrels of unleaded gas a day to PEMEX. Mexican demand for unleaded fuel is expanding as it attempts to reduce air pollution. Also, the two companies are discussing the expansion of the refinery to handle hard-to-produce Mayan crude oil.

* Glenview, Illinois-based *Zenith Electronics* reported deepening losses which will cause it to consolidate its manufacturing and reduce the number of its workers in Mexico. Earlier in 1992 Zenith decided to send the majority of remaining American television production to Mexico from Springfield, Missouri. In an effort to reduce costs, Zenith plans to reduce its workforce in Mexico, which currently stands at 20,000.

* Over the next four years *J.C. Penney Company* of Dallas, Texas plans to open three stores in Mexico City, one in Monterrey, and a store in Guadalajara.

* Pittsburgh, Pennsylvania-based *Alcoa*, the world's largest aluminum producer, sold its 44.3% interest in *Grupo Aluminio* for $50 million to *Grupo Carso of Mexico*.

* *Mrs. Fields Cookies, Inc.* and *Pasteleria el Molino S.A.*, a retail bakery chain in Mexico, signed a multi-unit licensing agreement which envisions opening 50 Mrs. Fields Cookie stores in Mexico over the next 5 years.

* In an attempt to take advantage of possible NAFTA opportunities, Oregon computer company, *Advanced Data Concepts*, announced plans to relocate and hire 600 workers in Orange County California by the end of 1993.

* In another example of Mexico's desire to win a market share in the U.S. through acquisitions, Mexico City-based *Real Turismo*, a luxury hotel chain, plans to obtain the landmark *Paso del Norte Hotel* in El Paso, Texas.

* *Pyle National*, a subsidiary of Connecticut-based holding company *Amphenol Corp.*, is planning to close its Chicago plant and transfer its equipment first to their New York plant and later to Mexico. This move, attributed to low Mexican wages, will result in the loss of 600 jobs for the Chicago workers.

* *Volkswagen A.C.* was forced to delay the introduction of re-designed Golf and Jetta cars for three months due to a five-week strike at its Puebla, Mexico plant during the summer of 1992. This occurred right after Volkswagen announced plans to invest $960 million in this plant in order to increase its capacity from 150,000 units per year to 400,000 units per year. This would cause it to play a larger role in the North American markets. German-based *BMW A.G.* plans to build its first car plant in the U.S. and initially invest as much as $400 million in it.

* *USX Corporation* of Pittsburg, Pennsylvania and *Armco Incorporated* of Parsippany, New Jersey announced that they will continue to own and operate *National Oilwell*. USX and Armco had previously agreed to sell their National Oilwell unit to *Empresas Lanzogrota SA de CV* of Mexico City for $214 million.

* *Southwestern Bell* decided to move its headquarters from St. Louis, Missouri to San Antonio, Texas mainly because of San Antonio's close ties with Mexico. Southwestern values these ties because of its recent investments there. In 1990 Southwestern Bell, *Grupo Carso* of Mexico, and *France Telecom* formed an alliance and bought a controlling interest in *Teléfonos de Mexico* (TELMEX), Mexico's telephone system. The group plans to spend billions more on rebuilding the telephone system. Southwestern Bell's 10% interest in TELMEX has nearly tripled in value.

* A jointly-owned construction and engineering company will be formed in Mexico City by *Fluor Daniel, Inc.*, the main subsidiary of *Fluor Corp.* of Irvine, California, and *ICA Industrial*, a large Mexico City construction company. Fluor is hoping to capitalize on the anticipated construction boom and increase in business brought on by NAFTA.

* *DESC Sociedad de Fomento Industrial* will acquire a 40% stake in a Mexico City joint venture from partner *Monsanto Company*.

* *American Express Company* announced the introduction of membership miles with *Aeromexico* in Mexico and *Qantas* in Australia.

* *Philip Morris Companies* announced it will purchase a 7.9% interest in *Foemtno Económico Mexicana SA*, a large Mexican brewery, bottler, and convenience store company, from *Citicorp International Holdings Incorporated*, an investment division of *Citicorp*, for an estimated $160 million.

* *K-Mart Corp.* announced its plan to form a joint venture with *El Puerto de Liverpool*, which runs 17 full-line department stores in Mexico. The deal foresees the construction and operation of combined grocery and general merchandise stores in Mexico.

* Columbus, Ohio-based *Banc One Corporation* and *Banco Nacional de Mexico*, Mexico's largest bank, are discussing a possible alliance to establish a Mexican credit-card processing program. Also, Banc One and the unit of *Grupo Financiero Banamax* are considering a possible joint venture to provide services throughout Latin America.

* Boston, Massachusetts-based *Liberty Mutual Insurance Co.*, has entered into a marketing agreement with Mexico's largest multi-line insurer, *Grupo Nacional Provincial, S.A.* (GNP). Through this agreement they began providing reinsurance for auto and truck fleets, loss prevention, health care and safety consulting for GNP's clients as well as for U.S.-based multinationals.

* The *Sara Lee Corporation*, the marketer of *Hanes* and *L'Eggs* pantyhose, bought *Mallorca S.A. de C.V.*, the second largest hosiery maker in Mexico. Mallorca markets its hosiery under the *Spanel* brand name. A week earlier Sara Lee acquired *Rinbros S.A.*, a Mexican maker of men's and boy's underwear. Also, Sara Lee owns *House of Fuller* in Mexico, which specializes in door-to-door sales of cosmetics, household and personal products.

* *Badger*, a unit of the *Raytheon Company*, acquired a contract with a Mexican construction company to build a *Petroleos Mexicanos* (PEMEX) refinery in Veracruz worth $40 million.

* A contract to build a 700-megawatt power plant in Mexico for \$500 million to \$600 million was awarded to a U.S./Mexican consortium. The members of the consortium are: *El Paso Natural Gas Co*; *Coastal Corp.*; *General Electric Corp.*; *Bechtel Group, Inc.*; and *ICA Industrial SA de CV*, of Mexico.

2. 1993 TRANSACTIONS[2]

* The Mexican manufacturing operations of *General Tire, Inc.* has merged with *Grupo Carso SA.* in an attempt to rival *Goodyear Tire and Rubber Co.* for tire sales in Mexico.

* *Grupo Situr*, a real estate and development company, and *Holiday Inn Worldwide*, a division of *Bass PLC*, announced plans to develop and operate hotels in Mexico.

* Houston, Texas-based *Vista Chemicals* is expected to join with *Petroleos Mexicanos S.A.* (PEMEX) of Mexico City in a linear alkylbenzene project.

* A letter of intent was signed between *Inland Container*, a U.S. packaging paper and container maker, and *Grupo Industrial*, a Mexican pulp and paper group, to set up a 50/50 partnership which would create the *Durango Island Co.* The new company would operate corrugated case converting plants in Mexico. These plants would have a combined capacity of 84,000 tpy.

* New York-based Blackstone Capital Partners L.P., a unit of the *Blackstone Group*, and Montreal-based *Unigesco, Inc.* announced their plan to obtain *Univa*, Canada's second largest supermarket chain, for about \$1.25 billion in cash and debt. Blackstone Capital, which is paying \$300 million for an 80% stake in Univa, has also agreed to liquidate its interest in Univa within seven years.

* *Aeromexico* reached an agreement to increase its stake in *Mexicana Airlines* from 11% to 55% pending approval by Mexico's Secretariat of Communications and Transportation. Aeromexico's parent company, *Aerovias de Mexico SA*, will exchange stock for the Mexicana stake held by *Corporación Falcon SA*.

---

[2] Preparation of this article was done through the use of various media and resource/research materials. The transactions have not been independently verified.

* The plan between Calgary-based *PWA Corp.*, the parent company of *Canadian Airlines International*, and Texas-based *AMR Corporation*, the parent company of *American Airlines*, to create an alliance appears to be in trouble. This is due to an April 2, 1993 decision by the Ontario Court of Justice which rejected PWA's bid to withdraw from the *Gemini* computer reservation system, a requirement of the PWA-AMR tentative alliance. The terms of the deal called for AMR to pay $193 million for a 33.3% stake in Canadian Airlines. In return Canadian Airlines was to have shifted its seat inventory system from the Gemini Group computer system to AMR's Sabre system.

* *Southern Pacific Transportation, Burlington Northern Railroad*, and *Ferrocarriles Nacionales de Mexico*, Mexico's national carrier, have agreed to team up in order to provide two-way service between Monterrey, Mexico and the United States. In this deal southbound traffic would consist of apples and peas from the Pacific Northwest for *Sun Country Transportation, Inc.* The northbound journey would carry frozen broccoli and orange juice.

* *PFT-Robertson Transportation* of Farmer City, Illinois is completing a $15 million buyout of a Montana flat-bed carrier in the hopes of extending its routes serving the western Canadian provinces. Robertson hopes to cash in on expanded U.S. trade after NAFTA is approved.

* In order to reduce costs, *Marquest Medical Products Incorporated*, a medical products maker headquatered in Englewood, Colorado, will close its plant located in Nogales, Mexico and integrate the employees and operations with its main facility in Colorado.

* *B.A.T. International*, based in West Valley, Utah, entered into a contract to manufacture and distribute electric vehicles in Mexico.

* *Ryland Trading Limited*, a subsidiary unit of *Ryland Group Incorporated*, and *Orendain Equipo Constructor SC* entered into an agreement to build homes in Guadalajara, Mexico.

* *Superior Industries International Incorporated* will build an aluminum wheel manufacturing plant in Mexico, which is estimated to cost over $30 million.

* Michigan-based *Durakon Industries, Inc.* joined with *Consorcio Larmo*, a Mexican auto parts company, to build truck bedliners in Mexico.

* U.S. brewer, *Anheuser-Busch Co.*, made its first major investment in a foreign brewer when it announced it would pay \$477 million to acquire 18% of *Grupo Modelo S.A.*, Mexico's biggest brewer and the producer of the popular Corona beer. The venture will not change export procedures for Corona or Budweiser. Grupo Modelo plans to use the cash from this deal to purchase its eighth brewery.

* The Milwaukee, Wisconsin-based *Miller Brewing Co.*, a unit of *Philip Morris*, paid \$273 million for a 20% stake in *Molson Breweries* of Canada's U.S. import operators, a joint venture between *Molson Co.* of Toronto and Australia's *Foster's Brewing*. Molson, which has a 16% share of the U.S. import market, ranks second only to *Heineken* in U.S. beer imports. In December 1992, Philip Morris purchased a 7.9% interest in Mexico's largest beverage company, *Fomento Económico Mexicano*.

* In anticipation of NAFTA U.S. realtors have entered the Mexican market. New York-based *Cushman and Wakefield* entered into a joint venture with Mexico's *Grupo Comercial Imobiliario* to open in Mexico City an office whose goal is to find office space for U.S. companies trying to expand into Mexico. Similarly, Englewood, Colorado-based *Re/Max International, Inc.* signed a master franchise agreement with *Grupo Plaza SA*, a Guadalajara-based real estate broker. Already Re/Max has signed up 20 franchise offices in Guadalajara, Monterrey and Mexico City. Re/Max expects to sell 100 franchises in Mexico by the end of 1993. In addition, Irvine, California-based *Century 21 Real Estate Corp.* has opened around 70 franchise offices in Mexico during the past three years.

* In anticipation of NAFTA a joint venture was formed between *Cone Mills Corp.* of Greensboro, North Carolina and *Compañía Industrial de Parras, S.A.*, Mexico's largest denim manufacturer. The deal calls for a new denim manufacturing plant to be constructed in Parras, Mexico by 1995. Both companies will share a 50% interest in this venture while Cone Mills will also make a 20% equity investment in Cipsa existing plant. The denim manufacturing plant in Mexico is expected to cost between \$80 million to \$100 million.

* *Pepsi-Cola International* announced that over the forthcoming five years it would invest \$750 million to expand its Mexican operations. During the first phase, Pepsi intends to spend \$115 million in joint ventures in: Guadalajara (where Pepsi acquired a 29% interest in local bottler *Grupo Embotelladoras*); Monterrey (where Pepsi obtained a 49% interest in the local bottling firm *Grupo Protexa*); and in the Mexico City suburbs of Toluca and Tlanepantla (where Pepsi purchased 20% of *Grupo Rello*, which includes a merger with Pepsi bottlers in the Gulf coast cities of Tampico and Tuxpan. Since 1990, Pepsi has already spent $300 million in Mexico, including: the establishment of 20 Mexican bottling lines; the purchase of 2,500 truck routes; and implementing returnable plastic bottle programs. Indeed, by becoming an equity partner in local bottling operations, Pepsi should gain greater influence on marketing, advertising, and distribution strategies.

* Austin, Texas-based waste management company, *Mobley Environmental Services, Inc.*, and *Cementos Mexicanos SA* (CEMEX), a cement producer based in Monterrey, Mexico, will invest a total of $20 million in a joint venture to form a new company that will build two fuel-blending plants in Mexico.

* *Transportación Marítima Mexicana* decided to enter a space sharing agreement with *Hapag-Lloyd AG* for a weekly Europe-to-Gulf Coast and Mexico service bringing it into the Trans-Atlantic Agreement. *Tecomar*, Mexico's second largest container line, jointly owned by Transportación Marítima Mexicana and a group of private investors, will also join the agreement.

* *IDB Worldcom* of Los Angeles, California, a subsidiary of *IDB Communications Group Incorporated*, a supplier of satellite transmission and distribution services, for radio, television, and datavoice industries, announced an operating agreement to offer international telephone services with *Teléfonos de Mexico SA* (TELMEX).

* The *Allen-Bradley Company*, a unit of *Rockwell International Corporation* of Seal Beach, California, announced the consolidation of two Mexican subsidiaries to form *Allen-Bradley de Mexico SA*. The two subsidiaries, *Eléctrica Allen-Bradley SA* and *Controlmatic Allen-Bradley SA* of Mexico City, will be responsible for the sales and support of the company's automation control and communications projects as well as for power products and motor control centers.

* *Xerox Corporation* of Webster, New York announced its plans to expand its assembly production of its printer and copier components currently purchased from suppliers in Asia and Mexico by establishing a new unit named, *Low*

Complexity Manufacturing Group Incorporated, which will be located in Utica, New York.

* *Degussa Corporation* of Ridgefield Park, New Jersey, a subsidiary of the Frankfurt-based *Degussa A.G.*, announced its intent to start production of emission control catalysts at its new plant near Mexico City. The production, set to begin in early 1994, will be in Degussa's third catalyst plant. Degussa already has a plant in Ontario and one in Kentucky. The new plant is intended to serve the Mexican automotive market.

* *Apple Computer, Inc.* announced that it was planning to establish a new marketing and distribution development office in Mexico, termed *Apple Computer Mexico*. This Mexican sales force would aid local sales, marketing service, and provide advice to Apple resellers, third-party software developers, and partners in Mexico. With the personal computer market in Mexico expected to reach $1 billion, with 24% annual growth through 1995, Apple views the nation as an important market. In November 1992, Apple Computer, Inc. expanded its distribution efforts in Mexico by adding other Mexican resellers: *Dicom*, *Edumac*, and *Vertex*.

* U.S. led *Proyectos Ecologicos S.A.*, composed of Houston-based *Valero Energy Corp.*, *Banacci S.A.*, *Infomin S.A.*, and *Dragados Cepsa S.A.*, have signed papers with *Petróleos Mexicanos S.A.* (PEMEX) which allow Proesa to build and operate a $300 million gasoline-additive plant in southern Mexico's Gulf Coast. This plant is expected to produce 15,000 barrels of MTBE daily from butane supplied by PEMEX.

* In an effort to remain the world's number one chip maker, *Intel Corp.* is planning to spend $1 billion to enlarge its semiconductor factory in Mexico and later in 1993, hopes to build another factory of a similar size.

* A Palm Desert, California company, *U.S. Filter Corporation*, announced that it has been selected to negotiate the design, manufacture, and operation of a waste water treatment plant for the city of Cuernavaca in Morelos, Mexico for use by May 1994. Initially, U.S. Filter is expected to invest $14 million in the project, designed to serve a population of approximately 550,000 people.

* *Quality Coils* moved operations from its new Mexican plant to its old plant in Stonington, Connecticut after announcing that the low-wage labor in Mexico was less productive than U.S. labor.

* Holland, Michigan-based *Donnelly Corporation*, which manufactures both components and complete exterior mirror assemblies, plans to invest around $5 million for plant and equipment at a manufacturing plant in Monterrey, Mexico. The plant, which is expected to be fully operational in July 1994, will produce exterior mirror components for North and South American markets. Apparently, this production facility will lead to the creation of between 60-70 Mexican jobs.

* *LTV Steel Company* announced that it is opening a sales office in Mexico City.

* As part of its North American expansion strategy, *McKesson Corporation*, a drug and food distribution concern, acquired a 23% interest in *Nadro SA de CV*, Mexico's leading pharmaceutical distributor for approximately $50 million, with an option to acquire an additional 9% of Nadro's common stock.

* Coca-Cola paid $195 million to purchase a 30% stake in the soft-drink division of *Fomento Económico Mexicano S.A.*, FEMSA, a Monterrey-based beverage giant which owns the largest coke franchise in the world. FEMSA is expected to use the needed capital to buy and establish a huge plant in Mexico City, another bottling plant in Oaxaca, and to upgrade distribution network and other bottling plants.

* *Grupo Bermudez*, a major industrial developer in Mexico, is participating in a joint venture with *Binswanger*, a Philadelphia, Pennsylvania-based commercial real estate company. Under this joint venture, the two firms will be able to offer a full range of real estate services in the two nations.

* *Sigma Alimentos* will be the exclusive distributor of *Oscar Mayer*'s products in Mexico. Oscar Mayer is a unit of *Kraft General Foods Corporation*.

* The U.S. environmental services company, *WMX Technologies, Inc.*, and Mexico's largest construction firm, *Empresas ICA Controladora S.A. de C.V.* formed an environmental services firm. WMX will own 49% of the new venture, while ICA will hold the remainder ownership. The newly formed company will offer services in such areas as non-hazardous waste collection,

transportation and recycling, landfill management and remediation, composting, street and beach sweeping, medical waste services and methane recovery to both public and private clients in Mexico.

* *Servilamina Summit Mexicana S.A. de C.V.* was established in December 1992 as a subsidiary of the major Japanese trading house, *Suitomo Corporation*. The new company plans to begin operations in November of 1993. The new facility is expected to process 24,000 metric tons of steel in its first year. The main purpose of the company will be to process steel coil and sheet for just-in-time delivery to the expanding auto and electronics market in North America.

* *Allied Signal Incorporated* acquired *Filtram SA* from *Proeza Group*. Filtram SA manufactures Allied Signal's Fram filter products in Mexico.

* Mexican firm *Grupo Protexa* and *Forest City Development*, a unit of Cleveland, Ohio-based developer *Forest City Enterprises Incorporated*, entered into a joint venture agreement to build shopping malls in major cities in Mexico.

* *Dell Computer Corporation*, which entered the Mexican market for personal computers in 1993, plans to establish a production plant in Toluca, Mexico. At the new facility, it is expected that final custom configuration work on Dell's desktop personal computers and advanced server systems will take place. Nearly 30 employees are expected to work at the new facility.

* *Aerovias de Mexico S.A.* and *Mexicana Airlines*, Mexico's two largest airlines, have agreed to merge their cargo operations under the name *Aeromexpress*. Aeromexpress, based in Mexico City, will control the cargo activities of *Aeroperu*.

* *Galloway, Romero and Associates*, an Aurora, Colorado-based engineering firm, acquired a $500,000 contract from a small group of investors to re-design 30 of their recently purchased Mexico City service stations.

* In an effort to double the cellular telephone capacity of Mexico, *L.M. Ericsson Telefon* of Sweden signed a contract with *Radiomovil DIPSA* of Mexico for more than $100 million.

* As part of a $10 million expansion program Mexico-based *Mangino Industrial Group* acquired *F.F.R. Industries*, a Houston, Texas-based customizing

company from Rick and Michael Raney. F.F.R. conducted business as *Anaheim Industries*.

* *Roadway Services Incorporated* announced a joint venture between its Roadway Express unit and *Transportes de Nuevo Laredo*.

* The nation's third-largest seller of canned vegetables, *Stokley USA Incorporated*, announced plans to sell four plants located in Mexico, Michigan, Ohio, and Texas due to large losses.

* Minneapolis, Minnesota-based *Home Depot, Inc.* announced that it was pursuing the possibility of expanding its operations into Mexico. The home-supply corporation is expected to open 5 stores in Canada by 1995. While Home Depot, Inc. plans to have 264 stores in the U.S. by the end of 1993, it expects to have nearly 645 by January 1, 1997.

* *Atchison, Topeka and Santa Fe Railway* has struck a deal with *Ferrocarriles Nacionales de Mexico*, the Mexican national railroad, in which 125 new freight cars will be shipped from *Bombardier*, a Mexican manufacturer, to Santa Fe. In return for this Santa Fe will provide $1.4 million in components to build the freight cars. The application of the deal will achieve the settlement of a disagreement between the two over numerous items including per-diem charges and bridge tolls which have been in dispute since the early eighties. Earlier in 1993 the two railroads signed two contracts aimed at improving service between the U.S. and Mexico. The contracts included agreements to offer direct rail service between several Santa Fe terminals in California and the Midwest, and Chihuahua. Also, they agreed on a weekly dedicated double-stack container train between Los Angeles and Mexico City through the El Paso, Texas Gateway.

* *S & H Fabricating & Engineering* announced that it would close its air-conditioning component factory in Walled Lake, Michigan and transfer production to Mexico. In eliminating approximately 100 U.S. jobs, the move would result in a sharp reduction of costs. Prior to the closure, S & H Fabricating & Engineering employed nearly 1,000 in the U.S. and 200 in Mexico.

* *General Motors* announced that in 1994 it plans to move some production of its Chevrolet Cavelier subcompact and its Pontiac Sunbird from Mexico to Lansing, Michigan creating 1,000 new jobs at the Lansing plant.

* St. Louis, Missouri-based *Madison Brothers Stores, Inc.* decided to open 10 *Men Lova* apparel stores in the Mexico City area.

* *GE Plastics*, a subsidiary unit of *General Electric Company*, purchased the commercial ABS resin operations of *Industrial Resistol*, a major Mexican ABS supplier. GE Plastics announced it will conduct business from its manufacturing plants located in Mexico City, Tampico, and other cities.

* *Lean Power Corp.*, a small research and development company which specializes in automotive emissions, plans to begin production of a device which will reduce the amount of pollutants emitted from old cars in Mexico. The device employs a small computer to obtain more efficiency from the carburetor, and to induce a more complete burn from the air-fuel mixture and fewer tailpipe emissions.

* *Burlington Northern Railroad Co.* and *Grupo Protexa* of Monterrey, Mexico entered into a joint venture named *Protexa Burlington International S.A. de CV.* This venture carries railway cars on barges between Galveston, Texas and the Mexican ports of Altamira, Coatzacoalcos and Veracruz. This project now operates two 54 car capacity barges on a weekly schedule between these ports. Grain is expected to be the principle commodity to be shipped on this new route. This venture is the model for a similar venture being discussed by *CSX Transportation, Inc.*, which would operate out of either New Orleans, Louisiana or Mobile, Alabama and sail to the ports of Altamira and Veracruz.

* Akron, Ohio-based *Bridgestone/Firestone, Inc.* intends to expand its Cuernavaca, Mexico tire plant to raise its production by 38%, from 4,400 car and light truck radial tires daily to 6,050.

* *Diebold* plans to buy 80% of a Mexican distribution business from *Hidromex SA de CV*. Hidromex is the distributor of automated teller machines made by a Diebold-IBM joint venture.

* Houston, Texas-based *Trimac Transport System, Inc.*, a unit of the Calgary conglomerate, *Trimac Ltd.* entered a joint marketing agreement with *InterMex*,

a large Mexican bulk hauler. This agreement requires them to interchange cross-border equipment at Brownsville, Texas.

* *FFE Transportation Services, Inc.* became the first carrier to offer less-than-truckload service into Mexico on August 15, 1993, when it began this service in partnership with a Mexican motor carrier. FFE will obey the current Mexican law by dropping their trailers at the border for delivery by the Mexican carrier to points throughout Mexico including Monterrey, Guadalajara and Mexico City. Before this, shippers were forced to use air service or pay expensive full-truckload rates. FFE recently began a similar service to Eastern and Central Canada.

* *Aeromexico* and *Delta Air Lines, Inc.* formed a preliminary arrangement on sharing flight information and passenger bookings. More specifically, their marketing arrangements would include joint code sharing in their respective reservation systems and flight schedules. In addition, the airlines agreed to pursue block-space arrangements on U.S.-Mexico City flights.

* Due to increased Mexican and South American demand for plastics compounding *A. Schulman, Inc.*, a Fairlawn, Ohio-based company, will build a $15 million plant in San Luis Potosi. The 50,000-square foot plant, which should open during the second half of 1994, will initially have 55 employees and 2 production lines. Schulman, which previously supplied its Mexican customers from its Ohio plants, will utlize the new plant for Mexican & South American sales. Among Schulman's customer base are automotive, packaging, and appliance firms.

* *Seguros La Comercial*, Mexico's fourth largest insurer, and *Seguros America*, Mexico's second largest insurer are planning a merger which will create Mexico's largest insurance company, occupying about 25% of the market. The two companies will continue to operate independently following the merger in which Seguros La Comercial will hold 60% control and Seguros America the other 40%. Seguros La Comercial's niche is in property and casualty insurance while Seguros America's emphasis is on life insurance.

* Office supply producer *Smead Manufacturing*, which is based in Hastings, Minnesota, announced that it will transfer a portion of its office supply lines from plants in Hasting and River Falls, Wisconsin to Mexico. The shift of the company's production to Mexico of its bulk-priced file pockets and selected

expanding files is due to reduced production costs. Nevertheless, the remainder of Smead's 2,200 products will be produced in the U.S.

* Many U.S. insurers have begun obtaining Mexican partners in anticipation of NAFTA. *Reliance National Insurance Co.* of New York paid $3 million for a 30% stake in *Seguros Protección Mutua S.A.* This venture underwrites auto, fire, credit, accident and health coverage as well as providing auto insurance for U.S. citizens traveling in Mexico. While Warren, N.J.-based *Chubb Corp.* bought a 30% share in *Seguros La Equitativa S.A.*, Mexico's twenty-sixth largest insurer with $13.2 million in premiums, Philadelphia's *Cigna Co.* has acquired 49% of *Seguros Progreso S.A.* with $10.5 million in premiums and renamed it *Seguros Cigna S.A.*.

* In an estimated $100 million deal, *Lear Holdings Corporation* of Southfield, Michigan purchased *Ford Motor Company's* automotive seat-trim business and its seat design engineering unit. Included in the purchase is the Juarez, Mexico-based *Favesa SA de CV*, which produces seat and seat covers for nearly 11 of Ford's North American assembly plants.

* *Crowley American Transport*, the linear division of *Crowley Maritime Corp.* of Oakland, California will begin direct service to Mexico with weekly sailings from Port Everglades, Florida to the Mexican Gulf ports of Progreso, Veracruz, and Tampico beginning October 9, 1993.

* *Aerovox, Inc.* is planning to replace the building it currently occupies by leasing a larger building in Juarez, Mexico to accommodate new markets that have opened up in Mexico and Central America.

* *Pillsbury Company* obtained a 49% stake in *Pacific Star de Occidente*, which is a distributor of refrigerated foods in Mexico. The deal sought to double Pacific Star's distribution network to more than 1,400 Mexican supermarkets in the first year.

* Michigan-based *Blue Water Plastics, Inc.* and Tultitan, Mexico-based *CAMPCO de Mexico S.A. de C.V.* formed a joint venture agreement. The firms are both custom molders of plastic components for the auto, transport, office equipment, institutional seating and other industries.

* Minnesota-based *Cargill*, the largest grain trader, acquired a large meat-packing plant in Saltillo, Coahuila.

* *Johnson & Higgins*, the U.S. insurance firm, purchased 25% of the shares of *Brockman y Schuh*, Mexico's biggest insurance broker, for an undisclosed sum.

* *Hecla Mining*, based in Idaho, intends to invest $20 million in its La Choya mine in Mexico, enabling the firm to raise its proven and probable gold reserves by 320% and silver reserves by 80%.

* Boise-based *Morrison Knudsen* and joint venture partner *Grupo Automotriz y Industrial del Norte* obtained a letter of intent from *Ferrocarrilles Nacionales de Mexico*, for a $360 million contract to overhaul and maintain freight locomotives for the railway's northeast region.

* *Communications Technology Corp.*, a subsidiary of U.S.-based *Acme-Cleveland Corp.*, has entered into a telecommunications joint venture with *CIMA Sistemas* of Mexico City.

* Indiana-based *Imperial Petroleum, Inc.*'s wholly-owned *Ridgepoint Mining Co.* entered into an arrangement with an undisclosed seller to purchase a 55% interest in Lance and Trega gold mines in Mexico.

SELECTED UNITED STATES-MEXICO-CANADA CROSS-BORDER INVESTMENT AND TRADE DEALS: 1994

by Dean C. Alexander*

According to Mexico's Ministry of Commerce and Industrial Development, during the first half of 1994, foreign investment in Mexico rose by 34% over the previous year to $7.033 billion. Of this amount, $3.319 billion was direct foreign investment, while portfolio investment reached $3.466 billion. Of the $3.319 billion discussed above, 50.3% was targeted into services, 33.8% into manufacturing, 9.9% into commerce, 4.5% into construction, 1.3% into transport and communications, and 0.2% into mining.

1. 1994 TRANSACTIONS[1]

* *J.C. Penney Co., Inc.* plans to establish an import/export trading branch in Mexico City called *J.C. Penney Comercializadora S.A. de C.V.*

* *Liberty Mutual Insurance Company* established an office in Mexico City to provide occupational health and safety services and safety consulting services and products.

* *Grupo Financiero Banamex-Accival* and *MCI Corp.* entered into a $1 billion joint venture to provide long distance telecommunications services in Mexico.

---

*   Director, The NAFTA Research Institute, Washington, D.C.
[1]   Preparation of this article was done through the use of various media and resource/research materials. The transactions have not been independently verified.

Under this arrangement, Banacci will contribute $550 million for a 55% stake, while MCI will provide $450 million for 45% of their new firm. The companies intend to create a fiber-optic network that ultimately will link all of Mexico.

* Mexican construction company *Grupo Gutsa* and California-based *Scripps Hospital* announced their intention to construct an eighty-bed Scripps Hospital de Mexico in the State of Aguascalientes.

* The international project and construction management firm *Lehrer McGover Bovis, Inc.* opened an office in Mexico City, *Bovis de Mexico S.A. de C.V.*

* The U.S. firm *Mrs. Baird Bakeries* formed a joint venture with Mexico's largest baker, *Grupo Industrial Bimbo*. Under this arrangement, Bimbo will purchase 50% of Mrs. Baird. While Mrs. Baird's has 11 plants in Texas employing 3,200 people, Bimbo has sales of $1.4 billion, employing 40,000 workers in 30 plants in Mexico.

* U.S. firm *AMC Entertainment International* and real estate developer *Reichmann International Mexico* entered into an agreement to open a multiplex cinema in Mexico City's Santa Fe development area. The cinema, scheduled to open in 1995, will have 24 screens and be the largest in Mexico City. *Reichmann International Mexico* and Mexican construction company, *Empresas ICA Sociedad Controladora SA de CV*, announced that they will create a 30-building development in the Santa Fe areas called the Centro Oeste project. Centro Oeste will include hotel, shopping, restaurant and entertainment facilities, as well as an office and residential complex.

* Ireland-based *Kerry Dairy Group* will invest $25 million to buy *Productos Vegetales de Mexico* from the U.S. company *Basic Vegetable Products*.

* U.S. firm *Carroll Foods Corp.* planned to invest $7 million to establish a complete pork production cycle in Mexico. The investment is expected to create 700 jobs in Veracruz and that in five years; it will raise the state's pork output by 135%.

* *Sara Lee Corp.* entered into a joint venture agreement with *AXA S.A. de C.V.* to invest in its subsidiary. The subsidiary owns *Kir Alimentos*, an important name in the Mexican processed meat market. In addition, Sara Lee and Kir

agreed to terms where Kir would distribute selected Sara Lee meat products in Mexico.

* U.S. agriculture giant *ConAgra, Inc.* paid $25 million to obtain 20% of *Univasa S.A.*, the Mexican poultry, pork, and animal feeds company.

* U.S. seasoning firm *McCormick & Co.* announced that it had purchased *Grupo Pesa*, a Mexican seasoning company which was a leading flavoring supplier to Mexico's food processing industry.

* Michigan-based *Siemens Automotive* took over a $60 million automotive electronics manufacturing facility in Guadalajara.

* U.S. snackfood giant *Nabisco* invested $30 million in its pasta division, including the acquisition of a pasta production plant from *Anderson Clayton Company* in Tultitlan, Mexico.

* North Carolina-based *Verbatim Corp.* opened a plant in Tijuana to manufacture and format computer tape products.

* Mexican financial conglomerate *Grupo Financiero Interacciones* purchased 100% of *Laredo National Bank*, a leading U.S. bank involved in financing U.S. trade to Mexico.

* For an additional $60 million the U.S. company, *Aetna Life and Casualty*, increased its shares in Mexican insurance holding firm *Vamsa* from 30% to 44.5%.

* Chicago-based *A. Epstein & Sons International, Inc.* entered into a joint venture with *Latisa*, a leading Mexican achitectural, engineering, construction firm.

* U.S.-based *United Artists* and *Bufete Industrial de Mexico* entered into a contract to construct movie theater complexes in six Mexican cities, including Cuernavaca, Guadalajara, Hermosillo, Mexico City, Monterrey, and Puebla.

* In late 1994 or early 1995 German chemical company *BASF Group* will invest $100 million and open a chemical plant in Altamira, Tampico.

* *Servicios de Viaje Bancomer*, the travel subsidiary of Mexican bank Bancomer, was purchased by Pennsylvania-based *Rosenbluth International Travel*.

* British producer of paints, explosives, acrylics, and polyurethanes, *Imperial Chemical Industries*, will invest $5 million in capacity expansion and new product development in Mexico. The firm already has four operations in Mexico: *ICI Mexicanos, Atlas de Mexico, Explosivos Mexicanos, and Nitroamonia de Mexico*. ICI intends to build a new explosives accessories plant in Mexico.

* Leisure firm *Club Med* invested $40 million in Mexico to obtain a controlling interest in Club Med villages and sites (save the Sonora Bay location) that it managed and were under majority ownership of *Fonatur* (the tourism development arm of the Mexican Ministry of Tourism).

* Akron, Ohio-based supplier of plastic compounds and resins, *A. Schulman*, is constructing a plant in Mexico.

* Macon, Georgia-based school bus manufacturer, *Blue Bird Corp.*, acquired a location in Monterrey to construct general transportation buses for the Mexican market.

* *Honda Motor Company* plans to build an automobile production plant in the Mexican State of Jalisco. The plant, which is expected to result in the production of 15,000 units annually, will commence operations in late 1995 and employ 200 workers. The site will be next to Honda's existing motorcycle and automobile parts factory in Es Salto, Jalisco.

* *Rockwell Automotive* opened a new plant in Queretaro, Mexico to manufacture hoods, window components, and other parts for *Chrysler* and *Volkswagen* in Mexico. The facility will support Brazilian, Canadian, Mexican, and U.S. markets.

* Korean electronics firm, *Goldstar*, intends to spend between $5 to $10 million to transfer its television production facilities from Huntsville, Alabama to Mexicali. As a result, Goldstar will double its Mexican production. Presently, nearly 98% of Goldstar's Mexican production is for export to the U.S.

* Germany's *Temic Telefunken Mikroelectronik GMBH* began production at a manufacturing plant for automotive components and microelectronics in Cuautla, Mexico.

* A controlling interest in Colorado-based *Candy's Tortilla Factory* was obtained by the Mexican company *Gruma, S.A.* It is forseen that Gruma will obtain property contiguous to Candy's key manufacturing facility.

* German automaker *BMW* announced its intention to invest $600 million in car assembly, automobile parts and distribution operations in Mexico. BMW will own 60% of the operation, a Mexican group, Bavaria, will own the remaining 40%. Construction of the plant is expected in the State of Mexico.

* Japanese motorcycle manufacturer *Suzuki* intends to open a plant for the assembly of a subcompact car in Mexico. Production will be sold in the NAFTA nations.

* New Zealand-based *Broken Hill Pty.* obtained a stake in Mexico's *Grupo Ferrominero*, a firm which owns the majority of *Compañía Autlan*, a Mexican manganese ore miner and ferro alloy smelter.

* *General Motors de Mexico* is constructing a truck assembly plant in Silao to replace its aging Mexico City site. The plant, expected to be in operation by 1995, will build vehicles solely for the Mexican market.

* *Elásticos Selectos de Mexico* plans to construct a plant in southern Texas to make men's and women's underwear.

* Indiana-based *Alpine Electronics Manufacturing* formed a Mexican subsidiary, *Alcom Comunicaciones de Mexico S.A. de C.V.*, to produce audio equipment and electronic components for North American auto manufacturers and auto importers. The items will be produced at a facility at the Del Norte Industrial Park. Alpine invested $7 million in the facility and intial employment will be 300 workers.

* U.S. firm *Tenneco, Inc.* has constructed a plant in Calaya, Mexico which will produce automotive parts.

* Vancouver-based *Severide Environmental Industries, Inc.* obtained a commitment from authorities from the State of Baja California to provide a facility for the initial production of electric buses. *Dina Camiones de Occidente* plans to distribute and service these buses in Mexico. Severide will establish its electric bus manufacturing operations in Mexico under the name *S.V.E. Transportes Eléctricos, S.A.* In 1995 a new facility will be built to manufacture the buses, thereby creating between 350 to 400 jobs.

* Canadian film company *Beacon Group* and the Mexican firm *Grupo Situr* commenced plans for a tourist development in Baja California. The facility, to be located in Bajamar, is expected to be valued at $55 million.

* *Grupo Textil San Marcos*, a subsidiary of Mexican conglomerate *Cydsa*, will enter into a joint venture with U.S. firm *Crown Crafts, Inc.* Under the arrangement, Crown Crafts will market in the U.S. woven acrylic blankets produced by San Marcos in Mexico. Concurrently, San Marcos will distribute in Latin America bedding, cotton throws and other products produced by Crown Crafts in the U.S.

* In its creation of the first seamless, all-digital wireless network in North America, U.S.-based *Nextel Communications* intends to invest $165 million to acquire 22% of Mexican cellular provider *Mobilcom SA de CV*. Also, Nextel signed an investment arrangement with Canadian firm *Clearnet*.

* The largest beef and pork processor in the world, *IBP*, announced that it would open offices in Mexico in an attempt to increase its operations. Also, it was reported that IBP might form joint ventures with Mexican firms.

* U.S. electronics and telecommunications giant *Motorola Corp.* and Mexican industrial company *Grupo Protexa* entered into a joint venture to provide cellular phone services linking half of northern Mexico. Under this deal, an initial investment of $1.5 billion is expected. Moreover, this arrangement will connect the northeast part of Mexico where Protexa has a cellular license with central states Chihuahua and Durango, where Motorola has a license.

* *Wheeling-Pittsburg Steel Corp.* entered into a joint venture with Mexican steel producer *Hylsa* in which Mexican steel will be forwarded to Wheeling, whereby it will be processed into hot-rolled products.

* Mexican steel producer *ISPAT Mexicana* will purchase Canada-based steel producer *Sidbec-Dosco* for nearly $33 million plus adjustments for 100% of Sidbec-Dosco's capital.

* Mexican firm *Grupo Industrial Alfa* and U.S.-based *Shaw Industries, Inc.* formed a new joint venture to manufacture, distribute, and market carpets and related products in Mexico and South America.

* *Corporación Hotelera Boyce S.A. de C.V., Inmobiliaria Bear S.A. de CV* and *Holiday Inn Worldwide* formed an arrangement to construct a new Holiday Inn Crown Plaza Hotel in Mexico City. The new project is expected to include a $70 investment.

* *United Parcel Service* intends to invest $100 million to ameliorate its services in Mexico.

* *Grupo Cementos de Chihuahua*, a Mexican cement maker, purchased a cement plant near Albuquerque, New Mexico from *Holnam, Inc.* for $42 million.

* Mexican firm *Consorcio Grupo Dina, S.A. de C.V.* acquired 100% of the outstanding shares of a publicly held U.S. firm, *Motor Coach Industries International, Inc.* The value of the merger was $300 million.

* Mexico's biggest steel firm, *Amsa*, and U.S. firm, *Inland Steel Industries*, formed a 50%/50% joint venture to provide materials and management services to Mexican industrial products and construction markets.

* U.S.-based *Minnesota Mining & Manufacturing (3M)* will invest $27 million in Mexico in order to increase its exports from Mexico to Latin America.

* Canadian brewing company *John Labatt Ltd.* spent $510 million to obtain a share in *Fomento Económico Mexicano S.A. (Femsa)*. Femsa controls about half of the Mexican beer market. U.S.-based *Anheuser-Busch Companies* owns 17% of Mexico's other leading brewer *Grupo Modelo*.

* Toronto-based *Campbell Resources, Inc.* acquired the Santa Gertrudis gold mine located in Sonora, Mexico from subsidiaries of *Phelps Dodge Corp.* for $10 million.

* New Jersey-based *Blessings Corporation* acquired 60% of *Nacional de Envases Plásticos S.A. de C.V. (Nepsa)* in exchange for $41 million in cash and 200,000 newly issued shares. Nepsa is Mexico's leading manufacturer of extruded, printed and converted plastic film.

* U.S. television network *NBC* and Mexico's second-biggest television broadcaster, *Televisión Azteca*, entered into a strategic alliance which would establish broad cooperation between the firms in programming, management, and technology. Also, under the arrangement, NBC has a three-year option to purchase between 10%-20% of Televisión Azteca for between $170 million - $240 million.

* Japanese electronics giant *Sanyo* entered into a joint venture with *Mabe*, a Mexican home appliance corporation, to produce refrigerator compressors. The deal is valued at $48 million.

* Valve maker *Kitz Corp.* and Japanese trading firm *Nissho Iwai Corp.* will spend $15.2 million to construct a plant to manufacture steel-casting valves for the petroleum industry.

* Japanese electronics maker *Matsushita* intends to move production of its television manufacturing unit to Mexico from the United States.

* U.S. retail giant *Wal-Mart* and Mexico's largest retailer, *Grupo Cifra*, plan to invest $900 million during the next three years to open 91 new Sam's Club stores, Walmart Supercenters, and Aurrera Warehouse Outlets throughout Mexico.

* Japanese multinational *Hitachi* is transferring its television parts plant to Mexico from Malaysia.

* *Ryder Systems, Inc.* intends to open its Mexican operations during 1994, with locations in Guadalajara, Mexico City, and Monterrey.

* *Bell Atlantic* raised its ownership in Mexican cellular telephone firm *Grupo Iuscell*, from 23% to 42%. Bell Atlantic, which obtained the initial ownership in the Iusacell in October 1993 for $520 million, will raise its total ownership to almost $1.4 billion.

* The U.S. firm *Spalding Co.* and Mexico's *Empresarios Unidos de Jalisco* invested $5 million in their joint venture, *Causamex*, to produce auto parts.

* By mid-1995 Japanese firm *Toshiba Corp.* will transfer its U.S.-bound production of television parts to Mexico from Singapore in order to take advantage of lower tariffs under NAFTA. Toshiba assembles television sets at its U.S. plant in Tennessee.

* Swedish telecommunications giant *Telefon AB L.M. Ericsson* sold its 51% interest in *Conductores Latincasa S.A.*, the Mexican cable company, for $55 million.

* U.S. firm *Genuine Parts Co.* and *Auto Todo* agreed to establish a joint venture, Auto Todo Mexicana, to sell replacement parts in Mexico.

* Four Mexican investment groups and *La Quinta Inns, Inc.* entered into an arrangement to build 22 hotels in Mexico.

* *Kenwood Corp.*, the Japanese sound equipment manufacturer, established an operation in Ciudad Juarez to manufacture audio amplifiers for use in cars. Production is expected to commence in March 1995.

* Korean electronics giant *Samsung* intends to build in Tijuana a television manufacturing plant, valued at $100 million. In contrast to a current television assembly plant in Tijuana which utilizes imported parts, the new plant will manufacture its own components.

* U.S. firm *Royal Crown Cola* and Mexican company *Consorcio Aga* formed a joint venture to bottle RC Cola in Mexico.

* *Kentucky Fried Chicken* intends to triple its franchises in Mexico by the end of the 1990s and reach 450 restaurants.

* Japanese firm *Hosiden Corporation* plans to establish a plant for producing parts for personal computers in Mexico in March 1996.

* Mexican glass giant *Vitro* and French beverage can manufacturer *Pechiney International* entered into a $70 million deal to establish a company to

manufacture aluminum beverage cans in Mexico. Each firm will have a 50% ownership in the deal.

* Chihuahua, Mexico-based *Internaccional de Ceramica SA* is building a $76 million bathroom tile manufacturing plant in Garland, Texas.

* *Scott Paper Company* announced that its Mexican affiliate, *Compañía Industrial San Cristobal S.A.,* which is half-owned by Scott, will spend $148 million to expand plants in Mexico. The expansion includes a newspaper machine for a plant in Morelia, Michoacan, and a recycled fiber plant and facial tissue line at its factory in Ecatepec de Morelos-Mexico.

* U.S.-based *Amser, Inc.* entered into an arrangement with *Derivados Metal-Organicos SA de CV* of Monterrey, Mexico to design and implement a chemical transportation system.

* U.S.-firm *Motor Wheel Corp.*, an automotive wheel and brake manufacturer, will form a joint venture in Mexico with *Nissan Motor Co.* to manufacture automotive brake components. Motor Wheel will own 75% of the venture called *Motor Wheel de Mexico.* Nissan units *Kiriu Machine Manufacturing Co.* and *Nissan Trading Co.* will hold 25%.

* *Dillard Department Stores, Inc.*, *Wal-Mart Stores, Inc.*, and *Cifra* entered into a joint venture to build and operate 50 Dillard retail stores in Mexico. Dillard will be a 50% partner; the remaining portion will be owned by Wal-Mart and Cifra. The first store is expected to open in late 1995 in Monterrey, Mexico.

* *U.S. Electricar, Inc.* entered into a joint venture with *Grupo Industrial Casa* to create entities to market electric industrial vehicles and buses in the Americas. U.S. Electricar is a growing U.S. electric vehicle manufacturer, while Grupo Industrial Casa is Mexico's largest bus body manufacturer. Casa makes numerous types of diesel transit buses that are used in mass transit throughout Latin America. Under the deal, two jointly owned corporations will be created. A U.S.-based company will handle all U.S. and Canadian bus sales, while a Mexico-based firm will target products manufactured for Latin America. Company officials said the approach aims to take advantage of anti-pollution needs in both countries and trade benefits flowing from NAFTA.

* *Nissan Motor Co.* intends to transfer all its business operations for Central America and South America to *Nissan Mexicana SA de CV* from early 1995. Currently, about 60% of all Nissan unit sales in Central and South America are now of Nissan Mexicana-made vehicles.

* *Toyota Motor Corp.* will stop exporting Corolla sedans to the U.S. and Canada from Japan in the latter half of 1997. Rather, *Toyota* will raise production capacity at its Canadian factory to take over production of the model. *Toyota Motor Manufacturing Canada, Inc.* will increase capacity from the current 85,000 Corollas a year to 120,000 units by August 1997.

* Mexican-based *Empresas La Moderna*, a leading cigarette producer, purchased the vegetable seed division, *Asgrow Seed Co.*, of *Upjohn Company*. Asgrow is the among the world's top five seed companies in the world, with sales of $270 million.

* One of the largest prizes for the Mexican economy was the announcement by *AT&T Corporation* of its $1 billion alliance with Mexican partner *Grupo Industrial Alfa S.A.* Under this arrangement the firms will provide long distance telephone services when the present government-approved monopoly ends in 1997. This deal came as a surprise to many analysts as Alfa, a giant industrial group, apparently has little telephone experience. It was expected that AT&T would choose Telmex as its partner. Previous U.S. telecommunications deals with Mexican firms include: *MCI Communications Corp.* and *Grupo Financiero Banamex-Accival*; *Sprint* Corp. and *Grupo Iusacell*; and *GTE Corp.* with *Grupo Financiero Bancomer* and *Valores Industriales SA.*

TEXT OF THE INVESTMENT CHAPTER OF NAFTA

CHAPTER ELEVEN
INVESTMENT

SECTION A - INVESTMENT

Article 1101: Scope and Coverage

1. This Chapter applies to measures adopted or maintained by a Party relating to:
    (a) investors of another Party;
    (b) investments of investors of another Party in the territory of the Party; and
    (c) with respect to Articles 1106 and 1114, all investments in the territory of the Party.
2. A Party has the right to perform exclusively the economic activities set out in Annex III and to refuse to permit the establishment of investment in such activities.
3. This Chapter does not apply to measures adopted or maintained by a Party to the extent that they are covered by Chapter Fourteen (Financial Services).
4. Nothing in this Chapter shall be construed to prevent a Party from providing a service or performing a function such as law enforcement, correctional services, income security or insurance, social security or insurance, social welfare, public education, public training, health, and child care, in a manner that is not inconsistent with this Chapter.

Article 1102: National Treatment

1. Each Party shall accord to investors of another Party treatment no less favorable than that it accords, in like circumstances, to its own investors with respect to the establishment, acquisition, expansion, management, conduct, operation, and sale or other disposition of investments.
2. Each Party shall accord to investments of investors of another Party treatment no less favorable than that it accords, in like circumstances, to investments of its own investors with respect to the establishment, acquisition, expansion, management, conduct, operation, and sale or other disposition of investments.

3.   The treatment accorded by a Party under paragraph 1 and 2 means, with respect to a state or province, treatment no less favorable than the most favorable treatment accorded, in like circumstances, by that state or province to investors, and to investments of investors, of the Party of which it forms a part.

4.   For greater certainty, no Party may:

  (a) impose on an investor of another Party a requirement that a minimum level of equity in an enterprise in the territory of the Party be held by its nationals, other than nominal qualifying shares for directors or incorporators of corporations; or

  (b) require an investor of another Party, by reason of its nationality, to sell or otherwise dispose of an investment in the territory of the Party.

Article 1103: Most-Favored-Nation Treatment

1.   Each Party shall accord to investors of another Party treatment no less favorable than that it accords, in like circumstances, to investors of any other Party or of a non-Party with respect to the establishment, acquisition, expansion, management, conduct, operation, and sale or other disposition of investments.

2.   Each Party shall accord to investments of investors of another Party treatment no less favorable than that it accords, in like circumstances, to investments of investors of any other Party or of a non-Party with respect to the establishment, acquisition, expansion, management, conduct, operation, and sale or other disposition of investments.

Article 1104: Standard of Treatment

Each Party shall accord to investors of another Party and to investments of investors of another Party the better of the treatment required by Articles 1102 and 1103.

Article 1105: Minimum Standard of Treatment

1.   Each Party shall accord to investors of another Party treatment in accordance with international law, including fair and equitable treatment and full protection and security.

2.   Without prejudice to paragraph 1 and notwithstanding Article 1108(7)(b), each Party shall accord to investors of another Party, and to investments of investors of another Party, non-discriminatory treatment with respect to measures it adopts or maintains relating to losses suffered by investments in its territory owing to armed conflict or civil strife.

3.   Paragraph 2 does not apply to existing measures relating to subsidies or grants that would be inconsistent with Article 1102 but for Article 1108(7)(b).

Article 1106: Performance Requirements

1.   No Party may impose or enforce any of the following requirements, or enforce any commitment or undertaking, in connection with the establishment, acquisition, expansion, management, conduct or operation of an investment of an investor of a Party or of a non-Party in its territory:

  (a) to export a given level or percentage of goods or services;

  (b) to achieve a given level or percentage of domestic content;

  (c) to purchase, use or accord a preference to goods produced or services provided in its territory, or to purchase goods or services from persons in its territory;

(d) to relate in any way the volume or value of imports to the volume or value of exports or to the amount of foreign exchange inflows associated with such investment;

(e) to restrict sales of goods or services in its territory that such investment produces or provides by relating such sales in any way to the volume or value of its exports or foreign exchange earnings;

(f) to transfer technology, a production process or other proprietary knowledge to a person in its territory, except when the requirement is imposed or the commitment or undertaking is enforced by a court, administrative tribunal or competition authority to remedy an alleged violation of competition laws or to act in a manner not inconsistent with other provisions of this Agreement; or

(g) to act as the exclusive supplier of the goods it produces or services it provides to a specific region or world market.

2.   A measure that requires an investment to use a technology to meet generally applicable health, safety or environmental requirements shall not be construed to be inconsistent with paragraph 1(f). For greater certainty, Articles 1102 and 1103 apply to the measure.

3.   No Party may condition the receipt or continued receipt of an advantage, in connection with an investment in its territory of an investor of a Party or of a non-Party, on compliance with any of the following requirements:

(a) to achieve a given level or percentage of domestic content;

(b) to purchase, use or accord a preference to goods produced in its territory, or to purchase goods from producers in its territory;

(c) to relate in any way the volume or value of imports to the volume or value of exports or to the amount of foreign exchange inflows associated with such investments;

(d) to restrict sales of goods or services in its territory that such investment produces or provides by relating such sales in any way to the volume or value of its exports or foreign exchange earnings;

4.   Nothing in paragraph 3 shall be construed to prevent a Party from conditioning the receipt or continued receipt of an advantage, in connection with an investment in its territory of an investor of a Party or a non-Party, on compliance with a requirement to locate production, provide a service, train or employ workers, construct or expand particular facilities, or carry out research and development, in its territory.

5.   Paragraphs 1 and 3 do not apply to any requirement other than the requirement set out in those paragraphs.

6.   Provided that such measures are not applied in an arbitrary or unjustifiable manner, or do not constitute a disguised restriction on international trade or investment, nothing in paragraph 1(b) or (c) or 3(a) or (b) shall be construed to prevent any Party from adopting or maintaining measures, including environmental measures;

(a) necessary to secure compliance with laws and regulations that are not inconsistent with the provisions of this Agreement;

(b) necessary to protect human, animal or plant life or health; or

(c) necessary for the conservation of living or non-living exhaustible natural resources.

Article 1107: Senior Management and Boards of Directors

1.   No Party may require that an enterprise of that Party that is an investment of an investor of another Party appoint to senior management positions individuals of any particular nationality.

2.   A Party may require that a majority of the board of directors, or any committee thereof, of an enterprise of that Party that is an investment of an investor of another Party, be of particular nationality, or resident in the territory of the Party, provided that the requirement does not materially impair the ability of the investor to exercise control over its investment.

Article 1108: Reservations and Exceptions

1.   Articles 1102, 1103, 1106 and 1107 do not apply to:
 (a) any existing non-conforming measure that is maintained by
  (i)   a Party at the federal level, as set out in its Schedule to Annex I or III,
  (ii) a state or province, for two years after the date of entry into force of this Agreement, and thereafter as set out by a Party in its Schedule to Annex I in accordance with paragraph 2, or
  (iii) a local government;
 (b) the continuation or prompt renewal of any non-conforming measure referred to in subparagraph (a); or
 (c) an amendment to any non-conforming measure referred to in subparagraph (a) to the extent that the amendment does not decrease the conformity of the measure, as it existed immediately before the amendment, with Articles 1102, 1103, 1106 and 1107.

2.   Each Party may set out in its Schedule to Annex I, within two years of the date of entry into force of this Agreement, any existing non-conforming measure maintained by a state or province, not including a local government.

3.   Articles 1102, 1103, 1106 and 1107 do not apply to any measure that a Party adopts or maintains with respect to sectors, subsectors or activities, as set out in its Schedule to Annex II.

4.   No Party may, under any measure adopted after the date of entry into force of this Agreement and covered by its Schedule to Annex II, require an investor of another Party, by reason of its nationality, to sell or otherwise dispose of an investment existing at the time the measure becomes effective.

5.   Articles 1102 and 1103 do not apply to any measure that is an exception to, or derogation from, the obligation under Article 1703 (Intellectual Property - National Treatment) as specifically provided for in that Article.

6.   Article 1103 does not apply to treatment accorded by a Party pursuant to agreements, or with respect to sectors, set out in its Schedule to Annex IV.

7.   Articles 1102, 1103 and 1107 do not apply to:
 (a) procurement by a Party or a state enterprise; or
 (b) subsidies or grants provided by a Party or a state enterprise, including government-supported loans, guarantees and insurance.

8.   The provisions of:
 (a) Article 1106(1)(a), (b) and (c), and (3)(a) and (b) do not apply to qualification requirements for goods or services with respect to export promotion and foreign aid

programs;

(b) Article 1106(1)(b), (c), (f) and (g), and (3)(a) and (b) do not apply to procurement by a Party or a state enterprise; and

(c) Article 1106(3)(a) and (b) do not apply to requirements imposed by an importing Party relating to the content of goods necessary to qualify for preferential tariffs or preferential quotas.

Article 1109: Transfers

1. Each Party shall permit all transfers relating to an investment of an investor of another Party in the territory of the Party to be made freely and without delay. Such transfers include:

(a) profits, dividends, interest, capital gains, royalty payments, management fees, technical assistance and other fees, returns in kind and other amounts derived from the investment;

(b) proceeds from the sale of all or any part of the investment or from the partial or complete liquidation of the investment;

(c) payments made under a contract entered into by the investor, or its investment, including payments made pursuant to a loan agreement;

(d) payments made pursuant to Article 1110; and

(e) payments arising under Section B.

2. Each Party shall permit transfers to be made in a freely usable currency at the market rate of exchange prevailing on the date of transfer with respect to spot transactions in the currency to be transferred.

3. No Party may require its investors to transfer, or penalize its investors that fail to transfer, the income, earnings, profits or other amounts derived from, or attributable to, investments in the territory of another Party.

4. Notwithstanding paragraphs 1 and 2, a Party may prevent a transfer through the equitable, non-discriminatory and good faith application of its laws relating to:

(a) bankruptcy, insolvency or the protection of the rights of creditors;

(b) issuing, trading or dealing in securities;

(c) criminal or penal offenses;

(d) reports of transfers of currency or other monetary instruments; and

(e) ensuring the satisfaction of judgments in adjudicatory proceedings.

5. Paragraph 3 shall not be construed to prevent a Party from imposing any measure through the equitable, non-discriminatory and good faith application of its laws relating to the matters set out in subparagraphs (a) through (e) of paragraph 4.

6. Notwithstanding paragraph 1, a Party may restrict transfers of returns in kind in circumstances where it could otherwise restrict such transfers under this Agreement, including as set out in paragraph 4.

Article 1110: Expropriation and Compensation

1. No Party may directly or indirectly nationalize or expropriate an investment of an investor of another Party in its territory or take a measure tantamount to nationalization or expropriation of such an investment ("expropriation"), except:

(a) for a public purpose;

(b) on a non-discriminatory basis;

(c) in accordance with due process of law and Article 1105(1); and

(d) on payment of compensation in accordance with paragraphs 2 through 6.

2. Compensation shall be equivalent to the fair market value of the expropriated investment immediately before the expropriation took place ("date of expropriation"), and shall not reflect any change in value occurring because the intended expropriation had become known earlier. Valuation criteria shall include going concern value, asset value including declared tax value of tangible property, and other criteria, as appropriate, to determine fair market value.

3. Compensation shall be paid without delay and be fully realizable.

4. If payment is made in a G7 currency, compensation shall include interest at a commercially reasonable rate for that currency from the date of expropriation until the date of actual payment.

5. If a Party elects to pay in a currency other than a G7 currency, the amount paid on the date of payment, if converted into a G7 currency at the market rate of exchange prevailing on that date, shall be no less than if the amount of compensation owed on the date of expropriation had been converted into that G7 currency at the market rate of exchange prevailing on that date, and interest had accrued at a commercially reasonable rate for that G7 currency from the date of expropriation until the date of payment.

6. On payment, compensation shall be freely transferable as provided in Article 1109.

7. This Article does not apply to the issuance of compulsory licenses granted in relation to intellectual property rights, or to the revocation, limitation or creation of intellectual property rights, to the extent that such issuance, revocation, limitation or creation is consistent with Chapter Seventeen (Intellectual Property).

8. For purposes of this Article and for greater certainty, a non-discriminatory measure of general application shall not be considered a measure tantamount to an expropriation of a debt security or loan governed by this Chapter solely on the ground that the measure imposes costs on the debtor that cause it to default on the debt.

Article 1111: Special Formalities and Information Requirements

1. Nothing in Article 1102 shall be construed to prevent a Party from adopting or maintaining a measure that prescribes special formalities in connection with the establishment of investments by investors of another Party, such as a requirement that investors be residents of the Party or that investments be legally constituted under the laws or regulations of the Party, provided that such formalities do not materially impair the protections afforded by a Party to investors of another Party and investments of investors of another Party pursuant to this Chapter.

2. Notwithstanding Articles 1102 or 1103, a Party may require an investor of another Party, or its investment in its territory, to provide routine information concerning that investment solely for informational or statistical purposes. The Party shall protect such business information that is confidential from any disclosure that would prejudice the competitive position of the investor or the investment. Nothing in this paragraph shall be construed to prevent a Party from otherwise obtaining or disclosing information in connection with the equitable and good faith application of its law.

Article 1112: Relation to Other Chapters

1.   In the event of any inconsistency between this Chapter and another Chapter, the other Chapter shall prevail to the extent of the inconsistency.

2.   A requirement by a Party that a service provider of another Party post a bond or other form of financial security as a condition of providing a service into its territory does not of itself make this Chapter applicable to the provision of that cross-border service. This Chapter applies to that Party's treatment of the posted bond or financial security.

Article 1113: Denial of Benefits

1.   A Party may deny the benefits of this Chapter to an investor of another Party that is an enterprise of such Party and to investments of such investor if investors of a non-Party own or control the enterprise and the denying Party:

    (a)   does not maintain diplomatic relations with the non-Party; or

    (b)   adopts or maintains measures with respect to the non-Party that prohibit transactions with the enterprise or that would be violated or circumvented if the benefits of this Chapter were accorded to the enterprise or to its investments.

2.   Subject to prior notification and consultation in accordance with Articles 1803 (Notification and Provision of Information) and 2006 (Consultations), a Party may deny the benefits of this Chapter to an investor of another Party that is an enterprise of such Party and to investments of such investors if investors of a non-Party own or control the enterprise and the enterprise has no substantial business activities in the territory of the Party under whose law it is constituted or organized.

Article 1114: Environmental Measures

1.   Nothing in this Chapter shall be construed to prevent a Party from adopting, maintaining or enforcing any measure otherwise consistent with this Chapter that it considers appropriate to ensure that investment activity in its territory is undertaken in a manner sensitive to environmental concerns.

2.   The Parties recognize that it is inappropriate to encourage investment by relaxing domestic health, safety or environmental measures. Accordingly, a Party should not waive or otherwise derogate from, or offer to waive or otherwise derogate from, such measures as an encouragement for the establishment, acquisition, expansion or retention in its territory of an investment of an investor. If a Party considers that another Party has offered such an encouragement, it may request consultations with the other Party and the two Parties shall consult with a view to avoiding any such encouragement.

SECTION B - SETTLEMENT OF DISPUTES BETWEEN A PARTY AND AN INVESTOR OF ANOTHER PARTY

Article 1115: Purpose

Without prejudice to the rights and obligations of the Parties under Chapter Twenty (Institutional Arrangements and Dispute Settlement Procedures), this Section establishes a mechanism for the settlement of investment disputes that assures both equal treatment among investors of the Parties in accordance with the principle of international reciprocity and due process before an impartial tribunal.

Article 1116: Claim by an Investor of a Party on Its Own Behalf

1. An investor of a Party may submit to arbitration under this Section a claim that another Party has breached an obligation under:
   (a) Section A or Article 1503(2) (State Enterprises), or
   (b) Article 1502(3)(a) (Monopolies and State Enterprises) where the monopoly has acted in a manner inconsistent with the Party's obligations under Section A,
and that the investor has incurred loss or damage by reason of, or arising out of, that breach.
2. An investor may not make a claim if more than three years have elapsed from the date on which the investor first acquired, or should have first acquired, knowledge of the alleged breach and knowledge that the investor has incurred loss or damage.

Article 1117: Claim by an Investor of a Party on Behalf of an Enterprise

1. An investor of a Party, on behalf of an enterprise of another Party that is a juridical person that the investor owns or controls directly or indirectly, may submit to arbitration under this Section a claim that the other Party has breached an obligation under:
   (a) Section A or Article 1503(2) (State Enterprises), or
   (b) Article 1502(3)(a) (Monopolies and State Enterprises) where the monopoly has acted in a manner inconsistent with the Party's obligations under Section A,
and that the enterprise has incurred loss or damage by reason of, or arising out of, that breach.
2. An investor may not make a claim on behalf of an enterprise described in paragraph 1 if more than three years have elapsed from the date on which the enterprise first acquired, or should have first acquired, knowledge of the alleged breach and knowledge that the enterprise has incurred loss or damage.
3. Where an investor makes a claim under this Article and the investor or a non-controlling investor in the enterprise makes a claim under Article 1116 arising out of the same events that gave rise to the claim under this Article, and two or more of the claims are submitted to arbitration under Article 1120, the claims should be heard together by a Tribunal established under Article 1126, unless the Tribunal finds that the interests of a disputing party would be prejudiced thereby.
4. An investment may not make a claim under this Section.

Article 1118: Settlement of a Claim through Consultation and Negotiation

The disputing parties should first attempt to settle a claim through consultation or negotiation.

Article 1119: Notice of Intent to Submit a Claim to Arbitration

The disputing investor shall deliver to the disputing Party written notice of its intention to submit a claim to arbitration at least 90 days before the claim is submitted, which notice shall specify:
   (a) the name and address of the disputing investor and, where a claim is made under Article 1117, the name and address of the enterprise;

(b) the provisions of this Agreement alleged to have been breached and any other relevant provisions:

(c) the issues and the factual basis for the claim; and

(d) the relief sought and the approximate amount of damages claimed.

Article 1120: Submission of a Claim to Arbitration

1.   Except as provided in Annex 1120.1, and provided that six months have elapsed since the events giving rise to a claim, a disputing investor may submit the claim to arbitration under:

(a) the ICSID Convention, provided that both the disputing Party and the Party of the investor are parties to the Convention;

(b) the Additional Facility Rules of ICSID, provided that either the disputing Party or the Party of the investor, but not both, is a party to the ICSID Convention; or

(c) the UNCITRAL Arbitration Rules.

2.   The applicable arbitration rules shall govern the arbitration except to the extent modified by this Section.

Article 1121: Conditions Precedent to Submission of a Claim to Arbitration

1.   A disputing investor may submit a claim under Article 1116 to arbitration only if:

(a) the investor consents to arbitration in accordance with the procedures set out in this Agreement;

(b) the investor and, where the claim is for loss or damage to an interest in an enterprise of another Party that is a juridical person that the investor owns or controls directly or indirectly, the enterprise, waive their right to initiate or continue before any administrative tribunal or court under the law of any Party, or other dispute settlement procedures, any proceedings with respect to the measure of the disputing Party that is alleged to be a breach referred to in Article 1116, except for proceedings for injunctive, declaratory or other extraordinary relief, not involving the payment of damages, before an administrative tribunal or court under the law of the disputing Party.

2.   A disputing investor may submit a claim under Article 1117 to arbitration only if both the investor and the enterprise:

(a) consent to arbitration in accordance with the procedures set out in this Agreement; and

(b) waive the right to initiate or continue before any administrative tribunal or court under the law of any Party, or other dispute settlement procedures, any proceedings with respect to the measure of the disputing Party that is alleged to be a breach referred to in Article 1117, except for proceedings for injunctive, declaratory or other extraordinary relief, not involving the payment of damages, before an administrative tribunal or court under the law of the disputing Party.

3.   A consent and waiver required by this Article shall be in writing, shall be delivered to the disputing Party and shall be included in the submission of a claim to arbitration.

4.   Only where a disputing Party has deprived a disputing investor of control of an enterprise:

(a) a waiver from the enterprise under paragraph 1(b) or 2(b) shall not be required; and
(c) Annex 1120.1(b) shall not apply.

Article 1122: Consent to Arbitration

1. Each Party consents to the submission of a claim to arbitration in accordance with the procedures set out in this Agreement.
2. The consent given by paragraph 1 and the submission by a disputing investor of a claim to arbitration shall satisfy the requirement of:
   (a) Chapter II of the ICSID Convention (Jurisdiction of the Centre) and the Additional Facility Rules for written consent of the parties;
   (b) Article II of the New York Convention for an agreement in writing; and
   (c) Article I of the Inter-American Convention for an agreement.

Article 1123: Number of Arbitrators and Method of Appointment

Except in respect of a Tribunal established under Article 1126, and unless the disputing parties otherwise agree, the Tribunal shall comprise three arbitrators, one arbitrator appointed by each of the disputing parties and the third, who shall be the presiding arbitrator, appointed by agreement of the disputing parties.

Article 1124: Constitution of a Tribunal When a Party Fails to Appoint an Arbitrator or the Disputing Parties Are Unable to Agree on a Presiding Arbitrator

1. The Secretary-General shall serve as appointing authority for an arbitration under this Section.
2. If a Tribunal, other than a Tribunal established under Article 1126, has not been constituted within 90 days from the date that a claim is submitted to arbitration, the Secretary-General, on the request of either disputing party, shall appoint, in his discretion, the arbitrator or arbitrators not yet appointed, except that the presiding arbitrator shall be appointed in accordance with paragraph 3.
3. The Secretary-General shall appoint the presiding arbitrator from the roster of presiding arbitrators referred to in paragraph 4, provided that the presiding arbitrator shall not be a national of the disputing Party or a national of the Party of the disputing investor. In the event that no such presiding arbitrator is available to serve, the Secretary-General shall appoint, from the ICSID Panel of Arbitrators, a presiding arbitrator who is not a national of any of the Parties.
4. On the date of entry into force of this Agreement, the Parties shall establish, and thereafter maintain, a roster of 45 presiding arbitrators meeting the qualifications of the Convention and rules referred to in Article 1120 and experienced in international law and investment matters. The roster members shall be appointed by consensus and without regard to nationality.

Article 1125: Agreement to Appointment of Arbitrators

For purposes of Article 39 of the ICSID Convention and Article 7 of Schedule C to the ICSID Additional Facility Rules, and without prejudice to an objection to an arbitrator based on Article 1124(3) or on ground other than nationality:

(a) the disputing Party agrees to the appointment of each individual member of a Tribunal established under the ICSID Convention or the ICSID Additional Facility Rules;

(b) a disputing investor referred to in Article 1116 may submit a claim to arbitration, or continue a claim, under the ICSID Convention or the ICSID Additional Facility Rules, only on condition that the disputing investor agrees in writing to the appointment of each individual member of the Tribunal; and

(c) a disputing investor referred to in Article 1117(1) may submit a claim to arbitration, or continue a claim, under the ICSID Convention or the ICSID Additional Facility Rules, only on condition that the disputing investor and the enterprise agree in writing to the appointment of each individual member of the Tribunal.

Article 1126: Consolidation

1. A Tribunal established under this Article shall be established under the UNCITRAL Arbitration Rules and shall conduct its proceedings in accordance with those Rules, except as modified by this Section.

2. Where a Tribunal established under this Article is satisfied that claims have been submitted to arbitration under Article 1120 that have a question of law or fact in common the Tribunal may, in the interest of fair and efficient resolution of the claims, and after hearing the disputing parties, by order:

(a) assume jurisdiction over, and hear and determine together, all or part of the claims; or

(b) assume jurisdiction over, and hear and determine one or more of the claims, the determination of which it believes would assist in the resolution of the others.

3. A disputing party that seeks an order under paragraph 2 shall request the Secretary-General to establish a Tribunal and shall specify in the request:

(a) the name of the disputing Party or disputing investors against which the order is sought;

(b) the nature of the order sought; and

(c) the grounds on which the order is sought.

4. The disputing party shall deliver to the disputing Party or disputing investors against which the order is sought a copy of the request.

5. Within 60 days of receipt of the request, the Secretary-General shall establish a Tribunal comprising three arbitrators. The Secretary-General shall appoint the presiding arbitrator from the roster referred to in Article 1124(4). In the event that no such presiding arbitrator is available to serve, the Secretary-General shall appoint, from the ICSID Panel of Arbitrators, a presiding arbitrator who is not a national of any of the Parties. The Secretary-General shall appoint the two other members from the roster referred to in Article 1124(4), and to the extent not available from that roster, from the ICSID Panel of Arbitrators, and to the extent not available from that Panel, in the discretion of the Secretary-General. One member shall be a national of the disputing Party and one member shall be a national of a Party of the disputing investors.

6. Where a Tribunal has been established under this Article, a disputing investor that has submitted a claim to arbitration under Article 1116 or 1117 and that has not been named in a request made under paragraph 3 may make a written request to the Tribunal that it be

included in an order made under paragraph 2, and shall specify in the request:
  (a) the name and address of the disputing investor;
  (b) the nature of the order sought; and
  (c) the grounds on which the order is sought.
7.   A disputing investor referred to in paragraph 6 shall deliver a copy of its request to the disputing parties named in a request made under paragraph 3.
8.   A Tribunal established under Article 1120 shall not have jurisdiction to decide a claim, or a part of a claim, over which a Tribunal established under this Article has assumed jurisdiction.
9.   On application of a disputing party, a Tribunal established under this Article, pending its decision under paragraph 2, may order that the proceedings of a Tribunal established under Article 1120 be stayed, unless the latter Tribunal has already adjourned its proceedings.
10. A disputing Party shall deliver to the Secretariat, within 15 days of receipt by the disputing Party, a copy of:
  (a) a request for arbitration made under paragraph (1) of Article 36 of the ICSID Convention;
  (b) a notice of arbitration made under Article 2 of Schedule C of the ICSID Additional Facility Rules; or
  (c) a notice of arbitration given under the UNCITRAL Arbitration Rules.
11. A disputing Party shall deliver to the Secretariat a copy of a request made under paragraph 3:
  (a) within 15 days of receipt of the request, in the case of a request made by a disputing investor;
  (b) within 15 days of making the request, in the case of a request made by the disputing Party.
12. A disputing Party shall deliver to the Secretariat a copy of a request made under paragraph 6 within 15 days of receipt of the request.
13. The Secretariat shall maintain a public register of the documents referred to in paragraphs 10, 11 and 12.

Article 1127: Notice
A disputing Party shall deliver to the other Parties:
  (a) written notice of a claim that has been submitted to arbitration no later than 30 days after the date that the claim is submitted; and
  (b) copies of all pleadings filed in the arbitration.

Article 1128: Participation by a Party
On written notice to the disputing parties, a Party may make submissions to a Tribunal on a question of interpretation of this Agreement.

Article 1129: Documents
1.   A Party shall be entitled to receive from the disputing Party, at the cost of the requesting Party a copy of:
  (a) the evidence that has been tendered to the Tribunal; and
  (b) the written argument of the disputing parties.

2.   A Party receiving information pursuant to paragraph 1 shall treat the information as if it were a disputing Party.

Article 1130: Place of Arbitration

Unless the disputing parties agree otherwise, a Tribunal shall hold an arbitration in the territory of a Party that is a party to the New York Convention, selected in accordance with:
  (a) the ICSID Additional Facility Rules if the arbitration is under those Rules or the ICSID Convention;
  (b) the UNCITRAL Arbitration Rules if the arbitration is under those Rules.

Article 1131: Governing Law

1.   A Tribunal established under this Section shall decide the issues in dispute in accordance with this Agreement and applicable rules of international law.
2.   An interpretation by the Commission of a provision of this Agreement shall be binding on a Tribunal established under this Section.

Article 1132: Interpretation of Annexes

1. Where a disputing Party asserts as a defense that the measure alleged to be a breach is within the scope of a reservation or exception set out in Annex I, Annex II, Annex III or Annex IV, on request of the disputing Party, the Tribunal shall request the interpretation of the Commission on the issue. The Commission, within 60 days of delivery of the request, shall submit in writing its interpretation to the Tribunal.
2.   Further to Article 1131(2), a Commission interpretation submitted under paragraph 1 shall be binding on the Tribunal. If the Commission fails to submit an interpretation within 60 days, the Tribunal shall decide the issue.

Article 1133: Expert Reports

Without prejudice to the appointment of other kinds of experts where authorized by the applicable arbitration rules, a Tribunal, at the request of a disputing party or, unless the disputing parties disapprove, on its own initiative, may appoint one or more experts to report to it in writing on any factual issue concerning environmental, health, safety or other scientific matters raised by a disputing party in a proceeding, subject to such terms and conditions as the disputing parties may agree.

Article 1134: Interim Measures of Protection

A Tribunal may order an interim measure of protection to preserve the rights of a disputing party, or to ensure that the Tribunal's jurisdiction is made fully effective, including an order to preserve evidence in the possession or control of a disputing party or to protect the Tribunal's jurisdiction. A Tribunal may not order attachment or enjoin the application of the measure alleged to constitute a breach referred to in Article 1116 or 1117. For purposes of this paragraph, an order includes a recommendation.

Article 1135: Final Award

1.   Where a Tribunal makes a final award against a Party, the Tribunal may award, separately or in combination, only:

(a) monetary damages and any applicable interest;

(b) restitution of property, in which case the award shall provide that the disputing Party may pay monetary damages and any applicable interest in lieu of restitution.

A Tribunal may also award costs in accordance with the applicable arbitration rules.

2. Subject to paragraph 1, where a claim is made under Article 1117(1):

(a) an award of restitution of property shall provide that restitution be made to the enterprise;

(b) an award of monetary damages and any applicable interest shall provide that the sum be paid to the enterprise; and

(c) the award shall provide that it is made without prejudice to any right that any person may have in the relief under applicable domestic law.

2. A Tribunal may not order a Party to pay punitive damages.

Article 1136: Finality and Enforcement of an Award

1. An award made by a Tribunal shall have no binding force except between the disputing parties and in respect of the particular case.

2. Subject to paragraph 3 and the applicable review procedure for an interim award, a disputing party shall abide by and comply with an award without delay.

3. A disputing party may not seek enforcement of a final award until:

(a) in the case of a final award made under the ICSID Convention

(i) 120 days have elapsed from the date the award was rendered and no disputing party has requested revision or annulment of the award, or

(ii) revision or annulment proceedings have been completed; and

(b) in the case of a final award under the ICSID Additional Facility Rules or the UNCITRAL Arbitration Rules

(i) three months have elapsed from the date the award was rendered and no disputing party has commenced a proceeding to revise, set aside or annul the award, or

(ii) a court has dismissed or allowed an application to revise, set aside or annul the award and there is no further appeal.

4. Each Party shall provide for the enforcement of an award in its territory.

5. If a disputing Party fails to abide by or comply with a final award, the Commission, on delivery of a request by a Party whose investor was a party to the arbitration, shall establish a panel under Article 2008 (Request for an Arbitral Panel). The requesting Party may seek in such proceedings:

(a) a determination that the failure to abide by or comply with the final award is inconsistent with the obligations of this Agreement; and

(b) a recommendation that the Party abide by or comply with the final award.

6. A disputing investor may seek enforcement of an arbitration award under the ICSID Convention, the New York Convention or the Inter-American Convention regardless of whether proceedings have been taken under paragraph 5.

7. A claim that is submitted to arbitration under this Section shall be considered to arise out of a commercial relationship or transaction for purposes of Article I of the New York Convention and Article I of the Inter-American Convention.

Article 1137: General

Time when a Claim is Submitted to Arbitration

1. A claim is submitted to arbitration under this Section when:
   (a) the request for arbitration under paragraph (1) of Article 36 of the ICSID Convention has been received by the Secretary-General;
   (b) the notice of arbitration under Article 2 of Schedule C of the ICSID Additional Facility Rules has been received by the Secretary-General; or
   (c) the notice of arbitration given under the UNCITRAL Arbitration Rules is received by the disputing Party.

Service of Documents

2. Delivery of notice and other documents on a Party shall be made to the place named for that Party in Annex 1137.2.

Receipts under Insurance or Guarantee Contracts

3. In an arbitration under this Section, a Party shall not assert, as a defense, counterclaim, right of setoff or otherwise, that the disputing investor has received or will receive, pursuant to an insurance or guarantee contract, indemnification or other compensation for all or part of its alleged damages.

Publication of an Award

4. Annex 1137.4 applies to the Parties specified in that Annex with respect to publication of an award.

Article 1138: Exclusions

1. Without prejudice to the applicability or non-applicability of the dispute settlement provisions of this Section or of Chapter Twenty (Institutional Arrangements and Dispute Settlement Procedures) to other actions taken by a Party pursuant to Article 2102 (National Security), a decision by a Party to prohibit or restrict the acquisition of an investment in its territory by an investor of another Party, or its investment, pursuant to that Article shall not be subject to such provisions.

2. The dispute settlement provisions of this Section and of Chapter Twenty shall not apply to the matters referred to in Annex 1138.2.

SECTION C - DEFINITIONS

Article 1139: Definitions

For purposes of this Chapter:

disputing investor means an investor that makes a claim under Section B;

disputing parties means the disputing investor and the disputing Party;

disputing party means the disputing investor or the disputing Party;

disputing Party means a Party against which a claim is made under Section B;

enterprise means an "enterprise" as defined in Article 201 (Definitions of General Application), and a branch of an enterprise;

enterprise of a Party means an enterprise constituted or organized under the law of a Party, and a branch located in the territory of a Party and carrying out business activities there;

equity or debt securities includes voting and non-voting shares, bonds, convertible debentures, stock options and warrants;

G7 Currency means the currency of Canada, France, Germany, Italy, Japan, the United Kingdom of Great Britain and Northern Ireland or the United States;

ICSID means the International Centre for Settlement of Disputes;

ICSID Convention means the *Convention on the Settlement of Investment Disputes between States and Nationals of other States*, done at Washington, March 18, 1965;

Inter-American Convention means the *Inter-American Convention on International Commercial Arbitration*, done at Panama, January 30, 1975;

investment means:
  (a) an enterprise;
  (b) an equity security of an enterprise;
  (c) a debt security of an enterprise
      (i) where the enterprise is an affiliate of the investor, or
      (ii) where the original maturity of the debt security is at least three years,
      but does not include a debt security, regardless of original maturity, of a state enterprise;
  (d) a loan to an enterprise
      (i) where the enterprise is an affiliate of the investor, or
      (ii) where the original maturity of the loan is at least three years,
      but does not include a loan, regardless of original maturity, to a state enterprise;
  (e) an interest in an enterprise that entitles the owner to share in income or profits of the enterprise;
  (f) an interest in an enterprise that entitles the owner to share in the assets of that enterprise on dissolution, other than a debt security or a loan excluded from subparagraph (c) or (d);
  (g) real estate or other property, tangible or intangible, acquired in the expectation or used for the purpose of economic benefit or other business purposes; and
  (h) interests arising from the commitment of capital or other resources in the territory of a Party to economic activity in such territory, such as under
      (i) contracts involving the presence of an investor's property in the territory of the Party, including turnkey or construction contracts, or concessions, or
      (ii) contracts where renumeration depends substantially on the production, revenues or profits of an enterprise;
but investment does not mean,
  (i) claims to money that arise solely from
      (i) commercial contracts for the sale of goods or services by a national or enterprise in the territory of a Party to an enterprise in the territory of another Party, or
      (ii) the extension of credit in connection with a commercial transaction, such as trade financing, other than a loan covered by subparagraph (d); or

(j) any other claims to money,

that do not involve the kinds of interests set out in subparagraph (a) through (h);

investment of an investor of a Party means an investment owned or controlled directly or indirectly by an investor of such Party;

investor of a Party means a Party or state enterprise thereof, or a national or an enterprise of such Party, that seeks to make, is making or has made an investment;

investor of a non-Party means an investor other an investor of a Party, that seeks to make, is making or has made an investment;

New York Convention means the *United Nations Convention on the Recognition and Enforcement of Foreign Arbitral Awards*, done at New York, June 10, 1958;

Secretary-General means the Secretary-General of ICSID;

transfers means transfers and international payments;

Tribunal means an arbitration tribunal established under Article 1120 or 1126; and

UNCITRAL Arbitration Rules means the arbitration rules of the United Nations Commission on International Trade Law, approved by the United Nations General Assembly on December 15, 1976.

ANNEX 1120.1
SUBMISSION OF A CLAIM TO ARBITRATION

Mexico

With respect to the submission of a claim to arbitration:

(a) an investor of another Party may not allege that Mexico has breached an obligation under:

(i)   Section A or Article 1503(2) (State Enterprises), or

(ii)   Article 1502(3)(a) (Monopolies and State Enterprises) where the monopoly has acted in a manner inconsistent with the Party's obligations under Section A,

both in an arbitration under this Section and in proceedings before a Mexican court or administrative tribunal; and

(b) where an enterprise of Mexico that is a juridical person that investor of another Party owns or controls directly or indirectly alleges in proceedings before a Mexican court or administrative tribunal that Mexico has breached an obligation under:

(i)   Section A or Article 1503(2) (State Enterprises), or

(ii)   Article 1502(3)(a) (Monopolies and State Enterprises) where the monopoly has acted in a manner inconsistent with the Party's obligations under Section A,

the investor may not allege the breach in an arbitration under this Section.

ANNEX 1137.2
SERVICE OF DOCUMENTS ON A PARTY UNDER SECTION B

Each Party shall set out in this Annex and publish in its official journal by January 1, 1994, the place of delivery of notice and other documents under this Section.

ANNEX 1137.4
PUBLICATION OF AN AWARD

Canada

Where Canada is the disputing Party, either Canada or a disputing investor that is a party to the arbitration may make an award public.

Mexico

Where Mexico is the disputing Party, the applicable arbitration rules apply to the publication of an award.

United States

Where the United States is the disputing Party, either the United States or a disputing investor that is a party to the arbitration may make an award public.

ANNEX 1138.2
EXCLUSIONS FROM DISPUTE SETTLEMENT

Canada

A decision by Canada following a review under the *Investment Canada Act*, with respect to whether or not to permit an acquisition that is subject to review, shall not be subject to the dispute settlement provisions of Section B or of Chapter Twenty (Institutional Arrangements and Dispute Settlement Procedures).

Mexico

A decision by the National Commission on Foreign Investment ("Comisión Nacional de Inversiones Extranjeras") following a review pursuant to Annex I, page I-M-4, with respect to whether or not to permit an acquisition that is subject to review, shall not be subject to the dispute settlement provisions of Section B or of Chapter Twenty.

BIBILIOGRAPHY ON NAFTA AND INVESTMENT

by Dean C. Alexander*

Aparicio, Francisco J. & David J. Cibrian, *New Mexican Law and NAFTA Encourage Foreign Investments*, Los Angeles Daily Journal, March 28, 1994, at 7.

Arthur Andersen, *The Arthur Andersen North American Business Sourcebook*, Triumph Books (1994).

Baker & McKenzie, *1993 Guide to Foreign Investors in Mexico* (1994).

Berckholtz, Pablo, *Inversión Extranjera en America Latina: Aspectos Legales*, Hammurabi Press (1991).

Bryan, Gonzalez, Vargas y Gonzalez Baz, S.C., *Amendments to the Maquila Decree*, 16 International Lawyers' Newsletter 9-10 (1994).

Bryan, Gonzalez, Vargas y Gonzalez Baz, S.C., *Mexican Federation Enacts New Foreign Investment Law*, 16 International Lawyer 6 (1994).

Calvo, Nicolau Enrique, *Mexican Taxes on Foreign Investment and Trade*, 12 Houston Journal of International Law 265 (1990).

Camil, Jorge, *Mexico's 1989 Foreign Investment Regulations: The Cornerstone of a New Economic Model*, 12 Houston Journal of International Law 1 (1989).

---

* Director, The NAFTA Research Institute, Washington, D.C.

Camp, Jr., Hope H., Jaime Alvarez Garibay, & C. Lee Cusenbary, *Foreign Investment in Mexico From the Perspective of the Foreign Investor*, 24 St. Mary's Law Journal 775 (1993).

Carrillo, Arturo, *The New Mexican Revolution: Economic Reform and the 1989 Regulations of the Law for the Promotion of Mexican Investment and the Regulation of Foreign Investment*, 24 George Washington Journal of International Law and Economics 647 (1991).

Chayet, Zack C. & Eduardo A. Bustamante, *The Mexican Maquiladora Industry: Legal Framework of the 1990s*, 20 California Western International Law Journal 263 (1990).

Clayton, Tomas Anthony, Jose Humberto Diaz-Guerrero, Jose Trinidad Garcia-Cervantes, *Foreign Investment In Mexico: Mexico Welcomes Foreign Investors*, 12 Chicano Latino Law Review 12 (1992).

Diaz, Luis Miguel, *Globalización de las Inversiónes Extranjeras: Nuevos Aspectos Jurídicas*, Editorial Themis (1989).

DuMars, Charles T., *Liberalization of Foreign Investment Policies in Mexico: Legal Changes Encouraging New Direct Foreign Investment*, 21 New Mexcio Law Review 251 (1991).

Foreign Investment, *Mexico Business: The Portable Encyclopedia For Doing Business With Mexico*, World Trade Press (1994).

Gomez-Palacio, Ignacio, *The New Regulation on Foreign Investment: A Difficult Task*, 12 Houston Journal of International Law 253 (1990).

Hodgins, David B., *Mexico's 1989 Foreign Investment Regulations: A Significant Step Forward, But Is It Enough?*, 12 Houston Journal of International Law 361 (1990).

Hufbauer, Gary Clyde & Jeffrey J. Schott, *NAFTA: An Assessment*, Institute for International Economics (1993).

Hufbauer, Gary Clyde & Jeffrey J. Schott, *North American Free Trade: Issues and Recommendations*, Institute for International Economics (1992).

Jauregui-Rojas, Miguel, *Liberalization of Foreign Investment in Mexico: Present and Future Challenges*, Private International Abroad - Problems & Solutions in International Business, 2-1 (21) Annual 1992.

Kaye, Dionisio J., *Mexico: Liberalizing Foreign Investment*, 4 Temple International & Comparative Law Journal 79 (1990).

Kepner Jr., Hayden J., *Mexico's New Foreign Investment Regulations: A Legal Analysis*, 18 Syracuse Journal of International Law & Commerce 41 (1992).

Kimball, Jr., Dale A., *Secondary and Tertiary Petroleum Operations in Mexico: New Foreign Investment Opportunities*, 25 Texas International Law Journal 411 (1990).

Koslow, Lawrence E., *Mexican Foreign Investment Laws: An Overview*, 18 William Mitchell Law Review 441 (1992).

Marrero, Guillermo, *Mexican Reforms Under Way; Increased Foreign Investment is the Goal*, National Law Journal, December 6, 1993, at 25.

Mexican Tax, Customs and Foreign Investment Laws, CCH Incorporated (1994).

Mexico, Investment and Trade: Progress and Prospects, Practising Law Institute (1993).

Migrations Impacts of Trade and Foreign Investment: Mexico and Caribbean Basin Countries, Westview Press (1991).

Murphy, Jr., Ewell E., *The Dilemma of Hydrocarbon Investment in Mexico's Accession to the North American Free Trade Agreement*, 9 Journal of Energy & Natural Resources Law 261 (1991).

Nelson, Steven C., *NAFTA Provisions for Settlement of Investment Disputes: A Commentary*, American Conference Institute Program on NAFTA, December 1992.

Paul, Hastings, Janofsky & Walker, *North American Free Trade Agreement: Summary and Analysis*, Matthew Bender (1994).

Peres, Wilson, *Foreign Direct Investment and Industrial Development in Mexico*, Development Center of the Organization for Economic Cooperation and Development (1990).

Price, Daniel M., *An Overview of the NAFTA Investment Chapter: Substantive Rules and Investor-State Dispute Settlement*, 27 International Lawyer 727 (1993).

Rojas, Hector, *Governmental Approval of Foreign Investors Owning More Than a Minority Share in Mexican Corporations*, 19 Southwestern University Law Review 1179 (1990).

Rubin, Seymour J. & Dean C. Alexander, *Why Mexico Should Join The Multilateral Investment Guarantee Agency*, Trade & Culture, Winter 1993-94, at 117.

Sanchez, Fernando Ugarte, *Mexico's New Foreign Investment Climate*, 12 Houston Journal of International Law 361 (1990).

Sandrino, Gloria L., *The NAFTA Investment Chapter and Foreign Direct Investment in Mexico: A Third World Perspective*, 27 Vanderbilt Journal of Transnational Law 259 (1994).

Santamarina, Agustin V., *A Practical Outline of the Foreign Investment Laws, Regulations and Policies of Mexico*, Private Investors Abroad - Problems and Solutions in International Business, 6-1(30) Annual 1990.

Schechter, Cheryl & David Brill, Jr., *Maquiladoras: Will the Program Continue?*, 23 St. Mary's Law Journal 697 (1992).

Stephenson, Matilde K., *Mexico's Maquiladora Program: Challenges and Prospects*, 22 St. Mary's Law Journal 589 (1991).

Torres Landa R., Juan Francisco, *The Changing Times: Foreign Investment in Mexico*, 23 New York University Journal of International Law & Politics 801 (1991).

Turro, John, *Mexican Maquiladoras Provide Backdoor to U.S. Market*, Tax Notes International, October 1990, at 1013.

Twomey, Michael J., *Multinational Corporations and the North American Free Trade Agreement*, Praeger (1993).

U.S. Department of the Treasury, Office of International Trade, *NAFTA Limitation on Drawback, Elimination of Maquila Sales Restrictions and Export Performance Requirements* (1992).

U.S. General Accounting Office, *North American Free Trade Agreement: U.S.-Mexican Trade and Investment Data*, GAO/GGD-92-131 (September 1992).

U.S. General Accounting Office, *The Maquiladora Industry and U.S. Employment*, GAO/GGD-93-129 (July 1993).

U.S. International Trade Commission, *Production Sharing: U.S. Imports Under Harmonized Tariff Schedule Subheadings 9802.00.60 and 9802.00.80, 1988-1991*, U.S. ITC Pub. 2592 (February 1993).

U.S. International Trade Commission, *Potential Impact on the U.S. Economy and Selected Industries of the North American Free-Trade Agreement*, U.S. ITC Pub. 2596 (January 1993).

Voigt, David, *The Maquiladora Problem in the Age of NAFTA: Where Will We Find Solutions?*, 2 Minnesota Journal of Global Trade 323 (1992).
von Wobester, Claus & Kathleen Burguete, *New Mexican Foreign Investment Regulations*, 17 International Business Lawyer 519(5) (1989).

Whiting, Van R., *The Political Economy of Foreign Investment in Mexico: Nationalism, Liberalism, and Constraints on Choice*, Johns Hopkins University Press (1992).

ABOUT THE AUTHORS

Dean C. Alexander, an attorney, is the Director of The NAFTA Research Institute in Washington, D.C. He is co-editor of the *NAFTA Law & Policy Series* of Martinus Nijhoff Publishers and co-authored the book *Prospects of a U.S.-Chile Free Trade Agreement* (1994, Martinus Nijhoff Publishers).

Preston Brown is a partner at the Washington, D.C. office of the law firm Curtis, Mallet-Prevost, Colt & Mosle.

Luis Dodero is the Vice President and General Counsel of the Multilateral Investment Guarantee, the World Bank Group in Washington, D.C.

Kent S. Foster is Of Counsel at the law firm Sharretts, Paley, Carter & Blauvelt, P.C. and President of Global Communications Systems, Inc. in Washington, D.C. He co-authored the book *Prospects of a U.S.-Chile Free Trade Agreement* (1994, Martinus Nijhoff Publishers).

Carolyn Karr is an attorney with the U.S. Agency for International Development (AID) in Washington, D.C. Formerly she served as an associate at the Washington, D.C. office of the law firm Curtis, Mallet-Prevost, Colt & Mosle.

Tim Kennish is a partner at the law firm of Osler, Hoskin, Harcourt in Toronto, Ontario, Canada. He has written extensively on NAFTA and Investment.

Roberto L. Mayorga is a foreign legal consultant at the law firm Andrews & Kurth in Washington, D.C. and a partner at the Santiago, Chile law firm Urrutia & Co. Formerly, he served as Executive Vice President and General Counsel at the Foreign Investment Committee of Chile. He and Luis Montt co-authored the book *Foreign Investment in Chile* (1995, Martinus Nijhoff Publishers.)

Jorge Luis Ramos Uriarte is an attorney at the Ministry of Commerce and Industrial Promotion (SECOFI) in Mexico City. A Mexican trained attorney, he obtained an LL.M. degree from the National Law Center, George Washington University in Washington, D.C.

Rich Robins currently serves on the law faculty at the National Autonomous University of Mexico's Instituto de Investigaciones Jurídicas in Mexico City. He graduated from the University of Virginia School of Law, spent a semester on a fellowship with the law faculty at the University of Monterrey in Monterrey, Mexico before accepting his present one in Mexico City.

Seymour J. Rubin is Professor Emeritus at the Washington College of Law, American University; Senior Consultant and Honorary Vice President at the American Society of International Law; and Member, Inter-American Juridical Committee. He has written extensively on various aspects of international law. He is co-editor of the *NAFTA Law & Policy Series* of Martinus Nijhoff Publishers.

Jorge Witker is a licensed attorney serving as a NAFTA arbitration panelist. He also serves on the law faculty at the National Autonomous University of Mexico's Instituto de Investigaciones Jurídicas in Mexico City. In addition, he is a permanent member of Mexico's national organization of Investigadores of the Secretary of Public Education. Dr. Witker is widely-recognized as one of Mexico's leading authorities on foreign investment law.

INDEX

Agricultural sector, 148-151
  alcoholic beverages, 148
  citrus products, 148
  cotton, 148
  cut flowers, 148
  dairy products, 149
  fish, 149
  fruit, 150
  grains, 149
  livestock, 149-150
  lumber/wood products, 150
  meat, 149-150
  oilseeds, 149
  peanuts, 150
  poultry, 150
  sugar, 151
  vegetables, 151
Annex II exemptions, 28-30
Apparel, 157
Arbitration
  choice of options, 30-31
  precedents, 33
Automotive goods
  Mexico, 143-145

Automotive products, 152

Banking, 158
Bearings, 152
Bibliography, 237-244

Canada
  changing investment policies, 4
  cultural heritage, 8
  "direct" acquisition, 11
  FIRA, 5
  formation, 5
  historical background, 4-6
  ICA, 8-13
    exemptions, 9-10
    investments requiring review
    and approval, 10-11
  limits, 12-13
  loans from Great Britain, 5-6
  national identity, 8
  national legislation, 8-13
  "net benefit", 12
  notifications, 10
  Sensitive Sectors, 9

Canada-United States Free Trade
    Agreement, 15-18
    cultural industries, 17-18
    dispute resolution, 17
    national treatment, 15
    review thresholds, 16
    transfer of profits, 16-17
Canadian foreign investment laws
    and policies, 3-18
Canadian perspectives, 1-35
Ceramic floors/wall tiles, 152
Chemicals, 153
Chile, 179-184
    constitutional entities, 183-184
    enterprise regime, 180-181
    institutional bases of economic
        model, 179-184
    property regime, 179-180
    social market economy, 182-183
    state regime, 181-182
    treatment of foreign investment,
        179-184
Computers, 153
Construction, 158
Cultural industries
    meaning, 17-18

Electricity transmission, 153-154
Electronics, 153
Energy, 154
Engineering, 158
Environmental measures, 27

Flat glass, 154
Foreign investment in Mexico
    under NAFTA, 85-109
    constitutional framework, 86-87
    Execution of Treaties Law,
        90-92

Foreign Investment Law 1973,
    87-88
Foreign Investment Law 1993,
    92-98
    general rule, 93
    neutral investment, 94-95
    real estate, 95-97
    restricted activities, 93-94
    sanctions, 97
    transitory articles, 97-98
Foreign Investment Law
    Regulations 1989, 88-90
legal framework, 86-92
NAFTA, 98-108
    compensation, 106-107
    expropriation, 106-107
    foreign ownership, 101-103
    investment and the
        environment, 105-106
    investor-state dispute
        settlement, 107-108
    most-favored-nation treatment,
        100-101
    national treatment, 100
    performance requirements,
        103-104
    transfers, 105
rules prior to 1973, 87

General investment provisions,
    19-30
    Annex II exemptions, 28-30
    application, 19
    boards of directors, 22
    compensation, 26
    cultural industries, 28
    environmental measures, 27
    exceptions, 22-24
    expropriation, 26

formalities, 26
information requirements, 26
"investment", 19
"investors of a Party", 23
most-favored-nation treatment, 20
national security, 28
national treatment, 20
non-discriminatory treatment, 21
performance requirements, 21-22
reservations, 22-24
senior management, 22
social services, 24
transfers, 25-26
treatment in accordance with
  international law, 21
uranium mining properties,
  23-24

Household appliances, 154-155
Household glassware, 155

ICSID, 30-31
Industrial machinery, 155-156
Insurance, 159
  Mexico, 142-143
Intellectual property
  Mexico, 139-140
Investment
  meaning, 19
Investment Chapter, 1-2, 219-236
  boards of directors, 222
  compensation, 223
  coverage, 219
  definitions, 233-235
  denial of benefits, 225
  environmental measures, 225
  exceptions, 222-223

exclusions from dispute
  settlement, 230
expropriation, 223
information requirements, 224
minimum standard of treatment,
  220
most-favored-nation treatment,
  220
national treatment, 219-220
performance requirements,
  220-221
publication of award, 236
relation to other Chapters, 225
reservations, 222-223
scope, 219
senior management, 222
service of documents, 236
settlement of disputes, 225-233
  agreement to appointment of
  arbitrators, 228-229
  appointment of arbitrators,
  228
  claim by investor of party on
  behalf of enterprise, 226
  claim by investor of party on
  own behalf, 226
  conditions precedent to
  submission of claim to
  arbitration, 227-228
  consent to arbitration, 228
  consolidation, 229-230
  consultation, 226
  disagreement as to presiding
  arbitrator, 228
  documents, 230-231
  enforcement of award, 232
  exclusions, 233
  expert reports, 231

failure to appoint arbitrator,
    228
final award, 231-232
finality of award, 232
governing law, 231
interim measures of
    protection, 231
negotiation, 226
notice, 230
notice of intent to submit
    claim to arbitration, 226-227
number of arbitrators, 228
participation by party, 230
place of arbitration, 231
publication of award, 233
purpose, 225-226
service of documents, 233
submission of claim to
    arbitration, 227
special formalities, 224
standard of treatment, 220
submission of claim to
    arbitration, 235
transfers, 223
Investor dispute resolution, 30-34
arbitration procedures, 33
choice of arbitration options,
    30-31
eligibility requirements, 32-33
enforcement of awards, 34
exception for disapproved
    acquisitions, 34
finality, 34
preconditions to recourse, 32-33

Land ownership
Mexico, 129-130

Maquiladora, 7, 37-63
Article 1106 NAFTA, 63
background, 50-51
customs regulations, 39
Decree of 1989, 43-49
    administrative procedures, 44
    export quotas, 45
    immigration, 48
    import specifications, 45
    obligations, 46-47
    purposes, 43
    sales in domestic market,
        47-48
    sanctions, 48-49
    shrinkage, 45-46
    termination, 48-49
    transfers, 48
    waste, 45-46
    Working Program, 44
history, 37-40
Mexican regulation, 41-49
Mexican trade policy, and, 49-55
NAFTA, and, 52-55
    Chapter 3, 53-54
    Chapter 11, 54-55
    summary of provisions, 52-53
origin, 38
overview, 65-83
real estate, 60
regulation in Mexico after
    NAFTA, 55-59
    administrative procedures, 56
    currency requirements, 58-59
    Decree of 1989 as amended,
        55-59
    definitions, 55-56
    environmental matters, 59
    export quotas, 58
    import specifications, 58

sales in domestic market,
56-58
sanctions, 59
transfers, 59
Regulations before 1989, 41-43
structure, 40-41
taxes, 60-62
transformation under NAFTA,
37-63
Mexican foreign investment laws
and practices, 3-18
Mexico, 6-7
amendments to Maquila Decree,
79-81
bibliography, 81
attractive features for foreign
investors, 112-116
automotive goods, 143-145
cheap labor, 120-122
Constitution, 6-7
emerging market, 112-116
financial industry breakthroughs,
141-142
Foreign Investment Law 1993,
65-83
bibliography, 79
eighth title, 75-76
fifth title, 71-72
first title, 66-69
fourth title, 71
objective, 66-67
overview, 66
reserved activities, 67
second title, 69-70
seventh title, 73-75
sixth title, 72-73
specific regulation, 67-69
third title, 70
transitional provisions, 77-79

Foreign Investment Regulatory
Scheme, 111-145
foreign investment under
NAFTA. *See* Foreign
investment under NAFTA
foreign investments, 116
illiteracy, 121-122
insurance, 142-143
intellectual property, 139-140
lack of aperture, 128-130
lack of reliable data, 123
land ownership, 129-130
minerals, 126
NAFTA: catalyst for reform,
117-120
Calvo doctrine, 118-119
national treatment, 118-120
success of US, 117-118
National Foreign Investment
Commission, 72-73
national legislation, 13-14
national sovereignty, 128
new economic policies, 115
Pemex, 132-133
petroleum, 131-134
population, 113
post 1994 elections, 111-145
potentially less-stringent
environmentalism, 127-128
quality of products, 125
telecommunications, 136-139
Telmex, 136-139
trading partners, 114-115
transportation breakthroughs,
134-136
wages, 125
workers' rights, 121

Multilateral Investment Guarantee
  Agency (MIGA), 161-178
  advisory services, 171-172
  application for guarantee,
    168-169, 178
  breach of contract, 166
  civil disturbance, 166
  claims, 169-170
  contracts of guarantee
    outstanding, 176-177
  coverage of political risks,
    164-171
  criteria for eligibility, 167
  denial of justice, 166
  duration of guarantee, 168
  eligible investors, 168
  expropriation, 165
  guarantee program, 165
  inconvertibility, 166
  insurer, as, 164-165
  Latin America, and, 172-173
  meeting development objectives,
    167
  Mexico, and, 173-175
  national insurance agencies,
    170-171
  role in attracting foreign
    investments, 161-178
  sponsorship trust fund facility,
    171
  subrogation, 170
  transfer restrictions, 166
  types of investment, 166-167
  types of political risks covered
    by, 165-166
  underwriting, 169
  war, 166

NAFTA
  general investment provisions.
    See General investment
    provisions
  Investment Chapter, 219-236.
    See also Investment Chapter
National legislation
  Canada, 8-13
  Mexico, 13-14
  United States, 14-15
Natural gas, 160

Petroleum, 160
  Mexico, 131-134
Pharmaceuticals, 156
Primary petrochemicals, 156

Real estate
  maquiladora, 60

Social services, 24
Steel mill products, 157

Taxes
  maquiladora, 60-62
Telecommunications
  Mexico, 136-139
Telecommunications services, 159
Textiles, 157
Transport
  Mexico, 134-136
Transportation, 159

UNCITRAL Arbitration Rules, 31
United States
  national legislation, 14-15
  national treatment principle, 7
  US foreign investment laws and
    practices, 3-18

United States-Mexico-Canada
cross-border investment and
trade deals, 185-217
1992, 185-194
1993, 194-205
1994, 207-217

NAFTA Law and Policy Series

1. F.M. Abbott: *Law and Policy of Regional Integration: The NAFTA and Western Hemispheric Integration in the World Trade Organization System.* 1995   ISBN 0-7923-3295-4
2. S.J. Rubin and D.C. Alexander (eds.): *NAFTA and Investment.* 1995
                                                        ISBN 90-411-0032-6

KLUWER LAW INTERNATIONAL – THE HAGUE / LONDON / BOSTON